The Witness and the Other World

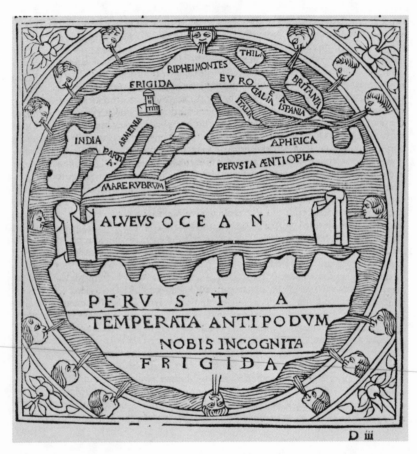

A "zone map" of the world as known to Europe for most of the Middle Ages.
From a printed edition of Macrobius's *De somnio Scipionis expositio*. Paris,
1519. Courtesy of the John Carter Brown Library at Brown University.

The Witness and the Other World

Exotic European
Travel Writing, 400–1600

MARY B. CAMPBELL

Cornell University Press

Ithaca and London

Cornell University Press gratefully acknowledges
a grant from the Andrew W. Mellon Foundation
that aided in bringing this book to publication.

First published 1988 by Cornell University Press.

International Standard Book Number 0-8014-2137-3
Library of Congress Catalog Card Number 88-47720
Printed in the United States of America
*Librarians: Library of Congress cataloging information
appears on the last page of the book.*

*The paper in this book is acid-free and meets the guidelines for
permanence and durability of the Committee on Production Guidelines
for Book Longevity of the Council on Library Resources.*

To my father, Kenneth L. Campbell, Jr.

Contents

Acknowledgments

This book was born in a graduate seminar on Middle English literature taught by Celia Millward at Boston University in the spring of 1978. She provided copious arcane materials and equal amounts of encouragement for the seminar paper on *Mandeville's Travels* that introduced me to the strangeness and charm of my subject; she continued to provide them for years to come as my dissertation adviser, often under very difficult circumstances. I owe a great deal to her steadfast support and friendship.

Institutions that have offered fellowship support and library resources for my research include Boston University's Department of English (and an anonymous donor who provided funds for a dissertation fellowship), the John Carter Brown Library at Brown University, and Columbia University's Society of Fellows in the Humanities. I owe particular thanks to Loretta Nassar, director of the Society of Fellows, and to two members of the staff at the John Carter Brown Library: Susan Danforth, the map curator, and Richard Hurley, the staff photographer, who is responsible for most of the prints reproduced here as illustrations. The remaining prints were supplied by the British Library and the New York Public Library, for whose permission to reproduce them I am grateful.

Several people have read and responded to drafts of the manuscript or parts of it; I have gladly taken advice and siphoned erudition from them all: my father, Kenneth L. Campbell, Jr., Gerald Fitzgerald, Emily Hannewalt, Robert Levine, Deborah Rubin, James Siemon, and Susan Winnett. Charles Rowan Beye and John Block Friedman offered especially attentive and useful responses to large sections of part 1. I have also been grateful for the generosity

Acknowledgments

and real helpfulness of my editor and readers at Cornell University Press, Bernhard Kendler, Percy G. Adams, and Christian K. Zacher. Many thanks to Robert Lamberton for first introducing my manuscript to them.

For help with translations, bibliographies, and footnotes and for giving me things to think about, I thank Carla Cappetti, Emily Hannewalt (again) and Bruce McBain (who read Egeria with me for a whole semester in spare time they didn't have), Pamela Raabe, Delia Sherman, Carol Smith, Nancy Stepan, and Gauri Viswanathan. The moral support of Marie Plasse and Helaine Ross kept the book alive when money dried up, libraries closed, or the temperature dropped below freezing. My grandmother, Mary Parker Campbell, offered financial assistance at several key points.

The book's most constant reader has been Laurence Breiner, to whose knowledge and imagination the book and I are happily indebted.

Where not otherwise credited, translations are my own.

M. B. C.

Cambridge, Massachusetts

The Witness and the Other World

And Marco's answer was: "Elsewhere is a negative mirror. The traveler recognizes the little that is his, discovering the much he has not had and will never have."

—Italo Calvino, *Invisible Cities*

Introduction

Of course the very first thing to do was to make a grand survey of the country she was going to travel through. "It's something very like learning geography," thought Alice, as she stood on tiptoes in hopes of being able to see a little further. "Principal rivers—there *are* none. Principal mountains—I'm on the only one, but I don't think it's got any name. Principal towns—why, what *are* those creatures, making honey down there? They can't be bees—nobody ever saw bees a mile off, you know—" and for some time she stood silent, watching one of them that was bustling about among the flowers, poking its proboscis into them, "just as if it was a regular bee," thought Alice.

—*Through the Looking Glass*

S oon after the Fall, human beings took their first jour-
ney—in this case, into exile from Paradise. We are, all of us, a displaced people. The movement of travel, whether it redeems or merely repeats that original displacement, belongs in the circle of elemental experience with "birth, copulation and death," as Eliot the expatriate should have known. Certainly Homer, Virgil, Dante, and the authors of Exodus and *Gilgamesh* knew it. And its presence in literature is attested at the figural level as well as the thematic. Ernst Curtius begins his treatment of metaphor ("the most important figure"; *European Literature and the Latin Middle Ages*, 128) with a section on nautical metaphors in which literary composition is likened to a sea voyage. Horace is the earliest writer he cites, but Homer's formula, "winged words," suggests a far earlier connection between the ideas of shaped language and travel. Indeed, *metaphor* itself is etymologically (and

I

metaphorically) a "change of place"; its equivalent in Latin rhetoric, *translatio*, was a word often used quite literally in this sense (and even now, Greek buses bear the label "metaphor").

Travel, then, is paradoxically a root—a radical. We find it in our myths of origin, in our earliest literatures, in our oldest critical terms for the most essential figure of speech. After we learn "to be" and "to have" in a new language, we learn "to go." During a period in which literary critics of all persuasions seem endlessly to find that writing is about writing, one might bear in mind that writing is travel and seek to investigate "travel" about travel. This book is such an investigation. It does not concern itself with frankly imaginative literature, but with the fraught project of translating one's own actual travel into a written record—with attempts, ranging from the devoutly earnest to the artfully mendacious, to "tell."

My desire to tell the story of travel literature did not begin from the perception that modern travel literature is a self-consciously artistic genre whose history needs telling, though that is true. It began with the perception that the literary situation, in any era, of the traveler who writes is an inherently interesting one—a limit case for such intertwined literary issues as truth, fact, figure, fiction, even genre. How, for instance, does one *distinguish* fact from fiction, either as writer or as reader, in the case of unverifiable records of private experience taking place in profoundly unfamiliar surroundings? How do the pressures of audience expectation and the writer's predispositions transform the language and content of such records? Are they records at all, or only literary occasions for compensatory fantasies on the part of the disillusioned, the nostalgic, the bewildered?

These issues are particularly clear for the modern reader of premodern travels—works, often of great charm, written by the ignorant for the parochial. Before the Renaissance, overseas travel was rare enough among Europeans that travelers could indeed "lie with authority," though they might not mean to. What, I wondered, happened to the genre in the Age of Discovery, when a sort of verification became possible and information from abroad came to have urgent practical uses? A history that bridged this rift in the *longue durée* would go some way toward explaining the genre's relationship to "truth" and provide as well a case study of the relations between writing and (literally) the world.

The travel book is a kind of witness: it is generically aimed at the truth. Neither power nor talent gives a travel writer his or her authority, which comes only and crucially from experience. The book exists to tell "some part of things that there be" (Mandeville, *Mandeville's Travels*, p. 3), to provide vicarious knowledge of the actual world to those who are "possessed by a desire to picture to their minds those things which they are not able to behold with their eyes" (Burchard of Mt. Sion, *Description of the Holy Land*, p. 4). But the traveler in foreign parts is faced with a world for which his language is not prepared: no matter how naïve the writer's understanding of language, the option of simple transparence, of verbal equivalences, is not open. In *Brazilian Adventure*, Peter Fleming explains his use of the Brazilian words *praia* and *urubú*: "the word sandbank, for instance, gives you a very niggardly idea of what a *praia* is, and the word *plague*, which conveys an image nearer the truth, has unsuitable associations. Similarly, an *urubú* is a far more scurvy and less spectacular creature than the popular conception of a vulture" (133). Medieval travelers tended to take another course, employing "similitudes" to frequently grotesque effect: Polo's unicorn-rhinocerous has "hair like the buffalo, . . . feet like the feet of an elephant . . . [and] one horn in the middle of the forehead . . . . It has the top of the head made like a wild boar" (Moule and Pelliot, 166). In neither case is the documentary ideal of transparency attained. In both cases, the truth thus rendered is an *exotic* truth, bearing witness to an alienated experience. But the medieval writer is more deeply shocked, or at least his shock is more rhetorically blatant.

This book, then, restricts it attention to premodern European accounts of travel outside Europe—more precisely, travel to Asia. The purely literary problems and solutions of travel writing stand out in clearest relief against an alien landscape, and for the period under discussion, the various landscapes of Asia were the most constitutively alien. Although Christopher Miller's recent book, *Blank Darkness*, makes a strong case for Africa as Europe's Other, there is no continuous corpus of travel accounts during the Middle Ages that take on Black Africa as an experienced and witnessed place: Egypt, then as now, was part of Asia, and Ethiopia was legend alone. Asia was both sufficiently "known" (witnessed, experienced) and unknown (Other) to provide the ground for dynamic struggles between the powers of language and the facts of life.

Introduction

To take accounts of Asia (which for our purposes includes America) as my focus is not, however, a simple geographical restriction: East and West have a rich and tragic historical relation—much of which is documented, some of which was even enabled, by the works we will be reading. Pilgrimage became crusade; the search for Marco Polo's Cathay ended in the conquests of Mexico and Peru. Many pilgrims were soldiers, many missionaries were military spies, most early explorers were conquistadores. So in following the early history of travel writing we will sometimes be looking at the linguistic shadows of European imperialism: several of the works examined here begin or end with explicit references to the future conquest of the lands or peoples described.

In speaking of a kind of literature defined by the circumstances of its writer and the experiences that form its subject, it becomes necessary to speak of circumstances and experiences as well as of literary texts themselves. Some of these circumstances and experiences are the very matter of history—the Crusades, the Mongol Empire, the discovery and conquest of America. But this book does not aim to be a cultural history. It is an investigation into the nature of a literary genre, a genre that gives historians many valuable documents to work with, but that conforms to the laws of *literary* nature and is not so transparent or reliable as parish registers or wills or charters.

Fact is important to the genre, but we will have occasion to look carefully at what might constitute a fact in the context of an autobiographical form concerned with the alien and unrecognizable. Marco Polo's unicorn is one of his facts—if we rename it "rhinocerous." Friar Odoric's pygmies are a fact. But they do not nowadays procreate at the age of five. The bird-centaurs of *Wonders of the East* belong to the genre of the fact, but they do not and never did exist—they were begotten of an error in scribal transmission. The total mosaic to which these facts contribute embodies as grotesque and fantastical a dream as Europe could imagine. But it was knowledge, too:

For I make you know that since our Lord God fashioned Adam our first father & Eve with his hands until this moment never was Christian, Saracen, nor pagan nor Tartar nor Indian nor any man of any kind who saw and knew or inquired so much of the different parts of the world and of the great wonders so much as this said Master Marc Pol searched out and

4

knows, nor had travelled through them . . . . And therefore he says to himself that it would be too great evil if he did not cause all the great wonders which he saw & which he heard for truth to be put in writing so that the other people who did not see them nor know may know them by this book. (Moule and Pelliot, 1)

The structure of this account is mimetic. The history of the travel book before the seventeenth century is, from our perspective, a *pre*history, a history of the slow assembling of the features that now identify a work as "travel literature." It is perhaps only from the armchair of the postcolonial twentieth century that these works can be seen as bearing a close enough family resemblance to constitute a genre. A chronological discussion of selected texts avoids some of the distortions of critical anachronism: each text is viewed, as it was written and initially received, in light of its own literary past and present. We find its future in another, later text.

Our point of origin, though, needs justifying: it is, like any point, imaginary. We begin in late antiquity, at the end of the fourth century, with the earliest known narrative of Christian pilgrimage written by a European. Why not begin earlier, with a pre-Christian work? Classical and Hellenistic Greek accounts of India and Persia are extant and will be referred to in these pages. The simple answer (elaborated more positively in the next chapter) is that travel literature is defined here as a kind of first-person narrative, or at least a second-person narrative (as in the travel guide: "thence you come to a pillar near the chamber of the holy sepulchre"). A history such as Herodotos wrote is a third-person narrative. The peripluses of Alexander the Great's pilots are almost narratives, but there is no "person" in the extant epitomes; the geography of Strabo or natural history of Pliny is not narrative at all. All these forms contributed matter and ideology to the form we will be watching, but so did the letter, the wonder book, the chronicle, the hagiography, the romance, the pastoral, the utopia. Attention will be paid to many contributing genres and "modes," but my focus is on such travel writing as bears a significant family resemblance to the modern genre, of which the first substantial instance is Egeria's account of Christian pilgrimage to the Holy Land.

Our history ends with a secular pilgrimage in search of a secular "Other World"—Sir Walter Ralegh's account of his search for El Dorado. Ralegh's book is characteristic of travel literature as we know it today: fully narrative, fully inhabited by its narrator, self-conscious about the problem of presenting difference in terms that neither inadvertently domesticate nor entirely alienate. Between Egeria and Ralegh, we will pay chronological attention to a series of texts that, though perhaps "subliterary," grapple with literary problems of presentation—self-presentation as well as presentation of the other and the external world—with an immediacy unmatched in other medieval prose genres.

I am primarily interested in travel literature itself, and this book is intended for those who share my interest. But the history of this form exemplifies its relevence to critics and historians of other literary (and not exactly literary) forms and even, perhaps, to theorists. This is a genre composed of other genres, as well as one that importantly contributed to the genesis of the modern novel and the renaissance of autobiography. It is a genre that confronts, at their extreme limit, representational tasks proper to a number of literary kinds: the translation of experience into narrative and description, of the strange into the visible, of observation into the verbal construct of fact; the deployment of personal voice in the service of transmitting information (or of creating devotional texts); the manipulation of rhetorical figures for ends other than ornament. Some of these demands are familiar to the "participant-observers" of ethnography, others to writers and critics of fictional realism or historiography. All of them are important to the analysis of travel writing.

As I have mentioned, the premodern history of travel writing is implicitly a history of Europe's relations with "the Orient" and the New World. For any to whom the European perspective on those relations is interesting, the texts considered here should be interesting, too. They are certainly not our only sources for retrieving this ancestral perspective, but taken together—as they have not been before now—they constitute an image of an image that flickered on the stage of political history, alluring and deceiving and inspiring the main characters of the tragedy. The alienation of Europe is bespoken in almost all of the rhetorical strategies (and silences) that present themselves for analysis. And the images of both self and other, Home and the Other World, which such strategies figure forth have some explanatory value when we consider the catastrophical historical climax of premodern European contact with the outside.

When Europe finally found the Other World for which it had sought throughout the East, that "earthly Paradise" became the scene of the hugest genocide the world has ever known: according to Todorov (depending on the demographic studies of S. Cook and W. W. Borah), the native population of the Americas fell from eighty million to ten million over the course of the sixteenth century. Estimates of these figures vary widely from historian to historian, and perhaps none can be trusted. Any scheme for reconstructing population counts in this context is inevitably colored by the political and national passions of the writer. But all agree that the destruction was vast and much of the violence premeditated. It was almost as if Europe felt the need to scour the map of all that was "satanic"—of all the chaotic, fertile, multitudinous splendors it had believed were "out there" and which threatened the hegemony of its conscious values. The story of how this discovery and extermination came to happen cannot be told simply through examination of the travel literature on which it only partially depended. And examination of that literature will tell us other things, more literary things, as well. The specter of the American holocaust will fade into the background of this study. But it haunts the whole.

Each of the texts to be considered could be said to represent a subgenre of the corpus, and as we move chronologically from book to book we will also be shifting from form to form. But these formal shifts have some relation to chronology as well: pilgrimage, for instance, was the most characteristic form of exotic travel during the early Middle Ages, as commercial exploration was during the Renaissance. And the topoi and structure of one sort can often be seen to infiltrate another: Mandeville's book mixes the Matters of the Holy Land and the End of the East, Ralegh's imposes the emotional structure of the pilgrimage on his exploration of the Orinoco. It is economical to take up the particularities of different forms of the travel account as we move through time: this should not, however, suggest that missionary accounts of the Far East *replaced* pilgrimage accounts in the thirteenth century (or indeed that anything ever replaced the *peregrinationes*—they are still being written).

Chapter 1 begins with the late fourth-century *Peregrinatio* of Egeria. Egeria is a clean slate: she has no known heritage on which to draw and is the most naïve of writers. We can see in her letter therefore the most elemental properties of the form achieve their simplest manifestations. Egeria's letter was written, it appears, to the members of the religious community to which she belonged and concentrates almost exclusively on the religious *monumentalia* of the Holy Land. Marvels, monsters, and the culture of the non-Christian Levant are entirely absent, but the assumption of Other World-liness about the land in which she is traveling is nevertheless fundamental to her account. Adamnan's rendition of Bishop Arculf's seventh-century journey extends the otherworldly vision to include nonscriptural features of the Holy Land: we see in his *De locis sanctis* the inclusion of the older, less holy supernature with which the writers of antiquity had imbued their East.

Chapter 2 is concerned with the most purely fabulous branch of literature about the East. The Alexander romances, familiar to medievalists, were the fictional vehicle of a mass of legendary and psuedoscientific matter—the Matter of the East—that descended from Herodotus and particularly Pliny through such (frequently vernacular) texts as *Wonders of the East* and *Alexander's Letter to Aristotle*. The popular material isolated in these latter works comes very close to fiction, but it was not necessarily received as fiction and was usually cast in the epistolary form that would continue to be seen as appropriate to "real" travel literature right up to the eighteenth century's various *Letters from Italy* and beyond. The Matter of the East itself, outside the family of genres elaborating Alexander's East, would also prove long-lived, reappearing in every travel book we touch on. The "wonders" are the most extreme and exquisite projections of European cultural fantasy: it is against their iconographic background of grotesque similes that a responsible literature of travel will develop, and it is among their images that Europe will find nourishment for its notions of "monstrous" savagery. The model (which finds its authority, though not its origins, in Pliny) of a world normal at its (European) center and monstrous at its (Asian and African) margins is easy to see as the self-image of a culture quite literally scared of its own shadow. I argue that the fear and loathing here influentially implicit became explicit—and murderous—when opportunity arose.

Chapter 3 treats the earliest (thirteenth century) accounts of travel to the Far East, chiefly those of the merchant Marco Polo and the missionary William of Rubruck (upon whose work Roger Bacon based his description of Scythia and Tartary in his *Opus majus*). These accounts exhibit both a freer sense of the importance and authority of first-person experience and a new interest in such secular topics as other human cultures. Circumstance accounts for the admission of secular material: the writers were not traveling in the footsteps of biblical persons. And circumstance makes room here for stylistic innovation, allowing the writers to establish rhetorics for describing what had only rarely been described before: alien human customs and beliefs. Their methods persisted for centuries, and even the content of their books hardened into immutable fact after communication with the East was severed again in the fourteenth century. (Sebastian Münster's *Cosmographiae universalis* [1544] plagiarizes Marco Polo as if history might have left Cathay untouched for 250 years.) In the account of Marco Polo—*Il milione,* to Italians—we have the most balanced and lush of all medieval re-creations of the East: the grotesque titillations of *Wonders* and the splendor and fertility of Paradise are here combined in a single comprehensive image. It was that "mirage" that drew Columbus to our shores.

In chapter 4 we are confronted with a complicated artistic climax, possible only in the circumstances of reduced travel and the consequent generic stabilization of travel writing that characterized the fourteenth century. *Mandeville's Travels*, the erudite invention of a man who may never have left Europe, combines the two formally distinct matters of the Holy Land and the Far East, as well as actual passages from encyclopedists, pilgrims, and merchant and missionary travel writers. "Mandeville" (whoever he may have been) inserts his own person into this patchwork of plagiarism more forcefully than any writer but William of Rubruck had before him, but what is even more notable, he manages for the first time to humanize the cultures he describes and to depict what he calls "that other half" as belonging to the same Nature as "our own." The rhetoric of his book is in a way a meditation on and corrective to the literature from which it was formed. Its remarkable cultural relativism may have been possible only to an untraveled man in a stay-at-home age, but it is nevertheless a bright spot in a picture that will almost immediately darken when the Age of Discovery begins. It was not the introduction of a human protagonist that humanized *Mandeville's Travels*, for the conquistadores and colonizers, though full of themselves in their writings, are rarely full of sympathy.

Ironically, Mandeville's fictional popularization of the idea of a circumnavigable and universally inhabited world was not uninfluential with the navigators and cartographers of the early discovery period. The man was a good writer, and he became an *auctoritas*. Columbus, Frobisher, Ralegh, Ortelius, Mercator: all read him, used him, believed him. But the message of his humane rhetoric was lost on Columbus, with whose first journal, and with the *Letter to Sanchez*, chapter 5 is concerned. Again we have a "first"— as Marco Polo was the first person to attempt a first-person description of the East, the West (imagined as Polo's East) comes to us first in the writings of Columbus.

With Columbus we see another confluence of Matters and manners. The Matters of both the biblical and the secular Easts are brought into alignment here with the landscapes, atmospheres, and values of chivalric romance and classical pastoral. Columbus's depiction of the Other World descends in part from the Alexander romances, in its focus on the fecundity and beauty of what he believes is the East, as well as in his own heroic relation to the territories he considers his. His journal is more emphatically narrative than any previous travel account but William of Rubruck's, and in the heroic figure of the Discoverer we are given, at last, a fully present narrator. And despite the tendency of recent commentators to isolate Columbus's statement in the *Letter* that he has found "no human monstrosities," the Matter of Alexander's East has left its mark. He passes on reports of monstrous races (anthropophagi, hairless men with tails, mermaids, Amazons) and tends to perceive his "Indians" in light of the half-admirable, half-contemptible gymnosophists whose weaponless and propertyless existence amused but did not compel the great Conqueror of India. The *Journal* and the *Letter* also conflate the Earthly Paradise of Mandeville's East with the pastoral *locus amoenus*: the result of all these mixtures is a Caribbean that belongs as much to the Other World of medieval geographic fantasy as it does to the map Columbus helped realize. Columbus believed literally in what the later Renaissance would come to see as metaphorical identifications, and he instructively compounds them in a letter to Pope Alexander VI: "This island is Tarsis, is Cythia, is Ophir and Ophaz and Cipangu, and we have named it Española." Such literal belief in the fantastic can seem charming to a modern reader, but may well have helped propagate the monstrous stereotypes through which the Spanish Empire perceived—and monstrously abused—its American "subjects."

In the last chapter we cross an imaginative meridian and find ourselves on the borders of the modern world. Although Walter Ralegh's *Discoverie of the Large, Rich, and Bewtiful Empire of Guiana* postulates for its unachieved destination the mythical land of El Dorado and includes hearsay accounts of Amazons and Mandeville's Acephali, it presents us with a Guiana that is both palpable and frankly subjective.

Ralegh's book is a fully detailed narration of a particular man's journey down a river that does not shroud itself in legend, displaced scriptural references, or beauties derived from travel formulas. In a sense it is another clean slate: stripped of the preordained, his account of a journey permits us a view of a writer struggling bare-handed with a thorny actuality. Nothing could be more alien from the English courtier's experience than this initial penetration of inland Venezuela, with its unnameable topography, its tropical drinking feasts, its armadillos, its pineapples, and its heat. Nor does Ralegh try to explain any of this as grotesque variation or supernatural exaggeration of the English norms in which his language has its roots. It is alien, and he says so, but with gusto and clarity: *chiarezza*. At last we see an actual man perform the feat that Mandeville so generously imagined: Ralegh talks to a monstrous savage as if he were a human being and records this conversation as though we might be interested in meeting him. The *longue durée* is ending. The Plinian model, of a world rimmed with the magical and monstrous fragments of a divided self, has broken up on the waters of the Orinoco, where Ralegh listens to Topiawari speak "as a man which had inward feeling."

This is not necessarily a happy ending, or rather it is only the very beginning of one—a literary beginning with which history has yet to catch up. I own a collection of tabloid articles about Asia which are as monstrous as anything in *Wonders of the East*, and they were all published in 1983. East and West remain dangerously divided, each side appearing so barbarous and monolithic to the other that we may each have to scour "that other half" again, and this scouring, if it happens, will be final. But in the travel book we have developed a literary instrument of consciousness, a genre of cultural translation which comes closer now than it once did to proving that such translation is possible at all.

"Asia, the second part of the earth, in the form of Pegasus." Heinrich Bunting. Magdeburg, c. 1585. By permission of the British Library.

PART ONE

THE EAST

I

The Scriptural East

Egeria, Arculf, and the

Written Pilgrimage

We take up the story of the European travel book with the earliest extant work devoted entirely to the account of a journey beyond the borders of Europe—the *Peregrinatio ad terram sanctam* of Egeria. But before examining that text, it is necessary to account in more detail for this choice of a starting point. Other critics treat the works of Herodotus and Ctesias as the first exemplars of European travel literature because they describe distant places on the basis (partly) of firsthand experience. But there is a crucial difference between such works as theirs and Egeria's: the traveling historians, geographers, and navigators of classical and late antiquity do not dwell in their books on journey or the self, but only on the data accumulated during the journey. Journey for them is a method of research; the self is a respectable "source" but not a subject whose human nature is or should be emphasized. As we will see, self remains problematic for Egeria, but becomes necessary as a rhetorical presence. And the idea of pilgrimage renders the journey important *as* journey: pilgrimage is significant journeying. Under its aegis the motion of travel becomes the action of quest, and so deserving of representation.

The East of pagan antiquity, the Matter encapsulated in the books of Herodotus, Ctesias, Arrian, Pliny and others, did not by any means fade into oblivion after the interruption of Christianity. From Herodotus to Pliny to Solinus to Isidore of Seville to Vincent of Beauvais to Sebastian Münster: each link of the chain binding the oriental lore of antiquity with that of the Renaissance is securely fastened to the next. But this continuity is one of manifest content above all, and in this chapter we are more concerned with form and rhetoric, with the structural innovations heralded by Egeria's letter. The East of antiquity was one in which Palestine figured very little (outside of Josephus's *Bellum Judaicum*). The literary existence of the Holy Land Egeria set out to describe was confined in the fourth century to the Bible and the writings of the Church Fathers.[1] Discussion of the wider pagan East will be postponed to chapter 2: it is not only irrelevant to Egeria's project, but was very likely unknown to her.

Egeria was the first Christian to render an account of a journey to the Near East, but not the first to write about its places. In his *Vita Constantini*, Eusebius Pamphili (260–340), bishop of Caesarea, had written extensively about the churches erected in and around the Holy Land by that emperor; he had also composed an *Onomasticon*, a book on the names of places mentioned in the scriptures. Jerome was soon to follow him with his *De situ et nominibus locorum Hebraicorum* (and Procopius would later do for the buildings of Justinian what Eusebius had done for Constantine's, in *De aedificiis*).

Eusebius, raised in Alexandria, was an apologist and admirer of the Neoplatonist Origen, in whose writings the science of Christian theology and the technique of allegorical exegesis were first formally established. His own mystical tendency and allegorical understanding of the material world render his architectural descriptions a matter of interest to critics of literature as well as to art historians; here, for instance, is his explanation of the design of a church erected by Paulinus at Tyre:

Building, then, in righteousness, he [Paulinus] distinguished by a due estimate the capacities of the whole people; for some merely surrounding the external enclosure having walled it round with unwavering faith [*sic*]. For of such a nature are a great number of the people, being capable of supporting no superior ediface. But to others he granted an entrance into the body

1. The seventh-century Gallician monk Valerius had this to say of Egeria's reading, in his "Letter in Praise . . . of the Most Blessed Egeria": "First with great industry she perused all the books of the Old and New Testaments, and discovered all its descriptions of the holy wonders of the world; and its regions, provinces, cities, mountains and deserts. . . . Then at length, moved by the longing for a pilgrimage to pray at the most sacred Mount of the Lord, she followed in the footsteps of the children of Israel" (*Analecta Bollandiana*, 29:394–95). The translation quoted here is from John Wilkinson, *Egeria's Travels to the Holy Land*.

of the church, bidding them stand at the doors and guide those who are entering in, these being not unfitly likened to the front entrances of the temple. Again, he supported others by the first columns which are round the rectangular court outside, placing them on those primal supports of the letter of the Four Gospels. And others again he sets on either side round the basilica, being as yet catechumens, and in a state of growth and progress, but not very far distant from the Divine vision of the faithful within. (*Historia ecclesiastica,* 10.4)

This habit of moralizing the inanimate, or reading into it an explanatory value, is a salient feature of the earliest pilgrimage literature as well: the perceived nature of the Holy Land lent itself to the development of a heavily allegorical topography. Jerome's account of his friend Paula's pilgrimage, which took place A.D. 382–84, reports that "she cared not to go to Cariathsepher, that is 'the village of letters,' because, despising the perishing letter, she had found the life-giving Spirit" (Jerome, "Pilgrimage of the Holy Paula," 10). Paula herself says, in her beautiful letter to Marcella (A.D. 386), "We shall go to Nazareth, and, according to the interpretation of its name, shall behold the flower of Galilee" (the Hebrew word *netzer* means "shoot" or "sprout"; "Letter of Paula and Eustochium," 15).

It is not just the habit of allegory that we are noticing here: it is a special kind of blindness and vision, expressed in a number of ways, to which any early Christian pilgrim to the Holy Land was susceptible. These writers were readers too—they read in the stones and fountains and caves of Palestine the narrative that had lured them there, the story of the Jewish people (whose holy places the Christian church was already beginning to appropriate through such architectural projects as Constantine's). Paula, in her invitation to Marcella, gives a spectacularly clear example of the kind of "sights" to which this early travel literature bore witness:

When will that day come, when we shall be able to enter the grotto of our Savior? to weep with our sister, and with our mother, in the Sepulchre of the Lord? . . . to see Lazarus come forth bound with grave clothes, and to see the waters of Jordan, made more pure by the baptism of the Lord? . . . To behold Amos the prophet even now lamenting on his rock with his shepherd's bugle-horn?[. . .]Thence we shall come to the Sea of Gennesareth, and shall see the five and four thousand men in the desert fed with five and seven loaves. (15)

This is not at all the sort of thing Herodotus saw in the Levant, nor the sort of seeing he recounts. Although he was a historian, as a traveler he was one who saw his surroundings in their present tense: "Thus far I have spoken of Egypt from my own observation, relating what I myself saw, the ideas that I formed and the results of my own researches" (*History*, 2:99). What he saw includes the alluvial and saline qualities of the Egyptian soil, the three Egyptian methods of embalming, the construction of Egyptian merchant vessels, "the peculiarities of the crocodile," the Egyptian custom of burying domestic and sacred animals. His gods had in fact made a number of important appearances in Egypt, which he recounts, but he betrays no sense at all of the land as "holy," or of his experience there as personal, a spiritual adventure.

Christianity is in fact the first Western religion in which the sacred territory is located emphatically Elsewhere.[2] As a result, Christian pilgrimages are the first to lead pilgrims abroad on their religious travels. Inevitably, the pilgrim's experience is intensified—by distance, by cultural alienation, by the sheer difference of the sacred territory from that of Home. The urge to bear witness is also intensified: the journey is too arduous and lengthy to be common, and most believers must forego it, substituting for it the vicarious experience of reading.

Beyond these practical and contingent reasons for the altered vision of the Christian travel writer, there is the fundamental metaphysical issue of "witnessing" itself. Not only does the individual "witness" assume a previously inconceivable importance, in light of the apostolic and evangelical origins of the new religion, but the nature of what the traveler is called on to witness has changed as well. The botany of Palestine, for instance, is of no concern: only such singular plants as the sycamore of Zacharius, the oak at the vale of Mambre, or the Burning Bush are notable. Engineering feats that Herodotus would have inspected and analyzed turn into commemorative miracles. Here is Antoninus Mar-

---

2. There are of course Eastern equivalents to this displacement of sacred territory. Far Eastern Buddhists, e.g., make pilgrimages to the modern Indian state of Bihar to visit and study at the place of the Buddha's Enlightenment, and there is a written tradition of Chinese "Journeys to the West" which parallels in some respects the Christian *peregrinationes*. The earliest extant account of travel to the Palestinian Holy Land by a European Jew is Rabbi Benjamin of Tudela's twelfth-century itinerary, translated in Wright, *Early Travels in Palestine*.

tyr (c. 565) on the syphon of an aqueduct at Rama: "At that very place I saw water come out of the rock in the midst of the road—I should say to the amount of nine pints—from which all men drink their fill, and yet the water is never more or less; and it is sweet to drink. It is said that this water sprang up because the Blessed Mary, when fleeing into Egypt, sat down in that place and thirsted" ("Of the Holy Places," 23).

The customs of alien people, recorded by Herodotus thoroughly and usually objectively, are irrelevant or demonic in this new kind of Holy Land which is inhabited mostly by unbelievers. The churches of Constantine, Helena, and Paulinus replace heathen temples ("dark shrine[s] of lifeless idols") on the holy sites, and "the emperor further gave directions that the material of that which was destroyed, both wood and stone, should be removed and thrown as far from the spot as possible. . . . Again, being inspired with holy zeal, he issued orders that, having dug up the soil to a considerable depth, they should transport to a far-distant spot the actual ground, earth and all, inasmuch as it had been polluted by the defilements of demon-worship" (Eusebius, *Vita Constantini*, 3). (Palestine is perhaps the first Holy Land in which worshipers feel the need to strip and discard the soil.)

Like an archaeologist, the Christian pilgrim is looking for the past, but it is a past made up of singular events and personalities, individual epiphanies, incarnations, and martyrdoms. Places are referred to as "witnesses" of those events and people, and pilgrims in turn are witnesses of those places seen *as* events. In Jerome's terminology, Paula "saw," "admired," or "revered" those places— as opposed to "visited." And once there she "remembered." Looking down on the desert,

what was once the country of Sodom and Gomorrah, . . . she remembered the cave of Lot, and bursting into tears, warned the maidens, her companions, to avoid wine, wherein is excess. ("Pilgrimage of the Holy Paula," 10)

Scarcely was the night past before she, with fervent zeal, came to the Jordan, stood on the bank of the river, and, as the sun rose, remembered the Sun of righteousness; how the priests stood on dry ground in the middle of the bed of Jordan; . . . and how, by His Baptism, the Lord cleansed the waters which had been defiled by the Flood and stained by His death. (12)

The agendum of the pilgrim-traveler is an agendum of moments of perception, and as we will see in more detail with Egeria, the pilgrim-traveler's written account of the journey is a testimony to the achievement of such perceptions. The religion of the Incarnate Christ and Doubting Thomas is one that has need of its Lazaruses who, coming back in person "to tell you all," are human witnesses to the reality of another life, an Other World.

With Christianity we find at last an *audience* for the first-person travel account and a metaphysic in which private experience is valued and self-consciousness imperative. The new religion and the foreignness of its holy places together make a fertile ground for the development of an experiential kind of travel literature virtually unknown before Egeria's *Peregrinatio*. As we will see shortly, *presentation* of self remained highly problematic for the traveler *ad terram sanctam*. Nevertheless, the shift from the third to the first person, from the land to the journey that reveals it, marks a tangible point of departure.

Egeria

Every sphere of human activity has its golden age, or at least leaves golden traces of its infancy. And nothing could be more golden, more full of pastoral innocence and single-minded purity, than the document left to us from the first age of Christian pilgrimage by Egeria. Her personal existence is almost trackless—scholars are not even sure of her name (Aetheria and Saint Sylvia are the favored alternatives to Egeria), and she has been variously supposed to have lived in Spain, Italy, and France, in the fourth, fifth, and sixth centuries, to have been an untutored, fragile young nun, a sturdy old abbess with royal connections and classical training, and a pious slut who had the habit on her journey "de rechercher que la compagnie des hommes" (Cabrol and Leclerq, "Etheria," in *Dictionnaire* 5:576). Her *Peregrinatio* allows the hungry biographer little scope for speculation, as Egeria is not interested in herself, or even in her experiences as far as they are merely hers. As Leo Spitzer has demonstrated in his rhetorical analysis of the *Peregrinatio*, the "I" of her story is a precursor of the medieval "didactic" or "representative I," that being who later found himself "in the middle of the journey of our life" ("Epic Style of the Pilgrim

Aetheria"). This idealized persona has a transpersonal goal in writing and a transcendent experience to record, which will come to seem inconceivable by the time of *Mandeville's Travels* and the excited propaganda of Renaissance pilgrims to the New World, with its more tangible but usually more elusive gold.

But inconceivable or not, Egeria's is the first narrative of travel produced by the Christian, European, Western world we still live in. Sylvia Wynter has pointed out in her article "Ethno or Socio Poetics" that it is in part the result of such travels and such narratives that we have come to see ourselves as "the West" at all—a world apart from and opposed to an Other World we call "the East." Egeria's record of her journey there reveals the extent to which the East was felt in the beginning of the Christian era as indeed an Other World. It speaks less of a journey through time and space than of a journey into another realm of existence, in which things and meanings bear a different relationship to each other.[3] But most importantly, it records a *journey*, an experience: in Egeria's *Peregrinatio* the subject of travel literature as we know it now is first circumscribed.

Nothing, however, could seem more remote from the modern experience of travel, or even of experience, than the monotonously litanized itinerary of Egeria's ideal pilgrim. She did not go to the Holy Land impelled by the *curiositas* with which the medieval pilgrim is traditionally associated (and which impels even the modern, reflexively iconoclastic tourist, with his secret desire to see how small Europe is, how barren Israel, how westernized Japan). She was not prepared to be shocked, and she was not shocked. Her horizons were not widened: how could they be? They

---

3. In *Image and Pilgrimage in Christian Culture*, the anthropologists Victor and Edith Turner have a great deal to say about this aspect of the experience of Christian pilgrimage (the purest form of which they reconstruct as the preinstitutional, voluntaristic travel "to a far holy place approved by all" most common before the granting of plenary indulgences for penitential pilgrimage began to absorb the experience into the sphere of official ritual). They liken the structured experience of distant pilgrimage to an "extroverted mysticism" (33): "The trials of the long route will normally have made the pilgrim quite vulnerable to such impressions [of imaginative entry into the "founder's" experience]. Religious images strike him, in these novel circumstances, as perhaps they have never done before. . . . The innocence of the eye is the whole point here, the 'cleansing of the doors of perception'" (11). As pilgrimage was by far the most common form of travel to the East before the Crusades, it is easy to see how the East itself became invested with the properties the Turners identify as belonging rather to the personal experience of the pilgrim.

were already wider than the physical universe. She went to see a
diorama of the Scriptures, and she found it, thanks to the like-
minded religious who inhabited the holy sites and through whom
all "ostendibantur juxta scripturas" ("were shown according to the
Scriptures").[4]

The famous mendacity of the traveler is impossible to Egeria, as
are the doubt and suspicion that distinguish some later travelers
from "travel liars" like Mandeville or dupes like Arculf. The logic
of her universe allows her to infer the authenticity of what she sees
(for example, the grave of Adam) from the theological necessity of
its being there. For Egeria, significance precedes existence, and in
the overwhelming earnestness of this attitude there is no room for
lying and no room for personality.[5] *Who* sees the places and objects
mandated by spiritual necessity is irrelevant; that they are seen is
significant only as a blessing, and the seeing itself is an act of
reverence, not of discovery. It is an experience only to the degree
that being present at the consecration of the Host is an experience,
an infinitely repeatable one in which the participant is absolutely
equivalent to all his fellow participants, an experience as nearly as
possible independent of its subject.

There are too few remaining accounts of pilgrimage in late antiquity for us to gauge Egeria's fidelity to any comprehensive set of
literary conventions. But her work is not an attempt at art, it is a
letter to friends or colleagues back home. It is unlikely then that
she was making any stabs at bold or problematic modes of percep-

---

4. This phrase is the fragment with which the only extant manuscript of the
Peregrinatio begins. It is repeated over and over again throughout the text, every
time Egeria stops at a site recorded in the Bible where there are guides to show her
around.

5. See Spitzer, "Epic Style of the Pilgrim Aetheria," 241–43. In an explanation of
Egeria's pleonastic and seemingly pointless use of the causal conjunction *nam* to
introduce such clauses as "hic est locus ubi," Spitzer suggests: "Aetheria works
with the following causal patterns:

| I am mentioning this place | } | *for* it has |
| This place was pointed out to me | } | significance. |

and even, perhaps, with the pattern:

This place existed, *for* it had significance."

He goes on to defend the postulate, which he admits may "seem overbold to the
reader," by adducing an explicit statement of this relationship in chapter 16: "Tunc
ego, ut sum satis curiosa, requirire coepi, quae esset haec uallis, ubi sanctus mon-
achus nunc monasterium sibi fecisset; non enim putabam hoc sine causa esse."

tion, and she is clearly a woman of average intelligence. The total effect of her narrative contains nothing that would suggest an eccentricity of attitude or training. It seems safe to assume that her method neither shocked nor bored her readers and that it can be held to reflect a state of mind and a conception of geography and the physical world that were commonly and contentedly shared.

The only extant manuscript of Egeria's *Peregrinatio* begins with the fragment "ostendibantur juxta scripturas." Here are the first two paragraphs of that manuscript:

I ... were shown according to the Scriptures. Walking meanwhile we came to a certain place where those mountains, among which we were going, opened and made an endless valley, vast, exceedingly flat and very beautiful, and across the valley appeared the holy mountain of God, Sinai. This place, moreover, where the mountains opened is joined with that place where are the Graves of Lust. 2. In that place therefore when one arrives, as those holy guides who went with us advised, saying "It is customary, that a prayer is made here by those who come, when from that place is first seen the mountain of God": and accordingly we did. It was moreover from that place to the mountain of God about four miles in all across that valley, which as I said is vast. II Now the valley itself is vast and beautiful, lying below the flank of the mountain of God, which as far as we could estimate seeing and as they said is almost sixteen miles in length; in width moreover they said it was four miles. So we had to cross this very valley in order to climb the mountain. 2. Now this valley is the vast and exceedingly flat valley where the children of Israel lingered, while holy Moses ascended the mountain of the Lord and was there forty days and forty nights. It is moreover this valley where the calf was made, which place is shown to this day: for a great stone set there stands in that very place. So this is that very valley, at whose head that place is, where holy Moses, as he fed the flocks of his father-in-law, God spoke to him a second time from the burning bush.[6]

Egeria's style, as Spitzer has so meticulously demonstrated, is based on the devices of repetition and recapitulation and is entirely indifferent to the number of streaks on the tulip. We are told that a valley is "vast and very flat" four times in the first two paragraphs,

6. For the original Latin, see *Itinerarium Egeriae*, ed. E. Franceschini and R. Weber. All subsequent quotation of Egeria will be translated from this edition, cited in the text by chapter and paragraph numbers. My gloss is dependent on the translation by George Gingras in *Egeria: Diary of a Pilgrimage*.

but not what grows there or whether it contains running water and is inhabited. Egeria wants to hold her reader's attention as any writer does, but she wants an unusual kind of attention. She wants us to concentrate on the fact of the physical existence of this plain, rather than to conjure up its particular image in precise and thus distracting detail. The plain matters as a sacred locale; what is describable about it is that it is "where the children of Israel lingered while holy Moses ascended the mountain of the Lord." That is what Egeria sees when she looks at it, not the shrubbery. And that as the only descriptive detail must be the reason why the plain is "very beautiful." Aesthetic judgments reflect her hierarchy of values, and beauty is a quality of essence, not of appearance. Those physical details she gives are details of extremity: the valley is not big but "ingens," not flat but "planissima." Like the long train or massive crown of a king, they seem to express the importance of the place rather than to be the sources of its importance.

Egeria is very interested in topography, but not because of her personal connection with it. Its beauties and difficulties are not mentioned unless they are directly expressive of some spiritually important quality. It is the Ideas that haunt the Holy Land, and not their individual forms, to which her spirit is really attuned. "In ipso loco," "in eodem loco": she repeats these formulas endlessly, populating her vision with sacred events and, when too pressed for time or skill to describe a place, telling the "venerable sisters" to whom she writes to look it up in Numbers. "It was too much, however, to write down each one individually, because so many details could not be retained; but when Your Affection reads the holy books of Moses, she will perceive, diligently [written], all that was done there" (v,8).

It is easier to say what Egeria is not up to than what she is—especially since the opening and closing of her letter are missing. Clearly she is not writing to amuse or fascinate, but almost as clearly she is not writing to inform her venerable sisters. Her repetitions and recapitulations, as Spitzer puts it, "are all destined to detain the pious reader—a second pilgrim as it were—and to fix his attention on particular stations" (233–34). The feature of the reading experience she is taking particular advantage of is its power to arrest and fix the reader's consciousness, even as hers is being arrested by the holy places themselves. And her experieence as a traveler bears a striking resemblance to the act of reading: the

Holy Land in all its physical and cultural fullness is for her only a map of its former self. It is the place where something happened *in illo tempore*, and her descriptions tend to render that other, sacred time and not her own.

Her narrative then is iconographic in nature: it is intended as a tool of meditation and directed toward imaginations less sensuous than ours. The images to which that zealous piety was attracted were limited in number and available from other sources, preeminently the Bible. What is the difference for the reader between touring the sacred spots with Egeria and touring them in the Bible with God himself? In part it must be the difference between Egeria and God. Egeria is our intercessor, opening a door for us in the wall between our place and the sacred places. She represents mere man (perhaps, in her intercessory function, even "mere woman") in a way that the canonical scriptures, transcribed but not inspired by men, cannot. Her "representative I" is a long way off from "myself am the matter of my book." But it begins, under the most awkward literary conditions, the history of the travel book's capitulation to egotism (an egotism that reaches its first apotheosis in the private, secular, and imaginary adventures of Robinson Crusoe on an island with no history to impinge on his own).

The first-person narrator of a journey like Egeria's is in a tricky position. The setting of the journey is overwhelmingly more important than the particular journey that reveals it to the narrator, and yet that narrator and that journey are so distractingly, a priori, interesting. *Curiositas* would never have become a sin if it were not first a temptation. It appears to be a fact of life familiar even to the idealized and, for the most part, depersonalized "I" of Egeria's story. She mentions her curiosity more than once, and it is in fact the only detail of her character that she notes at all ("Tunc ego, ut sum satis curiosa," or "I, therefore, who am curious enough"; xvi,3). So her literary task is somehow to depress the reader's interest in herself and the course of her journeying, while at the same time maintaining the presence of that inviting and intercessory first person which makes her meditative tool effective.

She does her job in part through the use of an extremely restricted vocabulary: not that her own vocabulary is necessarily small (Souter's dictionary, *Later Latin*, frequently cites her as the only source for a particular "later Latin" word), but she has made it formulaic. The formulas are her own in most cases, and they are not striking or memorable. They are simply formulaic. Her pleonastic repetitiveness gives to this account of what must have been high adventure something of the quality of a rosary being recited. Anyone can recite a rosary, and everyone sounds more or less the same doing it. This tendency is a matter of stylistic choice for Egeria; one has only to look ahead to Adamnan's *De locis sanctis*, an influential seventh-century text, to find that it is not necessarily characteristic of this kind of writing.

Those points at which Egeria mentions herself, or describes her spontaneous reactions to what she saw, are didactically selected. They are moments of awe, reverence, wonder, or gratitude. Thus they tend to reflect our interest back onto their objects, away from Egeria. This is not simply a function of early Christian *humilitas*. As F. C. Gardiner has pointed out in his discussion of medieval "letters of pure friendship," the idea of letters as both physical and metaphysical facsimiles of one's own presence, longed for by the absent friend, was strong enough to have produced and supported a fully conventionalized genre for several centuries. [7] The intensely personal tone of these letters, the particularity of the love they express, the private nature of the emotion communicated in what were at least semipublic documents—all this seems surprising next to Egeria's self-effacing epistle:

Oh, when will that time come when a breathless messenger shall bring us the news that our Marcella has reached the shore of Palestine, and all the choirs of monks, all the troops of nuns shall shout applause? We already are eager to start, and though no vehicle is expected, yet we wish to run to meet it. We shall clasp your hands, we shall behold your face, and shall scarcely be able to leave your long-wished-for embrace. ("Letter of Paula and Eustochium," 13–14)

I recollect by such a sweet reminder, most blessed Father, your love and intimacy, hoping that sometime a lovely occasion might come to me to embrace the neck of your charity with the light touch of my desires. Oh, if the translation of Habacuc were suddenly granted me, how I would rush with quick violence into your paternal embrace, and how with kisses embrace not only your eyes, ears and mouth, but even every separate finger and toe of your hands and feet, many times. But yet because by my

7. See Gardiner, *Pilgrimage of Desire*, chap. 2.

own fault it is not granted me to come to you, I send letters to you often in my rustic manner, so that in place of my words they might speak for me. (Alcuin, *Patrologia latina*, 100:141A)

I have included these passages from the letters of Paula and Alcuin only to stress that Egeria's culture did not exclude the option of emotive self-presentation. Seen in the context of this genre of letter writing, Egeria's composition is an anomaly, a document of deep reserve. But of course her letter does not belong there. It is a merging of two genres, perhaps the first such merger, surely one of the very earliest. Her predecessors as Christian "travel writers" are the compiler of the Antonine Itinerary and the "Bourdeaux Pilgrim," both of whose documents are barely more than lists of cities, *mansiones*, places of interest, and the approximate distances (given in *milia*) between them. Their works are in effect verbal charts, designed for the convenience of subsequent travelers, not for the reader's spiritual exaltation. Given the shifting political affiliations of the territory, and the consequent emergence and subsidence of new and old dangers, it was of some practical importance that such itineraries be updated from time to time. But Egeria has done more than that. She has married that objective form of record to the literary letter, and in so doing has created a chart not of the geography of the Holy Land, but of a particular, if universalized, experience of it. The potentially dynamic dimension of time has rumpled the flat surface of the chart. The difference between a journey of forty *milia* and a "two-day journey" is the difference, writ small, between geography and the novel.

Although the structure of the narrative half of Egeria's account is simple—perfectly linear and episodic, reflecting no inner process of transformation and no gradual accumulation of insight or depth of feeling—she introduced into the *itinerarium* a tension that would from then on be exploited or eluded. In the list, "all the places" are simultaneous and perpetual. They bear no relation to the traveler and only the spatial relation of distance to each other. The list is in no sense literature; it is an aggregation of data. Literature, anonymous or signed, "popular" or "serious," is the imprint of a human mind on such data, an imprint that imposes a pattern of relations, attempts to make sense. And making sense is the end result of making choices. How long should I stay in Nazareth? Should I describe the monastery or move the reader on to the next holy place? Why is that monastery there, anyway? Are the monks more holy, living so close to the actual footprints of Our Lord? When and whether to speak, when to amplify and when to summarize, when the narrative should move and when be still—a hundred such questions form the particulars of the fundamental question: How much should I be present?

Given the subject matter and the religious orientation of the writer, these questions are bound to be answered formulaically, passed through the grids of dogma and decorum. But for Egeria there is as yet no canon from which she can take her rhetorical cues. She must translate imperatives from other realms of art and experience into a decorum that will guide her in good conscience through the task she has set herself. What then are her principles of literary conduct? To what does her propriety refer?

In the inevitable zigzagging between the sacred map and the distortion it suffers through her temporal experience of it, her allegiance is chiefly with the map. This is clear in her suppression of almost all personal details of the journey: the names of the people she meets, the nature of the gifts she receives, the identities of her fellow travelers, the feelings evoked by what she sees.

But the map behind her verbal amplification is a very different thing from the neutral, valueless images of modern cartography. It is the map of a route, or routes, a picture of a particular itinerary, of a river of significance running through insignificant and consequently unmapped space. This is the conception that organizes her predecessors' itineraries too: a hieratic, undemocratic view of geography. Reconstructions of the lost initial chapters of her narrative indicate that her route essentially duplicates that of the Hebrew Exodus, though it is not continuous, as she frequently paused for long periods in Jerusalem and was willing to make detours to other holy places within more or less convenient distance of the route.[8] Places not appearing in the Scriptures are, to

8. In the critical introduction to his English translation of Egeria, George Gingras summarizes this reconstructive scholarship: "A partial reflection of the initial chapters of the *Diary* may be contained in the twelfth-century *Liber de locis sanctis* of Peter the Deacon, librarian of Monte Cassino, whose work is a compilation based on the Venerable Bede's earlier digest of travelogues recording trips to the East and on other anonymous sources. Gamurrini had recognized that the final pages of Peter the Deacon's book were composed of extracts from the first seven chapters of Egeria's narrative as we have it; but how much of the preceding material could reasonably be considered a summary of the missing chapters? Although Peter the Deacon does add considerable information to his borrowings from Bede, he

her, empty—as they will not be to the later pilgrim, Arculf, who devotes a whole chapter to the magnificence of Alexandria.

Thus the chronology that determines her narrative structure has not been itself determined by the arbitrary demands of convenience but by an established route that is the setting of some of the greatest and most significant travel stories of all time. By following such routes in her own story, she creates a topography that is, automatically, a series of incidents rather than a series of landscapes and objects. "This is the place where Melchisedech offered pure sacrifices of bread and wine to God, as it is written that he did" (XIII, 4). "This is the place where the Law of the Passover was received" (VII, 5). "This place is Horeb, to which the holy prophet Elias came when he fled from the face of King Achab, and where God spoke to him, saying: 'What are you doing here, Elias?', as it is written in the Book of Kings" (IV, 2). Two kinds of time have entered the itinerary: the experienced time which is seen here chiefly as a measure of distance ("From the city of Arabia we traveled for two whole days through the land of Gessen"), and a monumental past time in which events occurred that overshadow in their felt reality the contents of the mundane and merely personal present ("arriving at Tanis, the city where holy Moses was born"; IX, 5).[9]

Although Egeria has opened the door onto a new autobiographi-

---

slavishly follows the structure of the latter's text until he begins to speak about places in Egypt connected with the Exodus of the Hebrews. After a brief mention of Memphis and Heliopolis, he launches into a very detailed description of Clysma, near the present-day port of Suez, where according to the Christian tradition of late antiquity the Israelites' crossing of the Red Sea had occurred. He then describes the places a pilgrim would visit who wished to follow faithfully each stage of the Children of Israel's journey from the Red Sea to Mount Sinai. These passages blend smoothly into those extracts that can unmistakably be identified as borrowings from Egeria" (*Egeria: Diary of a Pilgrimage*, 16). Gingras's is the most abundantly annotated recent English translation of the *Peregrinatio*.

9. The linking of the two kinds of time apparent in this sentence was destined for a reversal of emphasis which will be charted in succeeding chapters but begins as early as the letter of Valerius, quoted above. He compares Egeria's devout and fearless behavior in the desert of Sinai with that of her "hardhearted" biblical predecessors, who despised the manna of the Lord and panicked. The current traveler's function as redemptive "type" or agent of prophetic fulfillment will be emphasized again by Fulcher of Chartres in his account of the First Crusade (see chap. 4, p. 131) and will rise to megalomaniac heights in Columbus's comparisons of his enterprise with those of Moses and David (see chap. 5, pp. 189–190 and note). This tendency does not necessarily constitute a direct line of development: it is perhaps primarily a reflection of recurrent periods of apocalyptic millenialism, which incorporates our time into *illo tempore* by eschatological means.

cal genre, she has opened it only a crack. Twenty-six of the forty-nine extant chapters of her letter are devoted to a description of the liturgical life of Jerusalem, almost entirely nonnarrative, written in the habitual present tense, and interrupted only once by a passage of description that insists on the writer's personal experience of what she discusses. This passage, which records with awe the lavish decoration of the churches in Jerusalem at the Feast of the Epiphany, is broken off as sternly as the one passage in her narrative in which she mentions a living person by name—the point at which she digresses for the first and last time from her account of pilgrimage to mention an ecstatic meeting with an old friend. That these two passages represent breaches in decorum is signaled by her overt rejections of them: "But let me return to the subject" ("Sed ut redeam ad rem"; xxiii, 4); "But let us return to the subject" ("Sed ut redeamus ad rem"; xxv,10).

It is not just Egeria's self-effacement and purely devotional orientation that separate her from the tradition she helped to engender. It is finally her ecstatic *contemptus mundi*. In a literary situation that to a modern sensibility would seem a magnet for description of all kinds, she chooses the general over the specific, the abstract over the concrete noun, the evaluative over the descriptive adjective, the passive over the active verb form, redundancy over variation, formula over rendering. This tendency is a result of an active choice: that she is capable (though not exactly brilliantly) of producing a sensuous impression is proved by her brief flurry of excitement at the splendor of Epiphany in Jerusalem:

There besides gold or gems or silk you see nothing else; for if you see hangings they are of gold-striped silk, if you see curtains they are likewise of gold-striped silk. Moreover every kind of golden vessel [covered with] gems is brought out on that day. Could the number or weight moreover of the candelabra and candles or lamps and the divers sacred vessels be estimated or written? 9. For what do I say about the embellishment of that same structure, which Constantine in his mother's presence, in as great a quantity as he had in his kingdom, adorned with gold, mosaic and precious marble, and, as in the major church [on Golgotha], so the Anastasis and the Cross and the other holy places in Jerusalem? (xxv, 8–9)

Even here she avoids details with an *occupatio* ("Could the number . . . be written?"), and the splendid present tense leads her to remember the past in which that splendor was established.

The marvels that the empty wilderness of the Holy Land fermented in the brains of later devout travelers are almost entirely absent from Egeria's account. She speaks of a sycamore tree "which was planted, it is said, by the Patriarchs. Those who are ill go there and take away twigs, and it helps them" (VIII,3). But her recounting is laced with *dicetur*s, and it is brief. If she cares little about the visible world, she cares less about its mirages. Already there was plenty of the merely marvelous to be seen in the Holy Land. The Bourdeaux Pilgrim had expanded his format slightly upon reaching Palestine to include notes on places of interest to be seen on the way to Jerusalem: among them are mentioned a miraculous spring "in which, if a woman wash, she becomes pregnant," Egeria's healing sycamore, the boot marks and bloodstains left in the temple after the slaying of Zacharius, the very oak at Mambre that sheltered Abraham when he "spoke with angels, and ate food with them," the Dead Sea which "turns over" any man who tries to swim in it.[10] Egeria neglects such sensational details, and in the case of the Pillar of Salt, often seen and described by later pilgrims, remarks to her venerable sisters that she "saw the place, but no pillar; I cannot deceive you about this matter" (XII, 7).

Two lines of development are heralded in Egeria's unbendingly idealist document: one of absolute interest in the external world, as in *Wonders of the East* or *Mandeville's Travels*, and one exploring the subjective and autobiographical capacities of the form—*The Booke of Margery Kempe* or *Robinson Crusoe*. Egeria has resisted both imaginative pressures. Neither the physical world outside nor the emotional one within is permitted to engage our interest or distract us, as so many later pilgrims and readers were distracted, from the transcendental goal.

That transcendental goal seems to overwhelm the sense of specific geographical destination one might expect in a tale of pilgrimage, and so Egeria avoids what has since become one of the determining tensions of travel accounts: that between the interest of the way there and the interest of the destination. What is the imaginative destination of the traveler? In the case of pilgrimage in the later Middle Ages, the answer is clearer than for any other form of travel: the climax is Jerusalem (or later still, Compostella or Rome).[11] The way there is a series of distractions and tempta-

10. See Bourdeaux Pilgrim, "Itinerary from Bourdeaux to Jerusalem," 17–27.
11. The shift from Jerusalem to European destinations was a result of the Islamic conquest of the Holy Land. "When access to the Holy Places was blocked for a time

tions—frequently quite successful ones, but always seen as such.
Egeria's kind of pilgrimage, undertaken in a less Jerusalem-cen-
tered era and before the age of shrines, does not make such a clear
distinction between route and destination. Her account therefore
does not contain the elements of suspense and climax that animate
many later examples of the *peregrinatio*, however quietly. But that
she does see her first twenty-three chapters as a narrative, in which
motion is the constitutive trope, is demonstrated by her separate
treatment of the churches and liturgy of Jerusalem. Rather than
work them into her story, she brings us to the end of her travels (at
the point of writing) and then offers, in a kind of flashback, descriptions of the religious environment of her most important destination among many.

Here we might expect a flamboyance and a warmth of style
denied to her earlier, when the most important qualities of the
landscape were invisible, the events of a consecrating and already
written past. But where formulaic speech and extreme objectivity
effaced the visual images of her journey, attention to the forms of
ritual replaces the physical and architectural detail we might
expect in her description of Jerusalem. As the past was more
important than the present in her journeying, so the ritual is more
important than the temple here.

The bareness of her style could be seen to reflect a bareness of
perception, but it could as easily manifest a kind of Platonic scorn,
not only of mimesis but of the phenomena that constitute its subject. Those places that are valid topics make up a world essentially
invisible, past, and transcendent. There are in fact no "places,"
only "places where." The Holy Land is a spectacularly effective
rosary, and Egeria desires that at every bead, "the proper passage
from Scripture would be read," a prayer recited, and if possible "the
sacrifice offered."[12] And that is what she does. Traveling along a
route sanctified by Scripture, she reads aloud from the Bible and
participates in sacramental rites at every site, working continually
to elevate her raw sense experience into a form of communion

---

by Islam, there developed a tendency to 'reduplicate' the Palestinian shrines in the
Christian countries of Europe, either by imitation or through claim to a direct,
supernatural translation of material relics from Palestine to Europe" (Turner and
Turner, *Image and Pilgrimage in Christian Culture*, 168)—as in the case of the
Virgin's house at Loreto.

12. See, e.g., IV, XI, XIV, XV.

with that sacred world which *in illo tempore* merged for a while with this one. Her journey is a kind of psychodrama; it is a prayer and an *imitatio* in a territory that is itself only an *imitatio*. "It would be superfluous," she says, "to describe how the churches are decorated . . . on that day" (xxv, 8). She goes on to try, but it is indeed superfluous, and she breaks off: the celestial Jerusalem is the object of her desire, and its geographical shadow only a spur to meditation.

Egeria was not a literalist. More acutely than some of her medieval successors, she felt a difference between soul and body, holiness and icon, faith and belief. In her time the doctrine of the Transubstantiation had not yet been established, and the granting of indulgences to pilgrims was a rare practice only fifty years old or so. The numinous had not yet been made corporeal: heaven was earned by personal goodness, the Eucharist was understood to be symbolic, and faith to be a mystery of the imagination—not, as it tended to become in the hands of later missionaries, a logical conclusion arrived at from the evidence provided by miracles. Egeria then was not drawn to the concrete or to its rendering. Her account makes the leap from itinerary to prayer, avoiding the literary concerns of mimesis and verisimilitude. But her subject matter lent itself too easily, both as an experience and as a literary topic, to a concern with the actual. While attention to the actual alienness of the civilizations of the East was a long time in coming, the next travel account we will look at, Adamnan's *De locis sanctis*, displays a much greater concern with the physical presences of the Holy Land and exploits our interest in the traveler in significant, if fleeting and subtle ways.

Arculf and Adamnan

In the late seventh century, about three hundred years after the most probable date of Egeria's pilgrimage, Bishop Arculf, a Merovingian Gaul, was shipwrecked off the west coast of Britain. During his ensuing stay with Adamnan, abbot of the monastery at Iona and author of the famous biography of its founder, Saint Columban, he related the story of his three-year pilgrimage to the Holy Land, and Adamnan eventually wrote the account *De locis sanctis* from his notes. In some ways the account is not comparable to Egeria's *Peregrinatio*: it was written by someone other than the traveler himself and from a point in time well after the completion of those travels. Furthermore, we have the whole thing—beginning, middle, and *explicit*: twenty-two manuscripts and fragments are known and cataloged.

But despite these differences of provenance and compositional circumstance, the general purpose of the work is that of Egeria's letter: to permit stay-at-home Christians imaginative entrance to the places and events of the Holy Land on which their thoughts so often fastened. And it was one of the most influential accounts of its type, forming the basis for Bede's *De locis sanctis* and still read by prospective pilgrims as late as the fifteenth century, when Felix Fabri refers to it in his *Wanderings*.[13] It is at least interesting to consider the prevalence of such mediated accounts in this genre, the appeal of which would seem logically to originate in the eye-witnessing behind the text. The three most famous and influential works of this kind in the Western corpus—Marco Polo's *Description of the World, Mandeville's Travels*, and the *Journal* of Christopher Columbus—are also secondhand accounts, one way or another. Marco Polo dictated his adventures to his cell mate, a Frenchman; Mandeville plagiarized most of his material; and the journal of Columbus's first voyage has only reached us as edited, abridged, and partly summarized by Las Casas. Adamnan's work could be seen as one of the first in a line of important pieces of what might be termed collaboration or reinterpretation. Our modern sense that the first-person is a generic prerequisite in this form developed very gradually indeed. Epitomes of both Egeria's and Adamnan's accounts appear without distinction of kind in Peter the Deacon's twelfth-century compilation, *De locis sanctis*.

We have little notion of how many such narratives were written and lost during the three centuries between Egeria's and Arculf's pilgrimages, and it would be foolhardy to make of Egeria's account a literary norm against which to look at Adamnan's. But given the worldview within which Egeria's letter was composed, the relations then conventionally assumed between reader and writer, experience and sacred history, texts and Scriptures, it would not be outrageous to consider it an archetype, an artifact so inevitable in

13. See Fabri, *Wanderings of Felix Fabri*, 1:408, 409; 2:37.

its form that deviations from it or variations on it would be worth considering in its light.

How then does the collaborative effort of Adamnan and Arculf differ from the *Peregrinatio*?

By the time of *De locis sanctis*, pilgrimage literature seems more or less to have arrived. We have besides Jerome's secondhand accounts of pilgrimages made by members of his circle, the "Epitome" of Bishop Eucharius, the anonymous "Breviarus," Procopius's six books on the churches of Justinian, and two firsthand narratives by European pilgrims, Anthony of Piacenza and the *"archdiaconus"* Theodosius.[14] These are doubtless the fragmentary remains of a larger body of literature—most of the writers refer to other writers and their "reading" about the Holy Land. The predominant format is that of description rather than of narration, except in the case of Anthony, whose tale, chock-full of marvels and mistakes, announces the imminence of the pilgrimage corrupted by *curiositas* and the accompanying tradition of accounts written from what Percy Adams calls "creative memory."

Arculf and Adamnan were both learned and pious men, as fortified as possible against the encroachments of the idle, secular curiosity and gullibility which mark Anthony's account and, eventually, divert the enterprises of both pilgrimage and travel writing into the sphere of the fantastic. Clearly, times have changed if two members of the intellectual elite can collaboratively produce an account so much more gullible and marvelous than Egeria's, whose status and literary pretensions were so much humbler.

Like the *Peregrinatio*, *De locis sanctis* attempts to encompass both the sites of the Holy Land and the traveler's experience of them. It is not, however, a chronologically structured account. It begins in book 1 with a description of Jerusalem and covers the major sites of the Holy Land in descending order of their importance. This importance seems to be based on their distance, in scriptural time or miles, from the Passion. Thus, book 2 discusses places sanctified by their roles in the Old Testament or in the private and public life of Christ up until the events of the Passion,

14. For translations of all of these early works, as well as those of Egeria ("Saint Sylvia") and Arculf, see *Library of the Palestine Pilgrims' Text Society*, vols. 1 and 2.

and book 3 describes Constantinople and its churches. The final chapter in book 3 crosses a boundary the literature has more or less carefully observed before this time and devotes itself to a rather sensationalized account of the volcanic isle of Mt. Vulgan, twelve miles from Sicily.

The work then is not, as Egeria's was at least in part, a story. Nor is it told in the first person. The distracting presence of the eyewitness narrator is not a problem with which Adamnan has to deal. The object before our eyes is not that complex confluence of time, space, and consciousness, the *peregrinatio*; it is merely a landscape, *locus sanctus*. And the landscape itself, three hundred years more distant from the touch of Christ's feet (whose footprints it nevertheless still retains), is beginning to acquire a present tense. It is no longer only a place where something happened, where shadows play on a cave wall, but a place where things happen now. And the cave wall itself interests both Arculf and Adamnan.

The first paragraph of book 1 enumerates and describes the gates of the city of Jerusalem, in traditional clockwise order from west to south, and the second plunges directly into enthusiastic description of a contemporary marvel:

On the twelfth day of the month of September, he says, there is an annual custom whereby a huge concourse of people from various nations everywhere is wont to come together in Jerusalem to do business by mutual buying and selling. Consequently it happens inevitably that crowds of different peoples are lodged in this hospitable city for some days. Owing to the very great number of their camels, horses, asses, and oxen, all carriers of diverse merchandise, filth from their discharges spreads everywhere throughout the city streets, the stench providing no little annoyance to the citizens, and walking being impeded. Wonderful to relate, on the night of the day on which the said bands depart with their various beasts of burden, there is released from the clouds an immense downpour of rain, which descends on the city, and renders it clean of dirt by purging away all the abominable filth from the streets. For the site itself of Jerusalem is so arranged by God, its founder, on a gentle incline, falling away from the northern summit of Mount Sion to the low-lying regions at the northern and eastern walls, that this great flood of rain cannot by any means lie stagnant on the streets, but flows like torrents from the higher regions to the low-lying. The flood of heavenly waters, then, pouring through the eastern gates, and bearing all the filth and nuisance with it, enters the valley of Josaphat, swells the torrent of Cedron, and after such a baptism of Jerusalem straightway the copious flood ceases. Thus one should carefully note the magnitude and character of the honor which this chosen and famous city has in the sight of the eternal father, who does not suffer it to remain soiled for long, but quickly cleanses it out of reverence for his only begotten son, who has the honored place of his holy cross and resurrection within the compass of its walls. (Meehan, *Adaman's "De locis sanctis,"* 41–43)[15]

The third and last paragraph of the chapter describes a hastily built Saracen prayer house erected on the site of the temple. The temple is not tied to the sacred past by a recounting of any famous incident that took place there; the prayer house is described in careful detail. The chapter contains no mention of the sacred past, except briefly to explain the cause of the marvelous cleansing, or in nostalgic indignation to point out an irony of present-day Jerusalem—that there is a Saracen prayer house "where once the temple arose in its magnificence" (43).

This first chapter is paradigmatic of the work. The emotions that move it are wonder and nostalgia, as opposed to Egeria's awe and carefully maintained focus on the vanished but living past. Wonder and nostalgia characterize a state of mind more susceptible to secular stimuli, and *De locis sanctis* contains a far greater number of references to places, objects, and events that are simply interesting.

It is difficult to know what to make of the miracles with which the book is filled. Jonathan Sumption's explanation of medieval credulity in this matter, though it concerns "educated men of the twelfth and thirteenth centuries," is applicable and persuasive:

If the majority . . . accepted the evidence for miracles, it was not because they were unduly credulous or irrational, still less because they cared nothing for the truth. It was rather because in assessing the evidence they applied criteria very different from those of David Hume. They may often have been misled by lying witnesses, but the fundamental cause of their

15. All quotations from Adamnan will be cited by page numbers from Denis Meehan's edition and translation, *Adamnan's "De locis sanctis."* Meehan gives the Latin and English texts on facing pages.

error was that they considered a miracle to be a normal, though nonetheless remarkable, incident of life. . . . Thus they did not require the same high standard of proof as the eighteenth century philosopher, and indeed they were inclined to attribute events to the intervention of the Almighty which could quite easily have been explained without. Men accepted the evidence for particular miracles because they passionately desired to believe in miracles in general. (*Pilgrimage*, 65)

This adequately explains Adamnan's acceptance of Arculf's story about the miraculous yearly cleansing of Jerusalem, but it does not quite explain Arculf's story itself. The story reads like an eyewitness account in its breathless expanse of detail, and Arculf, who lived in Jerusalem for at least nine months, was almost certainly there in September. Perhaps it rained after the fair that year, and local people, spotting him as a gull, invented the story of its regular occurrence for his entertainment. But again and again we hear of regularly occurring marvels the bishop has managed to experience himself. Every year on the anniversary of the Ascension, a high wind passes over the church of the Ascension on Mt. Olivet, knocking worshipers to the ground. And "he himself was actually present in the church on Mt. Olivet at the very hour when that intense blast rushed in on the day of the Lord's ascension" (*De locis sanctis*, 69). We would have to imagine an identical scenario to explain this experience, and then there is the Sicilian volcano that "thunders more on Fridays and Saturdays" (121), not to mention the improbable crocodiles that drag oxen into the water by one foot and devour them. That both Arculf and Adamnan are gullible is obvious from the secondhand accounts of miracles that Arculf passes on. But the kind of gullibility that creates a perception of miraculous experience in the observer himself is mysterious in its origin and function.

The Holy Land has begun to be sensationalized. Where the Holy Paula "by the eyes of faith . . . could see the Infant Lord, wrapped in swaddling clothes, wailing in the manger, the Magi adoring, the star shining above, the Virgin mother, the careful nursing" (Jerome, "Pilgrimage of the Holy Paula," 7), Arculf at the same spot sees a miraculous, but phenomenal, channel full of "the purest water," "the water of the first ablution of the Lord's little body after the nativity," which has filled the channel "from that very day up to our time" (Adamnan, *De locus sanctis*, 75–77).

"Our friend Arculf saw it with his own eyes and washed his face in it": the increased literalism of the pilgrim's expectations and perceptions is accompanied by Adamnan's stress on empiricism. Almost all sensational details are followed by the avowal that "noster Arculfus" saw, heard, or touched the miraculous event or object under discussion. Arculf is a gull because underneath he is a Doubting Thomas: "Wonderful to relate, to this day there remain in the marble column [where Saint George was flogged] the prints of [a hard-hearted unbeliever's] ten fingers inserted up to the roots, and into this place the holy Arculf inserted his own ten fingers, they likewise penetrating up to the roots" (115).[16]

The cumulative effect of this stress on Arculf as an eyewitness (despite his replacement by the narrating voice of Adamnan) is to make the text sound like evidence in the case for the supernatural and sacred. Of course, Britain was fairly recently Christianized and the Church was to some extent still actually involved in making such a case. Miracles were an important card in its hand. But the audience of Adamnan's work was bound to be an already converted one, as literacy in his time was almost entirely limited to the religious orders, and thus the sensational and experiential bent of the text must be seen to reflect a predilection shared by pilgrim, author, and audience alike.

Perhaps the far greater distance in time between Adamnan and Arculf and the events of the New Testament accounts for the anxiety this predilection betrays. This distance is certainly an emotional factor in Arculf's experience. The past in his eyes is a more ephemeral thing than it had been in Egeria's or Paula's "eyes of faith." They seemed to see it reenacted as they passed along; Arculf sees its ruins:

Chebron, which is also Mambre, once the metropolis of the Phillistines and the dwelling place of giants, and in which David reigned for seven

16. The reasonable question Why should an infidel "insert his fingers" into the relic? is not to be asked here. The infidels of such miraculous fables are frequently as eager as any Christian to touch or steal the relics of the Holy Land. Their function in the fables is to draw miraculous signs of the Divine anger with their blasphemous touch. The plausibility of their motives is irrelevant.

years, nowadays, as Arculf relates, has no surrounding walls; and amongst the ruined remains a few vestiges only are to be seen of the city long ago destroyed. There are, however, some crudely constructed streets and detached houses too, some inside and some outside the broken-down walls, all along the level ground. (79)

After the destruction of three cities on the same site, wonderful to relate, the house of Raab alone remained, the woman who hid the two spies that were sent over by Jesu Ben Nun in the upper room of her house by means of linen straw. Its roofless stone walls are still extant. Crops and vineyards cover the site of the whole city, which is bare of human habitation and without a single dwelling. Large palm groves lie between the site of the ruined city and the river Jordan, and in the midst of them, at intervals, are little clearings in which some very miserable folk of Canaanite stock have very numerous houses. (85)

The ruins Adamnan dwells on are another kind of evidence for the reality of the sacred. Though they are ruins they are palpable, and their palpability seems to stir a sadness in both the pilgrim, who noticed so much, and the author, who did not leave it out. They are evidence not only of the past but of its remoteness, of the fact that it is over. As sheer evidence they are no doubt comforting; as ruins, alienating and nostalgic.

That ruins should receive such full, detailed, and evocative treatment, per ruins, underlines the orientation of *De locis sanctis* toward the contemporary presence of the Holy Land. This will eventually blossom into a kind of primitive anthropological tendency in travel accounts (and, ultimately, into anthropology itself), but at this early stage it registers more pointedly the preoccupation of the early medieval church with alienation. F. C. Gardiner and Gerhart Ladner stress the importance of this topos as it appears in the religious writings of the Middle Ages, and the great age of the Irish religious exile was in full swing in Arculf's time.[17] Pilgrimage, as Gardiner points out, could be seen as an intensely ambivalent experience: the real destination, the celestial Jerusalem, is unreachable, and the arrival at what might have come to seem, from far away, sacred territory would only make more vivid

17. See Gardiner, *Pilgrimage of Desire*, and Gerhart B. Ladner, *"Homo Viator*: Medieval Ideas on Alienation and Order."

the absence of sacred events and presences from the mundane world of which, after all, it is a part.

The Irish purists avoided this ultimate disappointment in their refusal to search out any destination:

Their distinctive contribution to the spiritual life of the 'dark ages' was the idea of the aimless wanderer whose renunciation of the world was the most complete of which man could conceive. . . . By wandering freely without destination, the Irish hermit felt that he had cut himself off from every material accessory to life. In his eighth sermon Saint Columban dwells on the transitory nature of life and declares, 'I know that if this earthly tent of mine is taken down, I shall get a new home from God made by no human hands. It makes me sigh, this longing for the shelter of my heavenly habitation . . . for I know that while I am in my body I am traveling away from God.' The notion of a specific destination did not enter into Columban's thinking; his only destination was the heavenly Jerusalem. (Sumption, *Pilgrimage*, 95)

Adamnan, Saint Columban's successor and biographer, seems alive to this Celtic sadness and accentuates those aspects of Arculf's account which reflect its source. Of course there is a great spiritual gap between the aimless Celtic wanderer and the "sedulous visitor of holy places," as Adamnan calls Arculf. But the *contemptus mundi* of one seems the reaction of a more stoic temperment to the same daunted desire that provokes credulity in the other.

Egeria does not mention places that are not holy places or, for the most part, aspects of the holy places that are not connected with religion in some way. She seems to feel that there is something profane in attention to other topics, and not only in the context of her letter. In describing the conversation of a certain "sanctus episcopus" at Haran she says, "I do not want Your Affection to think of the monks that they ever speak of anything but the Scriptures of God or of the acts of the great monks" (xx, 13). The literary result of this attitude is a coherence in the image she projects of Palestine and Egypt which is lacking in Adamnan's work. Egeria's *Peregrinatio* is unified by a rigid selectivity; instead of sketching a living and palpable culture, she presents us with a museum in which the occasional darting appearance of a native of the Levant comes to seem like a glimpse of a derelict loiterer in the lobby.

Arculf noted and remembered, and Adamnan included in his text, data that often reminds us as much of this world as of the other. (It is noteworthy that one place where the fifteenth-century pilgrim Felix Fabri refers to Adamnan's book in his own is in a passage on the subject of the "wild honey" of the Palestinian desert.) The chapters "Concerning the vineyards and crops of Mt. Olivet," "Concerning the color of the Jordan," "Concerning locusts and wild honey," "Concerning Alexandria, the river Nile, and its crocodiles," "Concerning Mt. Vulgan," to name a few, represent a significantly altered idea of a subject matter that seems before Arculf and Adamnan to have acquired a certain stability in its topics. The consistently devotional orientation of previous writers had produced an imaginary spot on the world's atlas, a Holy Land with no life of its own, a penitential Paradise inhabited only by ascetics and visited only by pilgrims. Arculf is more of a true traveler, in the modern sense. Where Egeria vitalized the itinerary form by imposing a vision on its list of names and establishing relations between those names and human experience, Adamnan has implicitly added another set of relations, shattering and widening the frame of the vision. This new set of relations joins the Holy Land to the rest of the merely phenomenal world. The criterion according to which Adamnan includes or discards Arculf's data is that of strangeness, which reflects domestic assumptions in illustrating foreign deviations from the "normal." Neither Arculf nor Adamnan is consciously comparative. But with every note of wonder struck at the difference of Levantine flora, fauna, topography, or climate, one's impression grows stronger that this pilgrim has a home, a background that puts the wild honey and the crocodiles into such vivid relief that, to use Adamnan's formula, they "ought not, it seems, to be passed over" ("hoc . . . non esse pratereundum videtur").

There must be some further criterion according to which Adamnan limits the amount of secular data included in his book. What is allowable and relevant in a book called *De locis sanctis* and what is not? The most conspicuous absence in the work is the absence of "natives." Palestinians and Egyptians do not interest the writer, neither singly nor as cultural groups. Christians, "worshipers," the bodies of pilgrims rotting on "the plot which is called Aldemach," the Burgundian hermit Peter, who acts as Arculf's guide at Nazareth, and a few "believing Jews" receive mention, but not those exotic natives whose ways are irresistable topics to Marco Polo and Mandeville. Arculf's eye seems to have been for places, places made strange by miracles, by their connection with sacred history, or merely by their difference from Gaul. This difference may be a matter of exotic fauna, but never of exotic human customs. If the Other World has become phenomenal by the time of Arculf and Adamnan, it does not yet seem to provide a significant cultural complement to the West. It is a world both sub- and superhuman, in which there is no simply human reality but that of the amazed and alienated traveler himself.

The outer circumference of the work limits it to the Holy Land and its inner restrictions to places within the Holy Land made strange by miracles or exotica. The scope and perspective of *De locis sanctis*, once perceived, offer no surprises until the end. Adamnan was a writer interested in his craft. His sentences are involved and stylistically self-conscious; he quotes poetry and Scripture accurately, compares Arculf's accounts with those in his library, and retells the pilgrim's miraculous anecdotes with a flair for narrative. The work is almost fussily divided and subdivided into books and chapters: the divisions are logical, and the separate chapters maintain a fairly organic internal unity. The peculiarity of the last chapter is then worthy of speculation: it is not only not about a holy place; it is not about a place in the Holy Land. The art of closure was not forgotten in the "dark ages": why does Adamnan end a work like this with a chapter about a European volcano? He is perfectly aware that he is writing a conclusion. His final paragraph describes the circumstances and difficulties of the text's composition and begs us to pray for him and for Arculf. But the only connection the penultimate paragraph has with the idea of conclusion is that it describes what was apparently the last strange thing that Arculf saw on his journey.[18]

This gives the book a symmetry that may help to resolve the

---

18. Adamnan was not to be alone in choosing to close with a volcano, though he is the first to break the decorum of the pilgrimage account with one. We will come across another "burning mountain" in the next chapter, and medieval travel literature is prolific of them, turning them eventually into "mouths of hell" and, as Patch notes in *The Other World*, poetic images of the barrier by which we are kept out of the Earthly Paradise. (See chap. 2.)

aesthetic problem: the book begins by relating a marvel witnessed at the geographic climax of the journey and ends with a marvel seen as close to home as Arculf could get without having actually returned. A parallel is set up that to Egeria would have seemed sacriligious, if she had been able to perceive it at all. To Adamnan the parallel is logical and apparently pleasing, as indeed all parallels and symmetries were to medieval imaginations.

The common denominator among the places in *De locis sanctis* is not holiness, clearly, but strangeness. That most of what was strange was also holy validates the title of the work, but points out a new quality in the charm of the Holy Land. No longer simply a giant icon for the meditative consciousness, it is becoming a receptacle for imaginative projection. But that Other World, visible more recently through Keats's "magic casements" and Yeats's "collarbone of a hare," is not, to Adamnan, the merely posited desideratum of the melancholy Romantics; it is a place on this earth. It is tantalizing and frustrating to the pilgrim whose ultimate goal is a sight of the face of God, but as the magnetized center of that strangeness in which the medieval European glimpsed His existence most positively, it is accessible and encouraging and "ought not, it seems, to be passed over."

Strangeness, as we are about to see, had a demonic aspect as well, which appealed by way of the subversion rather than suggestion of the holy. The phenomenal strangeness of miracles and crocodiles lies midway between the holy strangeness of Egeria's time travel and the grotesque inversions and perversions of European nature imagined in the rhetoric of "wonder books." The grotesquery we will examine next has a largely pagan heritage and an unseemliness that kept it out of the pilgrimage narratives which provided the bulk of medieval travel writing before Marco Polo. But its formal qualities were long-lived and influential, and its single-minded focus on the monstrous and marvelous reminds us again that, whatever the particular purposes and decorums of medieval accounts of the world beyond Europe, strangeness was the central experiential fact. Egeria's experience (whatever it may have been) is so thoroughly spiritualized, and thus organized, in the *Peregrinatio* that the phenomenal alienity of Palestine is erased for the reader, although its numinous otherworldliness is extreme. What we will next observe is a world stripped of spirit and past, a world so merely phenomenal that even order is abandoned and nature is set free, not only of theology but of natural law itself. Theologians would try to interpret it, and natural historians to explain it, but, like anything grotesque, its allure precedes rationalization and eludes it.

A two-headed baby eyes some popular monsters of Eastern lore: Sciopod, Cyclops, Blemmyae, Doghead. Printed in Sebastian Münster's *Cosmographiae universalis*, lib. vi. Basel, 1554. Courtesy of the John Carter Brown Library at Brown University.

2

The Fabulous East

"Wonder Books" and
Grotesque Facts

To the great Matters of medieval literature—of Britain, of Rome, of Troy—it is time to add a recognition of the Matter of the East: an emphatically marvelous body of traditional lore and symbol available to anyone who undertook to set a narrative in Asian territories. The major difference in this case is that the Matter of the East—primarily geographical and ethnographic in substance, rather than a source of character and plot motifs—was just as likely to turn up in the ostensibly factual accounts of travelers and geographers as in romance. This lore was couched in the present tense and thus less distanced from the "real" world inhabited by those who chose to believe in it.

Wonders of the East is an early medieval vernacular avatar of the Matter of the East—which Matter naturally insinuates itself into the rhetorical development of the travel book. Although *Wonders* is apparently a Christian work (the earliest devoted exclusively or even predominantly to the natural marvels of this Matter), its link with the classical and pagan past is far stronger and more pertinent than is Egeria's. A brief outline of the Matter's history and of the wide range of its forms and applications must be articulated before we can examine the form in which it is transmitted by *Wonders*. This chapter will have to touch on texts from as early as the fifth century B.C. to as late as the era of scholasticism—a sizable expanse of what Braudel calls "social time." But there is barely an hour of intellectual time between Ctesias and the Renaissance scholar Lilius, who in 1493 could publish a serious tract called *Contra antipodes* while Columbus was reporting antipodal Amazons and mermaids from the old Macrobian "burning zone," where nothing was supposed to live.[1]

To the Greek historian Ctesias (fl. 400 B.C.) the East was India; to the author of *Wonders of the East* it was Egypt and Babylonia. "The East" is a concept separable from any purely geographical area. It is essentially "Elsewhere." All four cardinal points equally imply the word *far* when used as place names, and at different times and from different vantages, all four have been suspect (the North to imperial Rome, the West to the Chinese, and so on). The Greek authors who first promulgated the marvels material in Europe tended to concentrate on the Eastern "Elsewhere" for historical reasons: they saw more of Asia than of other distant areas and came into political conflict with it. Their medieval inheritors and plagiarists continued what had become a traditional identification of monsters with the East—partly, at least at first, out of habit.

The Matter belongs to many genres, by its presence tying together more or less responsible geography, the Alexander romances, parody such as Lucian's *A True Story* (and much later, *Mandeville's Travels*), the *periploi* of Greek and Alexandrian exploratory travel, and a spate of "wonder books." It appears as well in encyclopedias, bestiaries, herbals, and lapidaries and finds representation in the architectural ornamentation of churches, on world maps, and in the marginal illumination of all kinds of books. Although the romances merely exploit the appeal of this lore, and Lucian openly derides it, as a body of "fact" it raised serious issues (as we will see) for some of the finest minds of the Middle Ages. And its persistent appearance in documentary travel books helped shape for Europe a world picture that would inform the discovery and rediscovery of both the East and the New World (with practical and even dire consequences for many indigenous peoples).

From a modern perspective, discussion of *Wonders'* literary context might seem best broken down into discussions of early geography, early ethnography, and early historical romance. But that would be to some degree anachronistic: although modern critics distinguish sharply between the history of Herodotus, the "romances" of Ctesias, and the "anthropological data" of Agathar-

---

1. For a thorough survey of the Greek and Roman literary genres concerned with travel, exploration, and Indian lore, see James Romm, "The Edges of the Earth in Ancient Thought" (Ph.D. diss.). His last chapter deals with Renaissance fabulous-voyage texts as well.

chides, they all belonged together to the ninth-century epitomizer, Photius, in whose *Bibliotheka* all found a home (though, it is true, his remarks about Ctesias are not welcoming).[2]

If Ctesias fathered the travel romance whose greatest successor, according to some, was the "mendacious" Mandeville, his most recent French editor and translator credits him with more practical influences as well:

He created delights for collectors of marvels, but serious authors read him: among them, Plato, Xenephon, Ephorus and Plutarch, and Aristotle borrowed from him.

There is more.

The famous student of Aristotle, Alexander himself, seems to have been attracted by the accounts of Ctesias. Nearchus, his admiral, attests that [these] accounts of the Orient had exersized the imagination of the prince as much as that of his historians. If the spirits of Alexander and Ctesias met in Hell, I do not doubt that the latter claimed for himself the greater part of the initiative which raised up the expedition to Asia. Men willingly let themselves be guided by mirages, and if the realism which is commonly recognized in Alexander blossomed on the way of a little dream born of a marvelous tale of Persia or of India, we can say of Ctesias that he helped more to make history than he can help us to write it. (Henry, *La Perse, L'Inde*, 8)

The story of Ctesias's influence on the conqueror will be repeated over and over during the course of Europe's discovery of the East (and West). History and geography boil down to legend and lure the traveler or explorer abroad; he both corrects and adds to the material of the legend, is himself vulgarized in the popular imagination, and lures on the next wave of discovery. Ctesias is heavily dependent on Herodotus (although he claims to have witnessed, or heard from witnesses, most of what he recounts); following the "mirage" of his fabulous East, Alexander and his conquests opened the way for far more responsible treatments of the territories he entered. But the histories and *periploi* of such contemporaries as Callisthenes, Nearchus, and Clitarchus fed in their turn well over a millennium of ever more improbable romances, whose data infiltrated the documentary accounts of such later rediscoverers of the East as Marco Polo and Odoric of Pordenone. It

2. The works of Ctesias are extant only in the epitomes of Photius.

almost seems as though the more degenerate the source, the greater the Matter's appeal.

This should not be mysterious: the history of travel, exploration, and discovery is mainly an achievement of men of action and unlearned people—not of scholars like Photius and Lilius, who thought they could distinguish fact from fantasy and preferred the former. A truly well-informed Columbus would never have set out for the East by sailing West. The best authorities knew better than he how far away were the western shores of Cathay. The appeal of the mirage may have been responsible in the end for more new knowledge than the merely abstract satisfactions of truth.

The marvels material appears at the geographical limits of knowledge—at the borders of the map, the farthest reach of the journey. Even the most responsible geographical works can be seen to modulate into the rhetoric of romance as those limits are reached. Herodotus knew Egypt well and rationalized whatever he found there. His thoroughly documented crocodiles are interesting but not wonderful. They belong to nature. But as he gets closer to each of the extremes of the known world, legends and marvels accumulate in his text, and even his famous skepticism does not so wholly reject them as leave them out. North of Scythia,

the country is said to be concealed from sight and made impassable by reason of the feathers which are shed abroad abundantly. The earth and air are alike full of them, and this it is which prevents the eye from obtaining any view of the region. (III,7)[3]

In the extreme west of Africa is

the mountain called Atlas, very taper[ed] and round; so lofty, moreover, that the top (it is said) cannot be seen, the clouds never quitting it either summer or winter. [The natives] . . . are reported not to eat any living thing, and never to have any dreams. (IV, 184)

At the southern limit,

Arabia is the last of the inhabited lands towards the south, and it is the only country which produces frankincense, myrrh, cassia, cinnamon, and

3. It is only fair to add that in a later chapter he unravels this particular marvel by adducing for it an origin in metaphor: "the Scythians, with their neighbors, call the snow-flakes feathers because, I think, of the likeness which they bear to them" (IV, 31).

ledanum. . . . The trees which bear the frankincense are guarded by winged serpents, small in size, and of varied colours, whereof vast numbers hang about every tree. . . . The Arabians say that the whole world would swarm with these serpents, if they were not kept in check in the way in which I know vipers are. (III, 107–8)

After explaining how the Indians gather their gold by stealing it on camelback from the swift, dog-sized ants that dig it up, he makes a generalization that will be echoed (with various distortions) in maps and travel books for millennia:

It seems as if the extreme regions of the earth were blessed by nature with the most excellent productions, just in the same way that Greece enjoys a climate more excellently tempered than any other country. In India, which . . . is the furthest region of the inhabited world towards the east, all the four-footed beasts and the birds are very much bigger than those found elsewhere. . . . Gold too is produced there in vast abundance. . . . And further, there are trees which grow wild there, the fruit whereof is a wool exceeding in beauty and goodness that of sheep. (III, 106)

He is not always so complimentary—western Libya is full of "dog-faced creatures, and the creatures without heads" (IV, 191), and many of the Indian tribes are made to sound brutish: not only do they not bury their dead, they often eat them (III, 98–101). But on the whole, Herodotus is antiquity's most just and skeptical chronicler of the East.

Ctesias calls Herodotus a liar and glories in the monstrous and marvelous images that provoke the latter's doubt. A comparison between his *Indika* and the India of the earlier historian reveals an important fact about the marvels material—its mobility. Ctesias moves the dogheads (cynocephali) to India from Libya, and the gold-guarding griffins are transported there from northern Europe. This is historically the direction in which the chiefest among the marvels moved—to the furthest East, to die a natural death at last in the European colonial settlement of Columbus's "Cathay" and "Ophir."

The point at which knowledge gave out at last varied from book to book according to the gullibility and egotism of the author. What lay beyond that point was anyone's guess, but—oddly—few guessed. Herodotus, as always, is the most levelheaded in his attitude: "For my part, I cannot but laugh when I see numbers of persons drawing maps of the world without having any reason to guide them; making, as they do, the ocean stream to run all round the earth, and the earth itself to be an exact circle. . . . Till you reach India the country is peopled; but further east it is void of inhabitants, and no one can say what sort of region it is" (IV, 36, 40).

The author of the *Periplus of the Erythraean Sea* (c. A.D. 100) expresses a sense of the unknown destined for a more fruitful history than Herodotus's calm acceptance. The *Periplus* ends with this sentence: "The lands beyond these places, on account of excessive winters, hard frosts, and inaccessible country, are unexplored—perhaps also on account of some divine power of the gods" (57).

We are about to see this notion of taboo again in *Wonders*, and Christian topography eventually gives it a definite image by placing the forbidden territory of the Earthly Paradise in the farthest East. In his *Christian Topography*, Cosmas Indicopleustes, the earliest of medieval Christian cosmographers, places the Earthly Paradise in the circle of land he postulates as surrounding the impassable Ocean Stream and from which humankind was floated to the *orbis terrarum* during the Flood of Noah: "if Paradise did exist in this earth of ours [i.e., in the *orbis terrarum*], many a man among those who are keen to know and enquire into all kinds of subjects, would think he could not be too quick in getting there: for if there be some who to procure silk for the miserable gains of commerce, hesitate not to travel to the uttermost ends of the earth, how should they hesitate to go where they would gain a sight of Paradise itself?" (47).

What Cosmas signifies by placing Paradise across the Ocean Stream, other writers and theorists would signify by surrounding it with walls of flame and/or impenetrable rock, or with the "Vale Perilous," or by situating it on an unscalable height to which even the waters of the Flood had not reached. A surprising number of *itineraria* and *cosmographiae* end with the description of one or another "burning hill" (and "burning hills" becomes thus representative of the contents of such books in one Renaissance cosmographer's remarks).[4] *Wonders of the East* is no exception, and in

4. "By [cosmographie], in so small a lumpe, or piece of clay, beholding such strange formes of men, beastes, foules, and fishes: such diversities of times, such burning hills, such mervelous stones, metalles and plants, we are inforced to confesse th'omnipotncy, and wonderous worke of God." William Cunningham, *Cosmographical Glasse* (1559), Avr.

two of its three British manuscripts, this final volcano is followed by a warning spoken from his "magical books" by the biblical wizard Jamnes to his brother Mambres: "Hail brother; I am not unjustly dead, but truly and justly I am dead, and God's judgement stands against me because I alone was wiser than all other sorcerers."[5]

The limit of geographical knowledge, wherever located, was a point commonly charged with moral significance and, even in pre-Christian times, with divine dangerousness. (The Hades of the *Odyssey* and the Colchis of the *Argonautica*, for instance, are each located in their respective texts at the end of a long passage of geographical *descriptio*.) As we will soon see from an examination of *Wonders*, this dangerousness had an appeal that could neutralize the odium attached to intellectual overreaching (*curiositas*) by Christian mythology and dogma. The charm of the monstrous and marvelous data that accumulated magnetically around the borders of the known was not to be denied. And so it was moralized. By the time Rabanus Maurus revised the *Etymologia* of Isidore of Seville, attaching allegorical and eschatological meanings to the marvels, the practice of "reading" monsters and marvels was centuries old: in the *City of God* Augustine already speaks of it (though scathingly) as an art.[6]

This was to be the fate of the marvels in most medieval writings; from bestiary to lapidary, from the *City of God* to the *Gesta romanorum*, the material, which more and more exclusively belonged to the Matter of the East, was destined to be read and known as a kind of perverse Scripture, an upside-down map of the moral universe.

This Matter formed the licentious fringe of a geography that was itself amenable to interpretation, despite its status as a science. As

5. Gibb, *"Wonders of the East,"* 98. See note 8, below.

6. "Those who divine by such signs are often at fault in the predictions they base on them; or they may give true forecasts, under the influence of evil spirits . . . ; or else in the course of their many predictions they may from time to time hit upon some truth. How all this comes about, it is up to these interpreters to decide!" (21.8.983). Monsters and prodigies had, not surprisingly, formed material for the arts of prognostication at least as far back as Homer, and one can see a natural extension of that art in the Christian moralization of the monstrous races said to inhabit Asia and Africa. For an account of the art (and science) of teratology in antiquity, from Homer to Augustine, see Wendy Morgan's Ph.D. dissertation "Constructing the Monster: Notions of the Monstrous in Classical Antiquity," especially chapter 1, "Monstrum Quod Monstrat." My thanks to John Friedman for loaning me his copy of this fascinating study from Down Under.

Eusebius had moralized the architecture of Constantine, so the ecclesiasts and clerics who constituted most of the fully literate population were to moralize the shape of the earth, the division into three parts of its land mass (see fig. 1), the location of Jerusalem, the climate of Europe, and so on. For a number of reasons, geography in the hands of literate Christians was the most "wonderful" of medieval sciences, excessively rich in meaning and far poorer than pagan geography in empirical or mathematical data.

The symbolic equation of the moralizers worked in both directions: it could also create geographical formulations to fit a spiritual truth. Thus, to take an extreme instance, rather than choosing to moralize the round world inherited from pagan antiquity, Cosmas Indicopleustes substituted a rectangular world derived from the description of the Tabernacle in the Pentateuch. As this allegorical and oversignificant understanding of geography would have enormous staying power and is essential to an understanding of the development and decay of medieval travel literature, I quote his verbal map in full:

Yea, even the blessed Moses having been ordered on Mt. Sinai to make the Tabernacle according to the pattern which he had seen, said under divine inspiration, that the outer Tabernacle was a pattern of this visible world. Now the divine Apostle in the epistle to the Hebrews, in explaining the inner Tabernacle, or that which was within the veil, declares that it was a pattern of the heavenly—that is, of the kingdom of the heavens or the future state, taking the veil which divides the one Tabernacle in two for the firmament, just as the firmament placed in the middle, between the heaven and the earth, has made two worlds—this world namely, and that which is to come, into which world to come the first who entered was the forerunner on our behalf, Christ, who thus prepared for us a new and living way. Now in his description of the first Tabernacle, Moses places in the south of it the candlestick, with seven lamps, after the number of days in the week—these lamps being typical of the celestial luminaries—and shining on the table placed in the north of the earth. On this table again he ordered to be daily placed twelve loaves of shewbread, according to the number of the twelve months of the year—three loaves at each corner of the table, to typify the three months between each of the four tropics. He commanded also to be wreathed all around the rim of the table a waved moulding, to represent a multitude of waters, that is, the ocean; and further, in the circuit of the waved work, a crown to be set of the circumference of the palm of the hand, to represent the land beyond the ocean, and encircling it, where in the east lies Paradise, and where also the extremities of the heaven are bound to the extremities of the earth. And from this description we not only learn concerning the luminaries and the stars that most of them, when they rise, run their course through the south, but from the same source we are taught that the earth is surrounded by the ocean, and further that beyond the ocean there is another earth by which the ocean is surrounded. (*Christian Topography*, 42–44)

Cosmas takes the implications of the medieval world map to their logical end: not only is the "pattern of this visible world" understood to signify transcendent spiritual meanings, but the cosmographer's only and sufficient source of data is a passage from Scripture. The geographical "pattern" itself is derived from a sacred description of a sacred object.[7]

The spherical earth and inhabited antipodal regions of the pagan philosophers proved to be theological nightmares for Christian writers, especially during the long absence of Aristotle and Ptolemy, their most compelling expositors. Old Testament cosmography said nothing of a round earth, and the Gospels spoke of the Word of God as available to all men. How then could there be men beneath the burning zone, across which the inhabitants of the *orbis terrarum* could not pass to proselytize? Theological rigor necessitated the construction of a geography more literary than empirical, conforming at whatever cost to the literal and implicit cosmography of Scripture.

The built-in significances that resulted from the attachment of theology to geography, and of moral allegory to natural history, are of course decisive in any attempt to situate the corpus of premodern travel literature between the extremes of science and fiction. A more detailed discussion of this issue will be taken up in chapter 4. But for now we are especially interested in the Matter's other and more pagan side. The lore of the East depended ultimately, until Marco Polo, on pagan sources, and the literature of travel preserved the pagan, amoral, secular aspects of its appeal better than any other literary host. Even today, travel can be pilgrimage. But even yesterday, it could be escape as well. We are

---

7. Several world maps based on Cosmas's fundamentalist geography have been recently reproduced in volume 1 of *The History of Cartography, Cartography in Prehistoric, Ancient, and Medieval Europe and the Mediterranean*, ed. J. B. Harley and David Woodward.

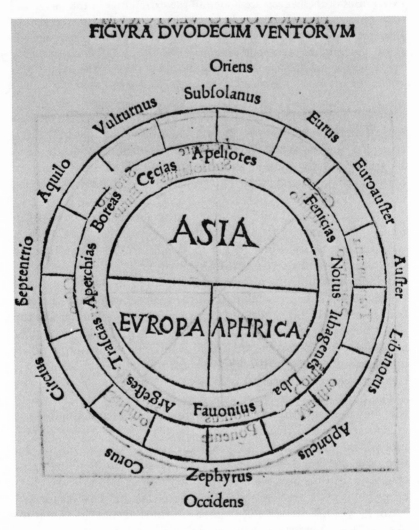

Fig. 1. A "T-O" type *mappa mundi*, showing the division of the world's land mass into three parts (one for each of Noah's sons). From an untitled collection of cosmographical works by Zaccherius Lilius. Florence, 1496. Courtesy of the John Carter Brown Library at Brown University.

about to take a look at the subversive side of travel literature, at the roots in legend and the grotesque of that secular exoticism which in *Mandeville's Travels* will turn at last to *charitas*.

Wonders of the East

The three British manuscripts of *Wonders of the East* (one in Latin, one in Old English, and one in both) are short collections of seemingly disconnected *descriptiones*, sketchily detailing a number of unusual human and animal "races," as well as a few strange plants and artifacts, vaguely located in the East. We will have to begin discussion of *Wonders* by treating the work as an apparent paradox: a transparent, denotative piece of exposition which is nevertheless organized symbolically and which can be best understood if we expand the term *grotesque* to include images of the actual. This paradox is made most concretely evident in the circumstances of the text's binding. Together with its copious and fantastic illustrations (see fig. 2 for an illustrated page from Cotton Tiberius Bv), all three of the British manuscripts are bound in miscellanies: two of them (Cotton Tiberius Bv, pt. 1, and Bodley 614) are basically scientific in theme. In the third and most famous of these codices, however, Cotton Vitellius Axv, *Wonders* is bound together with *Beowulf* and the Old English biblical poem *Judith*.[8] Because of this it has usually been treated, although with scorn until recently, as a (failed) literary work. Its latest American editor, Paul Gibb, has tried to appeal the verdict of literary failure: his edition includes a convincing structural interpretation which acquits the work of earlier charges that it is a mindlessly chaotic assortment of naïve and xenophobic rumors. But the problem runs

8. The combined Latin and Old English text of *Wonders* in Cotton Tiberius Bv is available in a magnificent photographic facsimile of that codex, published by Early English Manuscripts in Facsimile: *An Eleventh-Century Anglo-Saxon Miscellany*, ed. Patrick McGurk, Ann Knock, et al. The OE version in Cotton Vitellius Axv is in print in a diplomatic edition edited by Stanley Rypins for the Early English Text Society: *Three Old English Prose Texts in Cotton Vitellius A xv*. The Latin of Bodley 614 and Tiberius, together with all their Continental relatives, is printed in Appendix 2 of Paul Gibb's Ph.D. dissertation, "*Wonders of the East*: A Critical Edition and Commentary." I have translated the passages quoted in this chapter from Gibb's OE text, a conflation of Tiberius and Vitellius, and cited them according to his numbering. Further bibliographical information is available in McGurk, Knock, et al.

Fig. 2. Folio 85r of Cotton Tiberius Bv, part 1; on the right is one of the "women with hair down to their heels and oxen's feet." By permission of the British Library.

deeper than the solution of charging other medievalists with failure to recognize a literary structure. The medieval tendency,
already noted among the geographers, to regard all data as figurative and susceptible of allegorical understanding confounds the
modern urge to categorize written works into literary and nonliterary, imaginative and factual. And while literary theorists have
done much in recent years to educate us away from that urge, the
paradox of *Wonders* goes even deeper than the fact/fiction split,
confusing (in our terms, at least) the realms of the grotesque and
the actual.

Despite its close relations with genres and modes we now consider aesthetic in their primary effect, *Wonders of the East* is at
least superficially a work of information, heavily dependent on
Pliny's *Natural History*. But the work is not merely, or simply,
informational. Its depictions of the earth's margins can be
approached in connection with the grotesque and seen as both
parallel to and crucially distinct from the visual representations
recalled by its verbal images and formally mimicked in its rhetoric.
The issue of allegory comes up too: as Angus Fletcher notes, "any
fragmentary utterance . . . takes on the appearance of a coded
message needing to be deciphered" (*Allegory*, 107). The prose and
structure of *Wonders* are extremely fragmentary, and its closest
generic relative, the bestiary, was almost always read allegorically.

Was *Wonders* constructed (and justified) along allegorical lines,
or is it the random collection of distorted facts it sometimes
appears to modern medievalists? And if the latter is the case, how
are we to understand the "grotesque" appeal of its data for a medieval reader? The issues arising from the problem of category have
profound implications—moral, theological, epistemological—for
our understanding of the medieval relationship with alien cultures
and will lead us from a rhetorical consideration of this particular
text to the ethical and political aspects of the ideas assumed in its
rhetoric.

To a modern reader, the most significant of *Wonders'* relation-
ships is with the grotesque, and this is the relationship that is most
important to the history of exotic travel literature in a culture
suspended between two eras of imperial dominion. Though the
polite vision of the pilgrimage narratives and the demonic images
of *Wonders* seem mutually alien, their modes of seeing and telling
will finally be absorbed into a single tradition. To determine what

Wonders and its ilk contribute to that tradition we need to readjust our idea of the sphere in which the term *grotesque* seems applicable. Our more careful usages of the word restrict its application to the artificial: we consider it a kind of conceptual/aesthetic game playing performed in the neutral and marginal space of fantasy. *Wonders* not only resists our modern need to classify it as fictional before speaking of it as grotesque; it is anomalous as well in the cosmographical discourse of its own era. It is entirely unmoralized, empty of reference to Scripture, and only covertly allegorical. As we will see, it does not preserve enough distance from fact for us to be comfortable with its grotesque appeal, and yet it preserves so *much* distance from theology as to seem, in its own context, subversively literal.

Of course, the term *grotesque* itself is hardly unproblematic, now that its reference has been enlarged to include works of literature and of modern art. For use in this chapter we will have to develop an ad hoc sense of it that is slightly different from its current usages; first, however, a word about those usages is in order. In the years since World War II, Wolfgang Kayser and Mikhail Bakhtin in particular have put forth sharply conflicting definitions of the grotesque, especially as it applies to literature. Kayser sculpts his definition so as to account for the dizzying alienation embodied in modern works of grotesque art; Bakhtin, a cheerful Marxist, hears in the long medieval and Renaissance heyday of grotesque expression an antihierarchical laughter that binds all men together in a momentarily classless world. Bakhtin opposes grotesque images of the body to the idealized image characteristic of what he calls "official culture." This official or "classical" image, being normative, is easier to recognize and seems to have more verisimilitude. Though it changes over time, it is always centered on a kind of stick figure, healthy and complete but never excessive—with no goiters, beer bellies, or giant phalluses. The grotesque body, on the other hand, is an exuberant and often gigantic confusion of protrusions and orifices. He characterizes the opposition this way:

The essential principle of grotesque realism is degradation, that is, the lowering of all that is high, spiritual, abstract: it is a transfer to the material level, to the sphere of earth and body in their indissoluble unity.

. . . To degrade an object does not imply merely hurtling it into the void of nonexistence, into absolute destruction, but to hurl it down to the reproductive lower stratum, the zone in which conception and a new birth take place. (*Rabelais and His World*, 19–21)

Kayser places grotesque images in contrast to those of comedy and tragedy: to him they are images of man as an automaton, unworthy of or irrelevant to the seriousness of tragic and comic structures. To both critics, laughter is the definitive effect of the works and modes under discussion. Kayser sees the laughter as infernal and joyless, a defense mechanism; Bakhtin sees it as ambivalent, liberating, and even transcendent—Saint Francis of Assisi is its saint. Each definition tends to be exclusive, not only of the other but of the works the other critic chooses to treat. And both definitions seem to exclude *Wonders of the East* because it does not provoke laughter—at least not intentionally.[9]

Kayser warns of the ease with which the images of alien cultures can be felt as grotesque (and does not venture very far in time or space from the modern European world himself):

Those who are unfamiliar with the culture of the Incas will consider many of their statues to be grotesque, but perhaps that which we regard as nightmarish and ominously demonic, that is, the medium through which some horror, anguish or fear of the incomprehensible is expressed, is a familiar form that belongs to a perfectly intelligible frame of reference.

9. Geoffrey Harpham's recent book *On the Grotesque* seems to have been inspired in part by Kayser and Bakhtin's incompatibility. But his effort to rise above their mutual contradiction, by arguing that contradiction is precisely the essence of the grotesque, does not solve the problem considered here. Harpham tends to avoid the issue of intentionality, positing the grotesque as a type of experience rather than a type of artifact. From this angle, something actual or "natural" is just as capable as anything else of being grotesque. But that he is somewhat queasy about this position can be seen in the fact that he refers in his study only to works of art, and "high" art at that. Nor are there any reproductions of realistic representational art among the book's illustrations. Perhaps the question of whether the grotesque inheres in nature or in art is unavoidably answered differently in different eras. I ground my own position here in those of Thomas Browne and Montaigne—that "there are no Grotesques in Nature," and "what we call monsters are not so to God"—at least in part because they announce their positions during the era in which my story comes to a close, as if refuting a position that prevailed before them. In the heaven of pure critical consciousness there is no Right or Wrong, but one crucial narrative line of this study runs from a grotesque to a naturalistic rhetoric for the representation of the alien, and this development was seen as a triumph by those who achieved it.

Only our ignorance justifies our use of the word grotesque in such a case. (*Grotesque in Art and Literature,* 181)

This warning is certainly pertinent to a treatment of *Wonders* as part of the grotesque canon: the work *is* the product of an alien culture. Whether we "ignorantly" regard the distortions, exaggerations, and fusions of its images as nightmarish (under Kayser's definition) or liberating (under Bakhtin's), our reactions are inescapably conditioned by a spate of centuries in which the principle of the grotesque in art has been consciously invoked in practice and in commentary.

Kayser's warning is issued on the assumption that certain types of emotional response are automatically evoked by an artifact definable as grotesque and is meant to remind us that those responses are not necessarily appropriate to the work's conception. Certainly *Wonders* seems designed to evoke neither laughter nor fear. It is so strictly declarative, indicative, and informational in mood and tone that in Bodley 614 and Cotton Tiberius Bv it is bound together with serious scientific works, computational tables, maps, and geneological lists. The text does not seem intended to produce what we call an aesthetic experience. It functions to inform. But its information is grotesque in some sense that neither Kayser's nor Bakhtin's definition encompasses. They are concerned with the grotesque as a form of expressiveness, and *Wonders* is about as expressive as an annual report.

The grotesque qualities of *Wonders* are apparent on two levels: that of its hybridizing approach to the categories of natural history and that of the rhetorical techniques of its *descriptio.* The first, structural, level displays an extreme of disorganization suggestive of what Mary Douglas would call "impurity": that is, the distant Nature so represented seems to ignore all those biological and spatial category distinctions she sees as maintained by the taboos of cleanliness and dietary codes in *Purity and Danger.* (In her terms, the pagan and monstrous East can be seen to share in the "holiness" of the biblical East, for Douglas assimilates the unclean, the monstrous, and the anomalous to the general category of "the holy."[10]) Discussion of *Wonders'* structure, then, will lead us to

10. See particularly chapters 2 and 3 of Douglas, *Purity and Danger,* "Secular Defilement" and "The Abominations of Leviticus." Anthropologists such as Doug-

the topic of xenophobia, a mental state easily productive of the kind of grotesque representation we will confront later in considering the rhetorical aspects of the work.

The text of *Wonders* underwent such a long and complex process of translation, redaction, and dissemination throughout Europe that its literary form as stabilized in the extant British manuscripts is hard to pin down. Apparently it began its life in Egeria's genre: the British manuscripts descend from a redaction of a Continental Latin work usually called *The Letter of Farasmanes to Hadrian*. The eight extant Continental variants are all epistolary in format, that is, they begin with a salutation and contain a few uses of the first person. Gibb quite plausibly characterizes the work as psuedepigraphal, although Hadrian was in fact known to be fond of travel literature, and there was a real king named Farasmanes in Georgia during Hadrian's reign.[11] Gibb can date this Continental forebear no more precisely than between the second and sixth centuries: in terms of the medieval history of cosmography, somewhere between Pliny and Cosmas Indicopleustes.

The presence or absence of the salutation is of little account—the extant work has no narrative qualities in either its Continental or its Insular versions. Nor does it have even an implicit itinerary structure. The way it jumps around the map from Africa to Asia and back indicates that its focus is not on the East as a travelable

---

las can explain the symbolic necessity of marginalized anomalies, and even provide an apolitical and noncontingent reason for their location in or near a "holy land." In the Christian cosmography of the Middle Ages, as in any systematic arrangement of our knowledge of the world, there had to be a place for anomalies, hybrids, those impure beings that contradict our categorical sense perceptions and in so doing threaten category, perception, "sense" itself. It is not surprising that for the *summa* writers the monsters worked, ultimately, to support the stability and emphasize the central Power of the whole system. Nor is it surprising that such forms were considered marginal—they belonged epistemologically to the margins between perceptual categories, and their resulting "impurity" forced them out of the spaces of common life into the "outside"—the places of danger and holiness. Such places, however, in the cultures Douglas studies, are usually part of the local habitat. In casting their monsters into so remote an outer darkness that they are only accessible through verbal description and illustration, the system makers and wonderbook writers of the European Middle Ages created an unusually deep chasm between the clean and the unclean: the unclean was almost beyond experience itself, except for those temporary marginals, the travelers. The urge among the intellectuals to place the monsters outside the *oikumene*, in spaces not under the control of the local bishop or bailiff, brings the intracultural problem of pollution to the level, potentially, of international politics.

11. See Gibb, "Wonders of the East," 16–18.

geographic area, notable for its strangeness, but on that strangeness itself. Distances between places are often given, as in the *itineraria* and the travel accounts of pilgrims, but it is hard to say why, as the places are not described in an order suitable either to geography or to any conceivable journey. There are no practical directions for the would-be traveler, and, outside of a couple of references to places familiar from the Alexander romances, there is no mention of sites important in history, legend, or the Bible.

The form of the book as we have it is best described as a miniature encyclopedia in form (divided into roughly paragraph-length chapters in all but the Old English version). Plants, minerals, men, animals, and birds are jumbled together like ingredients for a casserole; it gives us, with distracting disorganization, a micro-summary of the minerology, botany, zoology, and ethnology of the East. These four sciences occupy themselves with four different kinds of physical existence: in one manner or another all cultures define them as separate. The grotesque quality of *Wonders* is most clearly apparent in the fusions it reports between these realms:

24. Then there is a golden vineyard near the rising of the sun which has berries one hundred and fifty feet long. On the berries are found certain pearls or gems.

27. Then there are women who have boars' tusks and hair down to their heels and oxen's tails growing out of their loins. These women are thirteen feet tall, and their bodies have the whiteness of marble, and they have camels' feet and donkeys' teeth.

17. . . . And *Homodubii* are begotten there, that is Double Ones [OE *twimenn*]. They have a human shape down to the navel, and from there on they resemble a donkey. They have long legs like birds and a gentle voice.

The Great Chain of Being seems here to have been melted down into that chaos that preceded God's orderly and rational Creation. There is much that should be threatening about this blurring of categories and distinctions. That God should break his own laws through the performance of individual miracles is one thing; that he should permit whole races and species of monstrous beings to flourish and multiply seems quite another. What Arculf saw on his journeys in the Holy Land was often alien, but the strangest things he reports are reassuringly absorbed into and validated by their connection with holy places and objects. He experiences the unfamiliar and the miraculous, but not the grotesque, the inverted world.

Ernst Curtius gives the name "the World Upside-Down" to a relevant topos he finds in both antique and medieval literature. Although he points to its origin as very early, in Archilochus (Fragment 74), he traces its rhetorical history in the Middle Ages to Virgil and quotes from the *Eclogues* (VIII, 52–55): "Now may the wolf of his own free will flee the sheep, the oak bear golden apples, owls compete with swans, the shepherd Tityrus be Orpheus." As modern examples he gives Breughel's painting *Dutch Proverbs*, and an unsettling lyric by Théophile de Viau (d. 1626) in which "un aspic s'accouple d'une ourse" and "cet arbre est sorty de sa place." Referring to Viau, Curtius says, "In the twilight of a distracted mind the 'world upside-down' can express horror," but he considers the medieval atmosphere of the topos to be satiric and parodic, and plots its satiric line between Lucian and Rabelais—two of the greatest writers of travel parody.[12]

This topos, however, could appear outside the properly literary and artistic spheres and enter the domain of science as well. The antique and medieval worlds were self-centered, and their ethnocentricity is reflected in the concentrically divided world of their maps and geographical writings. In the heavily illustrated medieval *mappae mundi*, images of the Plinian monstrosities are placed at the far edges of the world at the shore of the Ocean Stream, mostly in the North and South. Jerusalem occupies the exact geographical center of these disc-shaped images, and Europe is contained in the *oikumene* or inner circle. Macrobius's zone theory, based on the pagan assumption of a spherical earth, divided the world into habitable and uninhabitable climatic regions: our rather biased and inexact expression "temperate zone" descends to us from the Macrobian theory (see fig. 3). This view was anthropological as well as geographical. Nature and culture were held to be at their most reasonable in the reasonable and central climate of the northern Mediterranean inhabited by these authors and cartographers. The farther one got from Home, the temperate, reasonable mean, the more outlandish, *unheimlich*, became the bodies and manners of men.

Ranulf Higden, in his *Polychronicon*, articulates this attitude in

12. See Curtius, *European Literature and the Latin Middle Ages*, 94–98.

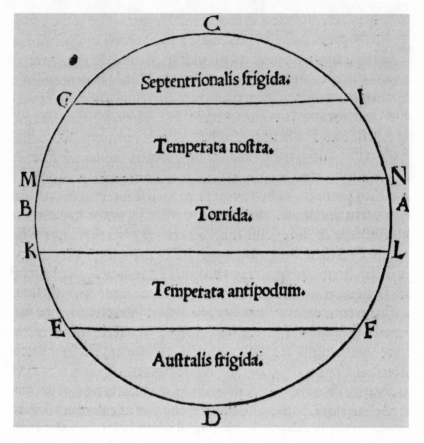

Fig. 3. Macrobian zone map. From Macrobius's *De Somnio scipionis expositio*. Paris, 1519. Courtesy of the John Carter Brown Library at Brown University.

its most benign dress, supporting Bakhtin's perception of the grotesque as carnival: "Note that at the farthest reaches of the world often occur new marvels and wonders, as though Nature plays with greater freedom secretly at the edges of the world than she does openly and nearer us in the midst of it" (1.34).[13] The Hippocra-

13. Quoted in John Block Friedman, *Monstrous Races in Medieval Art and Thought,* 43. Friedman's is the only book-length study of the history of monster lore in the European Middle Ages. In scope and depth of analysis it supersedes its more famous predecessor, Rudolf Wittkower's "Marvels of the East: A Study in the History of Monsters." I am in his debt, throughout this chapter, for his account of medieval discussion of the monstrous.

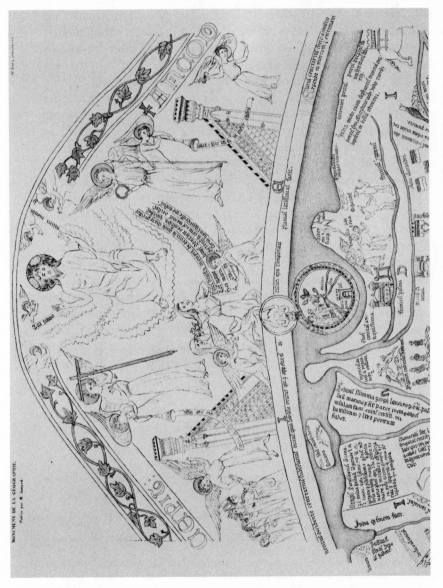

Fig. 4. The Earthly Paradise, at the extreme east of the Hereford Map, with the Celestial Paradise above it. From a facsimile. By kind permission of the Dean and Chapter of Hereford Cathedral.

tic treatise *Airs, Waters, Places* manifests a more phobic smugness about the superiority of the *oikumene.* "Difference" clearly carries a negative charge in this passage: "Growth and freedom from wildness are most fostered when nothing is forcibly predominant, but equality in every respect prevails. . . . For the seasons which modify physical frame differ; if the difference be great, the more too are the differences in the shapes" (1.12–13).

In the medieval world maps, the farthest East, where the Earthly Paradise is to be found, does not share the onus of the other extremes (see fig. 4). But the maps, images of the entire organic Creation, are more schematic and theologically determined than literary geography, which does not necessarily try to depict the whole world at once and which depends heavily on pre-Christian writings that need not sanctify the East.[14]

The European suspicion of distance in general is neatly symbolized in the *Odyssey,* in Tiresias's instructions to Odysseus: before he dies, the seafarer and island dweller is to make an inland journey that must end when he reaches a place where men are so ignorant of the sea that they mistake his oar for a winnowing fan. There he is to make ceremonial sacrifices to Poseidon, the god of his own domain (whose power perhaps does not stretch much farther from the sea than this), and turn directly homeward. Strangeness is dangerous; contact with what is truly alien forbidden. One Alexander legend expresses this taboo by having Alexander wall in the giants Gog and Magog in the Caucasus, in the far North, where they will remain, along with the host of "unclean peoples," until the Last Days.[15]

Alexander is the great hero of early European travel literature, and his role as *tamer* of the East is important. In *Wonders* he is said to have killed "the women who have boars' tusks and hair down to their heels and oxen's tails . . . because of their obscenity" (27). Pliny, in describing the icthyophagi, notes that Alexander "made

14. The Ebsdorf map depicts the world as literally "the body of Christ"—his head appearing outside the frame at the East, his feet at the West, and his left hand at the South, next to which, with sinister significance, the monstrous races are arranged in a framed band at the bottom of Africa.

15. The legend makes its way back into history when Matthew Paris interprets the appearance of the Mongol armies at the borders of Europe as precisely a fulfillment of this prophecy (see chap. 3). But catastrophic as this clash of alien cultures certainly was for eastern Europe, it was one result of an imperialist strategy that in fact reopened the East to Europe for over a century.

an order forbidding a fish diet to all the Fish Eaters" (*Natural History*, VI.xxv). The secular travel literature is obsessed with marvels, but tends to treat them either with kid gloves or the sword. They are to be eliminated, tamed, or merely observed from a distance, never dwelt on with the kind of empathetic interest that Mandeville will eventually display.

In *Alexander's Letter to Aristotle* (also included in Cotton Vitellius Axv), the democratic and jovial aspect of the grotesque is not much in evidence.[16] In the *Letter* there is less ambiguity of tone: mineralogical-botanical marvels are openly admired, zoological-anthropological marvels are feared or despised. The greed and hostility of the imperialist perspective on Elsewhere interfere with any more complex enjoyment of strangeness per se. But *Wonders of the East*, with its minimal reference to Alexander and its dryly factual tone, allows its audience an unadulterated and unmediated contemplation of the grotesque. It presents this element in a purer isolation than any other early medieval geographical or travel work and in so doing stands as an opposite pole to Egeria's personalized, normalized, spiritualized picture. It is her world that it inverts, or, to use Bakhtin's term, the body of her East that it "degrades."

To the extent that the phenomena of *Wonders* can be divided into the traditional categories of geographical literature—flora, fauna, landscape, and peoples—its rhetoric reflects a number of parallels with characteristic treatments of such subjects in grotesque visual art. The basic rhetorical pattern of the work is starkly simple: various regions of the East are described in one- or two-paragraph accounts of their most marvelous natural features. More often than not, those features are approximately human:

15. Then there is another island south of the Bryxontis on which are men begotten without heads, who have their eyes and mouths in their chests. They are eight feet tall and eight feet wide.

20. Then there is an island in the Red Sea where there is a race of men called by us Donestre. They are shaped like soothsayers from the head to the navel, and the other part is like a man's body. And they know all

16. This work is available, along with *Wonders of the East*, in Rypins, *Three Old English Prose Texts*.

human languages. When they see a man of foreign race, they address him and his relatives, [and] the names of acquaintances, and with lying words they beguile him and seize him. And then, after that, they devour him all but the head, and then they sit and weep over the head.

Animal life includes the dragon, griffin, and phoenix, as well as a few more obscure marvels characterized by gigantism or hybridization. The effect of hybridization is technically inescapable: in the context of describing the unknown, similitudes based on features of the known inevitably result in such perverse collages, destroying the coherence of the alien subject in order to transmit a visualizable image.

9. There are begotten there ants as big as dogs. They have feet like grasshoppers. They are of a red color and black.

14. Then there are on the Bryxontis wild animals which are called Lertices. They have ears of a donkey and wool of a sheep and feet of a bird.

Very occasionally, topography and vegetation appear. In addition to the golden vineyard with its 150–foot berries: "33. Then there is a land where vineyards grow most greatly, where there is a couch of ivory. It is three hundred and six feet long."

This secular East shares almost nothing with the East depicted in pilgrimage literature during the early Middle Ages. It has little landscape and few artifacts of civilization, while the pilgrim's Levant is almost entirely a matter of sacred topography and ecclesiastical buildings. As in the illustrations, landscape is reduced to a more or less detailed horizon line. *Wonders* often notes the size of various countries or "colonies," but topography is only included when necessary to the relation of a marvel—such as that of the horned snakes that guard the pepper fields. The three apparently human artifacts are a pair of pagan temples (one of them fashioned from wrought iron and brass) and the 306–foot ivory bed. The wrought iron temple and the ivory bed are empty; the other temple is inhabited, in one related continental manuscript, by a silent priest who lives on oysters. The social landscape is as absent here as the geographical landscape is in the depiction of organic marvels. Both the cultural and physical contexts of Eastern phenomena are, by implication, empty. Though again, this is determined technically, by the unavailability of data, the result for a modern reader resembles the isolation in empty, nonperspectival space of the grotesque images of Renaissance ornamental art.[17]

The features of the organic marvels manifest characteristically grotesque principles: hyperbolic dimensions, multiplication of body parts, and fusions of species:

11. Men are begotten there who are fifteen feet long, and they have a white body and two faces on one head, feet and knees very red, and a long nose and dark hair.

12. Their heads are maned like lions' heads and they are twenty feet tall and they have a great mouth like a winnowing fan.

14. Then there are wild animals on the Bryxontis which are called Lertices. They have ears of a donkey, wool of a sheep, and feet of a bird.

Grotesque representation of plant life usually limits itself to fusions of species, since it tends to appear most often in decorative art, where the size and scale of represented objects are not features, but in *Wonders* we have the "golden vineyard . . . which has berries one hundred and fifty feet long."

The hyperbolism seems to be a medieval accretion to the marvels material. Pliny rarely mentions the size of his monsters, nor does Herodotus. The classical writers exhibit an anthropological, if snobbish, interest in the manners and rituals of alien peoples; the author of *Wonders* presents iconographic images only, with one exception—he frequently describes the human and animal races in terms of their aggression or lack of it. They either chase and devour, or flee from the traveler. When there are no travelers to stimulate them into movement it would seem that they simply eat, sleep, and reproduce.

By "iconographic" I mean to suggest those qualities that have led some commentators to consider these depictions as mere verbal equivalents—even descriptions—of the more widely available

17. Of the illustrations in Cotton Tiberius Bv and Bodley 614, McGurk notes, "there is no attempt in the monochrome background to give an impression of space or atmosphere" (*An Eleventh-Century Anglo-Saxon Illustrated Miscellany*, 37).

visual images of Eastern or exotic *monstra*.[18] Such images, in both media, are missing the gratuitous detail of more frankly mimetic art and tend to convey, as a result, little information and much meaning. They resist amplification or variation over the years: they exist as self-sufficient totalities rather than as suggestive signifiers of complex and dynamic phenomena. Visual representations of the dogheads, for instance, remained as constant as verbal ones, throughout centuries of stylistic change in the languages of both visual and verbal mimesis. This is perhaps because a very bare minimum of features was necessary for definition, and once these features had been sketched or mentioned, the image "doghead" had been evoked to the limit of its usable significance.

Such iconographic images are sometimes curiously hard to visualize: the 150–foot berries, for instance, or the men who are "eight feet tall and eight feet wide" (15). The writer has given us only the marvelous facts themselves and no sense of even their immediate physical contexts. Are the vines proportionately thick? Are the men eight-feet wide from top to bottom, with no depth, like squares? The writing is not fully transparent after all: it isolates and atomizes its matter, so we are rarely if ever given the complete physical image of a monstrous being, never mind a cultural or geographical environment that might rationalize it.

This is a familiar trait in the grotesque fantasy writing of the twentieth century. H. P. Lovecraft's monsters are often little more than "huge and loathsome." In *The Palm-Wine Drinkard*, Amos Tutuola gives us a "half-bodied baby . . . with a lower voice like a telephone," and we spend pages in its company knowing no more than that. But, as noted before, *Wonders* is not fantasy writing. It is a kind of journalism, recognized as having what we would call documentary value by the medieval anthologists who bound it together with Bishop Sigeric's *itinerarium* of a pilgrimage to Rome, extracts from Bede, Macrobius, and other cosmographers, and Priscian's *Periegesis* (a geographical treatise in verse).[19]

It is in the nature of pictorial representation to freeze its subject in time: all painting is, in a way, still life. But when a verbal text, with its potential for narrative, with its resources of tense and

18. See, e.g., Wittkower, "Marvels of the East."
19. A complete listing of the contents of Cotton Tiberius Bv can be found in McGurk's introduction.

mood, elects the habitual present, the implications are significant. The most active of all the descriptions of dubious human races in *Wonders*, that of the man-eating Donestre, presents those peculiar polyglots in a state of apparently perpetual motion—addressing, beguiling, devouring, and weeping over the foreigner. But the action is an infinitely repeating one, like that of a peep show. It is the only action the Donestre perform, and it is not only unmotivated but self-contradictory: the final stage, of weeping over the butchered foreigner's head, reminds us of nothing so much as Carroll's Walrus weeping over his edible little friends, the Oysters. The image belongs to Nonsense, but not to the self-consciously delightful Nonsense of Carroll's Wonderland. It is delivered in the unadorned, declarative mode proper to information. The almost total absence of context surrounding each of the phenomena of *Wonders* greatly intensifies our experience of the grotesque, but at the same time the rhetorical starkness to which that absence belongs suggests for its depictions the status of fact.

The aesthetic term *grotesque* is recent, but, as anyone familiar with medieval illumination and sculpture knows, the representational mode itself is older and its effects accessible to an eleventh-century reader as well as to ourselves. We can see a problem beginning to emerge, then, in the case of descriptions like that of the Donestre, which seem to depict a grotesque actuality. The essential style of *Wonders*, as should be clear by now, is seductively similar to the ornamental grotesquery of Gothic and Renaissance visual art. Its similitudes parallel hybridization and skewed proportion; its lack of landscape or setting parallels the empty space of the margin or border; its absence of individuating detail draws our imaginations in the same way to the contemplation of form. It literalizes and holds still the fleeting incoherence of dreams, permitting us to entertain, while awake, the figures of the impossible. Its connection with the actual and normal is one of opposition, compensation—even competition. And this implies, in the context of factual discourse, that there is an opposed, compensatory, competing *world* out there somewhere, Elsewhere. This the visual grotesque does not imply.

As mentioned above, these static, compressed, and isolated images of monstrous life often sound like verbal descriptions of illustrations or carvings, and some of them may be so. But no matter how plausible a sculptor's rendering might be, his monstrous image has no inherent claim to historicity or literalness. A visual image predicates nothing; only words can do that. The predications of a text like *Wonders* claim a phenomenal actuality for the marginal world it represents.

Margaret Hodgen, in *Early Anthropology in the Sixteenth and Seventeenth Centuries*, complains of the stubborn longevity of these verbal schemata without suggesting an explanation:

Why was it that Isidore and Bartholomew, two men who were scholars in the Middle Ages, knew so little about their fellow human beings? Why were they content with their ignorance? Why their absorption, ethnologically speaking, in the abnormal, monstrous or trivial? Why their compulsive and tiresome reiteration of stale descriptions of fabulous peoples cribbed from predecessors, who in turn had cribbed from precursors all the way back to Roman and Hellenistic antiquity? (67)

If we were talking about the longevity of the dogheads or pygmies in the visual arts, Ernst Gombrich could help out with his "rhythm of schema and correction." With no opportunities for correction, the medieval illustrator of the East stuck with his "minimum stereotypes" and made free use of their grotesque appeal as conceptual elements. In the decorative context of his imagemaking, this usage was innocent: "If all art is conceptual, the issue is rather simple. For concepts, like pictures, cannot be true or false. They can only be more or less useful for the formation of descriptions" (Gombrich, *Art and Illusion*, 89). But predications, unlike pictures, or the concepts that lie behind them, *can* be true or false. Though we suspend our concern with this aspect of declarative sentences when reading most literary "art," *Wonders* and its progeny do not present themselves as fictional or poetic. And even such heavy clues to artistic intent as verse format or fantastic *materia* were not enough to prevent the clichéd outbursts against *mendacia poetarum* that punctuate medieval discourse about discourse.

I am not by any means claiming that its earlier readers all "believed" *Wonders*—only that they could judge it by the criterion of truth value, that its rhetoric is therefore one within which an actuality could be presented. It constitutes a set of credible schemata. There is a limited set of possible responses to it. Says Saint Augustine, of reported marvels generally, "It is open to anyone to withhold belief from them, and no one can justly be blamed for so doing" (*City of God*, xxi.7) Augustine, however, prefers to believe, and it is in the reasons for his preference that we may find a resolution to the problem of grotesque actuality.

Monsters and Meaning

Wonders of the East was not produced in a vacuum. Although its mixture of the grotesque and the informational provokes a certain amount of cognitive dissonance in the modern reader, its manner and matter can be seen to harmonize more easily if we take a harder look at medieval understanding of the monstrous in general. To provide the work with an intellectual context, however, is to raise more serious issues than cognitive dissonance and to find unsettling connections between rhetorical style, Christian theology, and man's inhumanity to man.

Both *Wonders* and the monstrous world it represents have been subject to the rationalizations of the exegete since at least the time of Augustine. The *materia* appeals to the exegete in all of us, and forces from many the kind of reading Angus Fletcher describes, in a discussion of literary allegory, as almost automatically interpretive: "By having a surrealistic surface texture allegory immediately elicits an interpretive response from the reader. The silences in allegory mean as much as the filled in spaces, because by bridging the silent gaps between oddly unrelated images we reach the sunken understructure of thought (the biblical exegete's 'underthought,' *hypnoia*, the Russian schoolboy's 'undertext.')" (*Allegory*, 107). The silences and surrealism of *Wonders* seem to have had just this effect on Paul Gibb, and when he adds a coherent allegorical *hypnoia* to the text, he removes some of the grotesque quality provided by its apparently empty spaces. An allegorical reading of the text shifts its grotesque aspect to the background, rendering its rhetorical features merely the natural concomitants of such a text's commitment to a hidden and transcendent "underthought." We are still, however, left with the problem of the text's simultaneous factuality—a problem inherent in the Matter of the East itself, wherever it is presented or imagined outside the safe confines of romance.

In Gibb's exegesis, the ordering of *Wonders'* monstrous *descrip-*

75

tiones suggests that it was written by a Christian. Although it avoids any mention of the holy places, and the only familiar figure it refers to is the pagan Alexander, it is apparently structured on the basis of the received exegetical meanings of its motifs. The Christian allegorical significances of ants, gold, serpents, horns, mountains, the griffin, the phoenix, as given in any of the medieval symbol dictionaries, provide what Gibb calls a "concatenative" structure for the work. Each section is connected to the one before it by means of a shared motif, which carries its *bonus* meaning in one section and its *malus* meaning in the next.[20]

What this structure adds up to, however, is a little difficult to say. After having translated all the passages of *Wonders* into their Christian significations, Gibb finds a movement in the work as a whole "from the temporal to the eternal, from the moral to the eschatological, from man to God" (*"Wonders of the East,"* 73). Since there is no geographical logic at work on the literal level of the text, no directional movement to which this spiritual movement could be analogous, the structure appears more than ordinarily extraneous to the immediate impact and appeal of the work. And though the period in which the extant manuscripts were copied (c. A.D. 1000–1100) falls a little short of the full flowering of the bestiary form, its ancestor, the *Physiologus*, dates to the period of *Wonders'* earliest origins. In the bestiaries, animals and monsters are always explicitly moralized; the absence of moralization in *Wonders* is a notable anomaly. Every piece of prose has some structure, if only associational, and Gibb is not unreasonable in thus rescuing *Wonders* from the charge of incoherence. But the esoteric perfunctoriness of this particular structure, which has eluded the imaginations of all medievalists until Gibb, suggests to me a motivation not purely aesthetic. Although his conjecture is persuasive and probable, it does not reveal so overwhelming an emphasis on meaning in the work as to block the titillating effect of its data and their presentation. To put the function of *Wonders'*

20. "In most cases the names of animals [given in medieval lists of symbols by Melito, Eucherius, and Rabanus Maurus] each have diametrically opposed meanings, one positive (termed *bonus* in the lists), the other negative (termed *malus*). Serpents, for example, can represent either Divine wisdom (*bonus*) or diabolical evil (*malus*). A lion can represent either Christ or the devil," etc. (Gibb, *"Wonders of the East,"* 69).

theological armature into perspective, we will have to consider the place of the monstrous in medieval theological discourse.

Grotesque realities present the theologian with a problem not so easily solvable as the related problem of pain. Pain has no life of its own. It is an experience within a life and as such can be converted to good: it can be perceived as a punishment or a stimulus and thus in effect *become* a punishment or stimulus. But to the extent that grotesque life forms are seen as ugly, in opposition to the forms of Bakhtin's "classical canon," where the idealized human body is in fact the image of God, they would seem to be direct evidence of error or carelessness in the Creation. They could even be seen as an anti-Creation, though this perception would be radically heretical. Theologians, particularly Augustine, took on the problem (or various parts of it) and defeated it with a logic that raises another, more serious issue. Among the reasons Augustine adduces for the existence of (and our belief in) monsters is the following:

The name 'monster', we are told, evidently comes from *monstrare*, 'to show', because they show by signifying something. . . . Now these signs are, apparently, contrary to nature and they are called 'unnatural'; and the Apostle uses the same human way of speaking when he talks of the wild olive being 'unnaturally' grafted on to the cultivated tree, and sharing in the richness of the garden olive. For us [i.e., Christians], however, they have a message. These 'monsters', 'signs', portents', and 'prodigies', as they are called, ought to 'show' us, to 'point out' to us, to 'portend' and 'foretell', that God is to do what he prophesied that he would do with the bodies of the dead [at the Resurrection], with no difficulty to hinder him, no law of nature to debar him from so doing. (*City of God*, 21.8.983)[21]

Augustine sees the monsters as merely God's way of proving his power, especially over anatomical nature: the resurrection of burned or dismembered bodies in a state of wholesome completeness will be no trouble for the God who brings us dogheads, pygmies, and headless men whose eyes are in their breasts.

21. The words in quotation marks in the last sentence of Bettenson's translation are puns in Augustine's Latin: "et [nobis] monstra ostenta portenta prodigia nuncupantur, hoc monstrare debent, hoc ostendere vel praeostendere, hóc praedicere, quod facturus sit Deus quae de corporibus hominum se praenuntiavit esse facturum, nulla impediente difficultate, nulla praescribente lege naturae" (Loeb edition, 56–58).

The discourse went on for centuries. Two scholastic philosophers, Alexander of Hales and the pseudo-Albertus of *De secretis mulierum*, taking off from Augustine's notion of *concordia discors*, present essentially aesthetic justifications for the existence of monsters. Pseudo-Albertus suggests that monsters were made "to embellish and to decorate the universe. For they say that just as diverse colors existing in a wall decorate this wall, so indeed, diverse monsters embellish this world" (*De secretis mulierum,* 23v-24r). Alexander says, with an oddly beautiful disregard for the question of the monsters' humanity: "So, just as the beauty of language is achieved by a contrast of opposites . . . the beauty of the course of the world is built up by a kind of rhetoric, not of words but of things, which employs the contrast of opposites" (*Summa theologica* 2.4.2.2.1.1.3.452).[22]

Augustine's argument is all very well in explaining miracles, and even monstrous flora and fauna, but he shares with the scholastics a tendency to see the human monsters far more easily as *exempla* than as living beings, diminishing their reality to the level of the equally portentous beasts and plants.[23] Their rarity and distance permit a perception of alien races as primarily significant—even rhetorical.

The move to an allegorical reading of the marvelous matter does not abolish—in fact, it depends on—the materials' factual nature. The monstrous life forms, it would seem, are facts and figures both: the facts of this world are the figures of God's composition ("Why, you're nothing but a sort of thing in his dream," as Tweedledum's insult to Alice goes). The monsters "embellish the world." Coincidentally, images of them embellish the misericord, the missal, the maps in the cathedral. Simultaneously (and, to the scholastics, invisibly) many of their prototypes carry on real lives of their own beyond the borders of Europe. The unicorn-rhinocerous cools off, in the mud of an actual Indian river, from the heat of a noonday sun only five or six hours distant from Britain,

22. Both quoted in Friedman, *Monstrous Races in Medieval Art and Thought,* 185 (author's translation).

23. In *City of God,* 21.8, Augustine takes up the crucial issue of "whether we are to suppose that [the monstrous races] are descended from the sons of Noah" (and thus from Adam). But he gets nowhere with it, concluding at last that "if such people exist, then either they are not human; or, if human, they are descended from Adam" (663–64).

and Donestres go fishing, get married, and suffer the burden of their immortal souls. The souls are missing in the world circumscribed by *Wonders*, and Augustine builds on this absence when he speaks of the *monstra* as bodies only: bodies that exist to prove God's power over *our* bodies at the Resurrection. What will he do with the dogheads at the Resurrection, or the pygmies? Will he turn them into Europeans?[24]

It hardly matters. The point is only that we are here confronted with an ontological order somewhere *between* the symbolic and the actual—a level of reality that resolves the confusion we began with. We might call it "minimum reality," an order in which beings can be conceived that exist only for the uses—psychological, theological, material—to which others can put them. The dogheads could exist here only for the Christians, only to prove "that God is to do what he prophesied that he would with the bodies of the dead." A human body with the head of a dog must be actual, as proof for Augustine's thesis, but the head need not have teeth for chewing or a mind to think with. And because for our purposes it need not, it does not.

Some of the same features that provoke a perception of *Wonders* as grotesque provoke the allegorical reading of it, but neither provides a real escape from the ethical problem of the work's factuality, nor does the remote allegorical *hypnoia* cancel out the appeal of its grotesque surface. The significance to medieval Christians of the text and its *materia* is one that depends on the factuality of both, and this is an ethically uncomfortable perspective for a citizen of the "global village." However it is read, *Wonders* has truth value, but the rhetorical schemata by which it represents its subjects describe, for us, a grotesque reality that we are able to reject as impossible. We reject it because, as far as we are sane, we

24. This question of the humanity of alien peoples or races will of course eventually take on a central importance, when the Renaissance reinvents colonialism. In 1550, Juan Ginés de Sepúlveda, in a long debate with Bartolomé de Las Casas over the proper method of spreading Christianity and Spanish hegemony in the West Indies and Central America, defended the method of brutal force on the basis of the Indians' questionable humanity. His arguments echo Albertus Magnus on the subject of the nonhuman and monstrous pygmies. Though Las Casas insisted on the Indians' full humanity, the history of Spanish behavior in the New World shows him to have lost the battle. (The issue is still alive in this century, and I am told was a topic of hot debate in the early 1960s, when the Jesuit magazine *America* raised the question of whether Christians were obliged to convert the extraterrestrial life forms we would soon be contacting.)

are now in a position to know that all real beings are equally real, dense, complex, soulful, interrelated. The life sciences have organized what we know about men and beasts and their habitats in such a way that "Caucasian" is (at least theoretically) just one category among many, and the rhinocerous belongs to the phylum of the pig. Meanwhile, the grotesque is a mode of vision we invoke for the purposes of entertainment: it is expressive, symbolic, shocking, but never mimetic.[25]

Although I would not deny the likelihood of *Wonders'* allegorical structure, it does not account for the work's appeal nor fully subordinate it to the uses of piety. The work belongs, after all, to the corpus of factual literature about distant places, and it is time we placed it there, in the context to which it makes its most important and long-lived contribution. *Wonders of the East* may be the black sheep of medieval travel literature, but it forms a crucial part of the picture available to medieval readers and writers of the world beyond their world. Perhaps we can best understand its perplexities by looking at it in relation to the rest of that picture as we have sketched it so far.

Exegetical rationalizations notwithstanding, there is something inescapably subversive in the grotesque. Its images speak of a world not yet finished, not quite organized, not thoroughly wholesome. This is agreeable and even necessary to Bakhtin, in whose eyes the picture of an organized and finished world *needs* subverting and is not whole. It is possible to see in the tradition to which *Wonders* belongs, the tradition of Alexander's *Letters* to Aristotle and to his mother Olympia, what Bakhtin broadly refers to as parody: in this case a parody of the accounts of the Holy Land brought back by such representatives of the "official culture" as Egeria and Arculf. But that would perhaps be stretching the idea of parody as a literary term past usefulness. A parody never hides its model as thoroughly as does *Wonders*.

25. The photographs of Diane Arbus might seem at first to present a counterexample, but in fact it is precisely the divorce between the grotesque and the actual that her images exploit. Her portraits challenge any glib tendencies we might have to reject the human reality of a face or body. Because they are untampered-with photographs of "our fellow Americans," they offer us grotesque images of people we must believe are as real as ourselves and force us to distinguish between grotesque schema and living motif.

This text has no formal relations with contemporary pilgrimage literature as direct as blasphemy or satire. Rather, it forms one term of an antinomy. In filling in the gaps left so noticeably by Egeria in her letter, it confronts the blinkered Christian perception of the East with the illicit but imaginatively opulent East of pagan tradition. The mutually exclusive divisions of the Matter of these two traditions will remain, until Mandeville, all but absolute— and for good reason. Despite its opulence, the presence of the monstrous is an indecorous "embellishment" in the ideal territories of Calvary, Bethlehem, and Eden. Perhaps the Christian subtext of *Wonders* outlined by Gibb is a structural apology on its author's part for his secular and problematic subject and for his single-minded focus on its most secular and problematic aspects. For certainly structure and surface seem to be at war here.

Augustine lumps miracles and natural wonders together when he defends God's ability to break the laws of nature. In doing so he implies that freaks of nature are to be subsumed under the category of miracles—the same category to which so many of Arculf's "wonders" belong. But miracles betray the interfering presence of a God, and the author of *Wonders* avoids the miraculous and the supernatural completely (until the closing cautionary tale of Jamnes and Mambre, which seems to function as a coda).[26] The gigantic ivory bed that looms over the land "where vineyards grow most greatly" (33) has an analogue in Pseudo-Callisthenes' *Alexander-Romance*, but there the gigantic bed is not empty— Dionysos is reclining on it. The absence of the god from the empty bed of *Wonders* (though probably due to the author's Christian piety) is paradigmatic of the marvelous world depicted in the text. It is a place without supernatural presences or gigantic powers; it is the realm of the inexplicable. It is a place that seems too far from the center to be under divine supervision.

26. This interpolation from the Apocrypha (which furnishes the Cotton Tiberius text with its final—and only full-page—illustration, of a scene from Hell) is probably best read as a traditional medieval retraction on the part of the uncomfortable Anglo-Saxon translator. After all, Jamnes is warning his brother that it was his "wisdom" that sent him to Hell—that same profane *curiositas* that Egeria so scrupulously avoids and for which later pilgrims and pilgrim writers were to be so frequently blasted from the pulpit. The interpolation is as close as we get to an explicit moralization of *Wonders'* contents, and it suggests that, for at least one medieval reader, the presence of an allegorical subtext could not rescue the work from the grotesque unseemliness of its surface.

Like the medieval manuscript and the medieval cathedral, the world itself has a margin, where the grotesque is free to frolic because it is perceived as somehow inherently beyond the power (or beneath the attention) of any integrative force. The question of whether these *twimenn* have souls, the disturbing alienness of 150–foot berries and gems that grow on trees: for the original audience these matters are relieved of their problematic nature by the simple fact that we are talking about the East. Once firmly located in a margin, the grotesque poses little threat to the central order. It *need* not be integrated.

Besides their implicit understanding of the East as belonging to a separate Nature—higher in Egeria's letter, lower in *Wonders*—the *peregrinatio* and the "wonder book" have one other attitude in common. In both works the eastern Elsewhere to which the reader's attention is directed contains no present-tense human reality. To Egeria the Holy Land is a vast shrine; to the author of *Wonders* it is a museum of unnatural history. Nothing in it moves but the European or Christian traveler—unless to run away or attack. Instead, both writers find hidden meanings in it: it is a sort of historical allegory to Egeria, a covert moral allegory to the author of *Wonders*. But the resemblance, though important as an adumbration of later missionary and colonialist attitudes, stops there. As works embodying the powers of literature, the two are radically dissimilar. Between them, they seem to split the work of the travel account as we know it now. It is as though the early European did not know how to travel, as though the idea had not yet been invented. Egeria maps a process, however static her vision of it may seem to modern eyes, and *Wonders* paints pictures, however incomplete. Egeria's *Peregrinatio* presents an experience almost shorn of its material mise-en-scène; *Wonders* records a mass of unsynthesized data shorn of any relation to an experiencing witness. The fusion of the two, the resolution of this implicit tension, is yet to come.

It is the lack of an intercessor between data and audience that makes *Wonders* so peculiarly hard to define or to treat as an example of the grotesque. Its declarative impersonality renders it voiceless and toneless. Nothing in it seems arranged or shaped in the interests of producing an effect or evoking any particular shade of imaginative response. True, the data have been selected by someone and embodied in sentences that are not Pliny's or the psuedo-

Callisthenes', but it is only in comparing the contents of this work with that of other works that the shadow of an author can be seen to fall across the page. Inside the boundaries of the work itself, we are in the hands of an omniscient information machine—not a traveler "come back to tell us all," but a conduit of facts. The facts, bare of any rhetorical amplification and lacking a context of explicit theological or scientific argument, are *in themselves* grotesque, and as such they are outside the purview of Bakhtin's or Kayser's criticism. As a body of transliterated facts, *Wonders* expresses nothing but the credulity of its audience; it is a measure of that audience's desire to believe in a grotesque actuality. Its closest modern analogues are the *National Enquirer* and *The Guiness Book of World Records*, but the parallel should not be pushed too far.

The surface literalism of the text is perplexing to the routinely skeptical modern reader, and it is made more so by its contradictory contexts—bound in one volume with scientific and practical compilations of data and in another with a great pagan epic and a biblical verse narrative. The apparent disjunction between these settings suggests an ambivalence in the minds of medieval readers and scribes about the nature of figurative speech. It should come as a reminder that modern distinctions between fact and *figura* are anachronistic when applied to the "technical" prose of an era that understood every phenomenon as figurative, that saw God precisely as an Author, history precisely as a fable, the hooting of an owl as an augury, the life of each man as an *imitatio Christi*. (In Emile Mâle's words, "The whole world is a symbol"; *Gothic Image*, 31.)

In this mode of apprehending the world, Augustine's explanation of monsters makes perfect sense, as does the exegetically determined structure of this brief encyclopedia of wonders. Significance is more important—even more striking—than existence. To the distant European onlooker, concerned with his own salvation, the conditions of being for monsters are not to be imagined: the spiritual radiance of facts is blinding. Facts have meanings. The writer does not create them: they are anterior to his use of them. He can arrange them so that the direction of his meanings has a meaning, as has the author of *Wonders*. This structure does not interfere with the informational status of his content. But given the rich symbolic resonance of such ideas as "journey" and "the East," it creates a complex problem of interpretation for the critic who has on his or her bookshelf both the *Odyssey* and Darwin's *Journal*.

For Hayden White and his followers, this might not seem so clearly problematic. Defining the "genre" of discourse (all prose that is neither logical demonstration nor "pure fiction") he says, "[The] process of understanding can only be tropological in nature, for what is involved in the rendering of the unfamiliar into the familiar is a troping that is generally figurative" (*Tropics of Discourse,* 5). This seems obviously true and permits us to speak of more more poetic ways of meaning in factual texts. But the fact remains that figuration in the modern world of discourse is something secondary, felt by its practitioners to be stylistic (thus we need a Hayden White to point out and expound its epistemological importance). We tend to imagine fact or data as prior to discourse, and as more central and solid than meaning, which is given to it by discourse. The more emphasis on meaning we feel in a work, the more likely we are to treat it as fiction. (*In Cold Blood* and *The Executioner's Song* are novels.) The medieval figure was more often primary, and self-consciously so. Augustine's pun on *monstrum/monstrare* is the justification for the existence of monsters, who exist in the service of his figure.

In the end, no effort of historical imagination will place *Wonders of the East* quite comfortably by the side of Egeria's or Arculf's East, or rationalize the carelessness of its attitude toward the immortal souls of the *twimenn.* That the particular kind of strangeness illustrated by *Wonders* had a strong appeal is attested by its eleven extant manuscripts, in Latin, Old French, and Old English, to be found in England, France, Italy, Spain, Germany, and Belgium. The Holy Places were strange too; Adamnan's chapters on crocodiles, wild locusts, and miraculous relics are evidence that their strangeness had its own appeal. But the strangeness of *Wonders* is of a different order: it points neither to the power of God nor to the fecund variety of rational nature. *Wonders* exposes the inverted, marginal world of a nature that can mean but not fully be. Its world can *signify* the patterns and temptations of life at the center, in the *oikumene,* but literally and first it stands in opposition to the world we know and the laws that govern it. Its subversive delightfulness lies in its stark presentation of what is Other, Beyond, and Outside. It promises to the credulous that there are more things in heaven and earth than are dreamed of, or at least fully accounted for, in the "official culture." It is a world that by its inexplicableness is set free of the terms in which the journeys of Egeria and Arculf are integrated into the rational order and justified. The documentary travel accounts of pilgrims and crusaders, as we have noted, included little or nothing of the monstrous until their journeys began to spill across the borders of the scriptural lands.

The usual tensions of Being in a religious climate, the anxieties that characterize "realness," are absent in this marvelous, marginal world. Presented as figures, motifs, and allegories, its monsters, when imagined as actual, must be conceived as existing in a sphere outside the moral and eschatological. No provision is made for them in the New Testament. There is no evidence of them at home. Their daily life does not include the concepts of salvation or damnation. As representations of real phenomena which the reader may choose to integrate into his image of the real world, they offer a more permanent release from the constrictions of nature than do the temporary stimulations of art.

Arguing against Kayser's gloomy conception of the grotesque as an alienated picture of our own familiar world, Bakhtin has this to say: "Actually the grotesque, including the Romantic form, discloses the potentiality of an entirely different world, of another order, another way of life. It leads men out of the confines of the apparent (false) unity, of the indisputable and stable. Born of folk humor, it always represents in one form or another . . . the return of Saturn's golden age to earth—the living possibility of its return" (*Rabelais and His World*, 48). Chapters 5 and 6 (particularly 5) will take up the matter of the golden age in its geographical form, in discussing accounts of voyages to the American "Earthly Paradise." The shift of the image from, as Henri Baudet puts it, "a distant past to a distant present" (*Paradise on Earth*, 15) is a shift from carnival to conquest.

There is a limit to the application of the term *grotesque*. One cannot appropriately respond to any natural living thing as grotesque (although the medieval writer and reader seem, inappropriately, to have done so); the word *must* refer to concepts, to ideas about the thing, and not the thing itself. And systems of concepts live in opposition to one another, dependent on such opposition for their very existence. The need for the world of *Wonders* was a conceptual need, and its data were important *as* objects of belief. No one has ever needed a griffin, only the idea of a griffin, or the idea of a world in which griffins are possible. The stark antirhetoric of *Wonders* frees its griffin from the inaccessible and merely pleasurable world of fable, poem, and romance: in a text without ornament the ornament must be substance.

The longevity of *Wonders'* rhetorical schemata was certainly abetted by a millennium of negligible opportunity for correction. But there was also a *use* for these frozen little data (as Edward Said implies when speaking of nineteenth-century orientalism's "unself-conscious bad innocence and the resistence of it to reality"; *Orientalism*, 116). *Wonders* and its rhetoric supported belief in a cosmos where density, reality, proportion, and self-sufficient being clustered in the geographical "center," while the margin sported the parodic or merely significant life whose image in art we call "the grotesque." Writers of geography and travel books would continue to employ for centuries this bare rhetorical simplicity in the description of marvels, with eerily charming results. But the beliefs supported by this style of presentation would become dangerous when the believers finally reached the marginal territories where the monsters were thought to make their homes. Grotesque ideas were then applied to a world as tangible as Europe, and a subversive and joyful intellectual construct worked to turn living Indians into signs and symbols. The erasure of such a sign is murder.

3

The Utter East

Merchant and Missionary Travels during the "Mongol Peace"

In the works of Marco Polo and the Franciscan friar William of Rubruck, the experiencing narrator born and bred in the pilgrimage accounts meets the fabulous and relatively unprescribed East of *Wonders* and the Alexander romances. One might expect this encounter between the eyewitness and the factitious to be a meeting of matter and antimatter, in which explosion a host of images will perforce be smashed. But images are hardier than that:

They have many wild elephants and they also have unicorns enough which are not at all by any means less than an elephant in size. And they are made like this, for they have the hair of the buffalo; it has the feet made like the feet of an elephant. It has one horn in the middle of the forehead very thick and large and black. . . . It has the top of the head made like a wild boar and always carries its head bent towards the ground and stays very willingly amongst lakes and forests in the mud and in the mire like swine. It is a very ugly beast to see and unclean. And they are not so as we here say and describe, who say that it lets itself be caught in the lap by a virgin girl; but I tell you that it is quite the contrary of that which we believe that it was. (Moule and Pelliot, 166)[1]

1. All but two quotations from Marco Polo are cited by chapter number from the critical edition of A. C. Moule and Paul Pelliot, *Marco Polo: The Description of the World* (1938). This work is a literal English translation based on the F text (Fr. 1116 in the Bibliothèque Nationale) but including all additions and variations from other manuscripts. It is the most complete printed edition of the book. Henry Yule's almost infinitely annotated English translation (*The Book of Ser Marco Polo*) conflates F and what he calls the "Remodelled French" texts (Bibl. Nat. Fr. 5631 and Fr.

Marco Polo has brought the West its first authentic rhinoceros, under cover of the same old unicorn, and very much in the style of *Wonders*.

Of course his book is radically different from *Wonders*, but it is not exactly a corrective. Amazon, unicorn, and doghead live on, witnessed and verified. The trees are full of flour, the desert is full of ghouls, the mountain streams flow with diamonds. The strangeness of his East is a familiar strangeness, nearly as familiar to his readers as the Holy Land was to the readers of Egeria and Arculf. Marco Polo travels across a landscape half created in advance of him, and at the appropriate moments his scribe, Rusticello the romancer, speaks in the voice that has been largely responsible for that creation.[2]

But whatever familiar features the landscape offers in isolated perspectives, its position relative to Europe and Home has changed. To Marco Polo and Friar William it is neither central nor marginal, and its emphasized quality is neither sacred nor grotesque. The Tartar conquests are a serious political reality, and the East is becoming dangerously palpable. In this East, according to Matthew Paris, Alexander's famous wall has been broken down and the "unclean peoples" have spread all over Asia, even to the Danube: "Swarming like locusts over the face of the earth [the Tartari] have brought terrible devastation to the eastern parts [of Europe], laying it waste with fire and carnage . . . it seemed that

---

2810); it includes in brackets important additions from Ramusio's sixteenth-century edition (based on a now lost manuscript sometimes thought to represent Marco's own revision). Moule and Pelliot's edition is more redundant and wordy than any original could have been, since it combines almost every word and phrase from every witness in an uninterrupted text; the resulting text balloons at times to almost unquotable proportions. Most ellisions among my quotations represent insignificant redundancies. I have occasionally cited Yule's simpler text to make points about particular Ramusian variations. Citations from Yule are by book and chapter numbers.

2. Ronald Latham summarizes the research of L. F. Benedetto, whose introduction to his critical edition of Polo's book is not available in English. Benedetto claims, for instance, that whole passages from Polo's accounts of the Tartar wars have been repeated almost word for word from battle scenes in Rusticello's Arthurian romances. Even "the dramatic account of the welcome accorded to the Polos on their second visit to Kubilai and the commendation of young Marco is closely modelled on Rustichello's previous description of the arrival of Tristan at King Arthur's court at Camelot" (Latham, *Travels of Marco Polo*, 17).

God did not wish them to come out; nevertheless it is written in sacred history that they shall come out toward the end of the world, and shall make a great slaughter of men."[3]

Although western Europe's initial terror of the Mongols dissipated rapidly, to be replaced by a desperate hope that a European-Mongol alliance might eliminate the Saracen menace, the Mongols' territory was no longer politically neutral, no longer a conveniently blank screen for imaginative projection. Friar William's journey to Karakorum was intended to open up at least a religious communication between the two civilizations, and the Polos hoped to open commercial relations. The two narratives belong then to a stupendous historical moment: in the second half of the thirteenth century the Eastern and Western limits of the *orbis terrarum* finally confronted each other in the flesh. The contact was not destined to last, but of course no one knew that.

Coming into European political history, the East was to some extent divested of its purely emblematic and psychological function: since the thirteenth century it has become both more and less than an eidolon. The images that comprised the merely legendary East survived, but the nature of the "lattice" in which they found their places altered significantly.[4] For one thing, the actual population of the East became a matter of interest and commentary.

---

3. *Chronica majora*, as quoted in William Rockhill, ed. and trans., *Journey of Friar William of Rubruck*, xvii.

4. "Lattice" is the term Curtius recommends in the epilogue to *European Literature and the Latin Middle Ages*: "Forms are configurations and systems of configurations in which the incorporeal things of the mind can manifest themselves and become comprehensible. Dante orders the blessed in circles of light and crosses of light. A crystal consists in a space lattice of electrons and molecules. . . . Literary forms perform the function of such lattices. As diffused light is concentrated in the lens, as crystals form, so the matter of poetry is crystallized into a configurational schema." The word could be used too, I think, to denote the "configurational schemas" of various Matters which are transmitted through nonliterary or unwritten means as well as by the relay of conventionalized literary tradition. The Matter of the East was handed down as much in conversation and informal storytelling as in books. A study of the "literary influence" of such conversation on the travel books of the Middle Ages and Renaissance would be worth making: it could help render more precise our notion of the degree to which rhetorical formalities can enforce the structures of "popular" mythology, and vice versa. (Todorov appears to be following a similar intuition when he theorizes, in "Origin of Genre," that all those "codifications of discursive properties" we call genres are amplifications and elaborations of various kinds of ordinary speech acts; "that literary genres have their origin, quite simply, in human discourse"; 169.)

Uninhabited territory was seen as exactly that: the absence of man and his products was a notable absence, and when encountered, neither marvel nor miracle was produced from the magician's empty hat. "When one leaves this province of Ghinghin talas of which I have told you above he goes riding continually ten days marches between sunrising and the Greek wind [i.e., east and northeast]. And in all this way there are no dwellings, or very few; and so there is nothing else which does to mention in our book" (Moule and Pelliot, 61). That "nothing" is precisely what Egeria, Arculf, and the author of *Wonders* filled their texts with, and those "dwellings" precisely what the early writers ignored.

At last the emphatic quality of the East has become its actualness, and the object to which its narrator would like to render himself transparent exists in the same way, along the same latitudes of the physical universe, as does the object Home. Many of the categories under which Home is describable are sensed as applicable to the East as well, and the objects and customs of Home enter the picture explicitly, not only in a fragmentation of similes but in analogies and comparisons:

For you may know quite truly that all idols have their proper days dedicated to them, on which days they make solemnities and reverence & great feasts in their names every year, as our saints have on the special days. (Moule and Pelliot, 75)

Wherever [these Iugar priests] go they are always in saffron coats, quite close-fitting and with a belt on top, just like Frenchmen, and they have a cloak on their left shoulder, hanging down in folds over the breast and back to their right side as the deacon wears a chausuble in Lent. (Dawson, xxv.4)[5]

5. All quotations but one from the *Itinerarium* of William of Rubruck are cited by chapter and paragraph numbers from the English translation "by a nun of Stanbrook Abbey," in *Mission to Asia*, ed. Christopher Dawson. The translation is based on the text edited by Anastasius van den Wyngaert in volume 1 of the *Sinica Fransiscana* (1929), which includes paragraph numbers: the Dawson text does not print these numbers, but follows van den Wyngaert's paragraphing exactly. I have also consulted the annotations to William Rockhill's edition and translation for the Hakluyt Society (1900). Rockhill's edition remains invaluable for its notes, but the translation is based on the now discredited Latin edition of Thomas Wright and Fransisque Michel (1839).

Such analogies demonstrate a sense, novel for medieval Europe, that the two worlds are both different *and* susceptible of relation to one another. From this point on we will be particularly concerned with charting the progress of that relation as it is both controlled and expressed in the literary "relations" of European travelers.

In the real world of a merchant it is the quotidian that matters. Marco Polo describes political and military structures, imports, exports, and mediums of exchange, religious customs, the protocols of marriage and burial, birds, beasts and countryside, the layout and architecture of cities. The phenomenal world is the only one we see here. Even when dealing with topics that might lead into metaphysical realms, Marco's eye is focused on the outward, public surface of things: on religious rites, not religious ideas, the outcome of battles, not the war of ideologies, the behavior of a nation, not its mythology.

Despite its reduction to more or less "hard" facts, the East has not escaped the network of symbolic geography. The conceptual division of the world into West and East is too useful a category of thought to disappear. But as a vehicle for metaphor it is used more consciously now. We know and feel the difference between the "East" of Hesse's *Journey to the East* and the East to which we are about to export nuclear technology or from which we buy cheap clothing. The reading audiences of Marco Polo and Friar William were only just beginning to conceive of a bare and practical, mundane and geographical East—an East from which real soldiers could come and besiege their cities. That East, with all its implications for theology and natural philosophy, was mainly accessible through the manuscripts of these travelers. They had an important task in hand: the transformation of an imaginative entity, previously more useful as figure or fantasy, into a topic for geography and history. The plethora of facts contained in the accounts of Eastern travel in the thirteenth century is random enough to elude their authors' capacities to characterize and rich enough to offer a compelling opportunity to later writers as well as to European culture at large. What literary organization does appear in their works, however, will have a confining and shaping effect on imaginations to come. What did Marco Polo and William of Rubruck make of their burden of new knowledge in carrying it back to Europe? How did they adapt the available powers of the written word to the task of turning fable into geography and history?

Marco Polo

Marco Polo's book was by far the more widely read and influential, although it is neither earlier nor indeed better than William's (and was preceded in Europe by three other firsthand accounts of the Tartar East). According to A. C. Moule, in the introduction to the Moule and Pelliot edition,

> The question of the true text of the book is a very curious and intricate one. . . . The book may have become popular, although Ramusio probably exaggerates when he says that "all Italy in few months was full of it." But this popularity resulted not in the preservation of it but in the destruction of the book in the form in which it left the author's hands, till there has survived no single known copy which can claim at all to be either complete or correct. . . . It was very long and not a little dull, the work of one who had, as has been said, "looked at everything and seen nothing"; it was written in an uncouth French much mingled with Italian which sometimes puzzled even contemporary interpreters; and so from the first each copyer omitted, abridged, paraphrased, made mistakes and mistranslations, as he saw fit, influenced naturally by his own point of view and immediate interests or purpose; and the result with which we have to deal is nearly 120 manuscripts of which, it is little exaggeration to say, no two are exactly alike. (40)

In line with the variorum spirit of Moule and Pelliot's edition, we will consider as part of Marco's book anything that has been believed to be so by medieval and Renaissance translators and readers. The book was in a sense the collaborative effort of a whole culture, enacting by its means its discovery of the Orient, and it is particularly as such an effort that it interests me here.

Even the urtext, whatever and wherever it may be, was not the work of a single individual. The essential originality of Marco's book is amazing when one considers that, of all the possible conduits for his memory, he chose as his ghostwriter Rusticello of Pisa, a man who had been a professional writer of Arthurian romances for the court of Prince Edward of England. But Rusticello's immediate impact on the work appears to have been relatively superficial. He is responsible for the language of romance that suffuses the narratives of the Tartar wars at the end of the work and perhaps for the more thoroughly fictional of the stories that replace data in chapters on cities Marco did not visit. The structure of the work, the selection of its material, and most of all the conception of the act of telling it displays are all Marco's—or, as that name renders a rather problematic voice, are at any rate not the contributions of Rusticello's genre. Would a professional romancer have said this: "And after we had begun about the Greater Sea then we repented of it . . . , because many people know it clearly. And therefore we will leave it then, and will begin about other things" (219)?

What is significant about the collaboration is not so much the degree to which the fiction writer adulterated the words of the documentarist, but the fact of the collaboration itself. To the extent that this autobiographical opportunity has not in the least been seen as such, we are still in the literary world of Egeria, whose "I" is only *an* "I," providing its text with little more than the brute context of eyewitnessing. In Marco's case, as in Egeria's, the only differentiating factor in the narrator's persona lies in the author's public identity. Marco is a merchant, and therefore he witnesses with the eye of a merchant, as Egeria had with the eye of a nun.

The similarities do not extend much further. For Marco's material is as open-ended and his topography as unlandscaped as Egeria's had been finite and prefabricated. Egeria had only to finger verbally the rosary beads of the already imaginatively tangible Holy Land. Marco had to turn into words a world that, for Europeans, was without a true history, a being. He had to do for the reality of Asia roughly what the Scriptures had done for Palestine.

No matter how undaunted his tone then, he must be aware that it is through him and the transcription of his experience that the East will receive its imprimatur. Unauthorized by God, unaided by a muse, politically and ecclesiastically uninvested, he must render the rest of the world in his own person, simply on the basis of his experience. Although William of Rubruck had come before him, the friar's account had been a letter to a king, and Marco's enterprise was a letter to Europe.

"There are two Armenies, one is called Armenie the Great and one Armenie the little" (20). The void behind this bald statement is hard to realize. A voice that can substantively predicate the mere existence of something as vast as a country is a voice with primal responsibilities and which sees itself as such. ("In the beginning God created heaven, and earth"; "All Gaul is divided into three parts.") This of course is also the voice of the textbook, but what textbook for adults begins by announcing the existence of anything the size of Armenia? And in the heyday of scholasticism, what private secular man would undertake to so essentially declare the truth of things?

Yet that is the mode of Messer Marco's "narrative." It is in fact *not* a narrative. It is a *descriptio* of unprecedented scope, confident enough to present itself as the equivalent of knowledge.[6] It is even less reportage than is Egeria's *Peregrinatio*. It is as declarative and impersonal in the majority of its sentences as *Wonders of the East*, although in its ostentatious basis in experience it places the ultimate source of authority firmly in the eyewitness.

The eyewitness cannot be just anyone, as Montaigne's speaker could have been—that would throw the emphasis of the work onto the nature and quality of the personal experience of travel (where in modern travel literature, and to some extent in Friar William's account, it mostly does lie). But this book is about "the different generations of men and the diversities of the different regions and lands of the world" (1). So while the eyewitness is the absolute prerequisite for a book about that which can only be known to others by hearsay, the personal aspect of Marco's experience is of negligible importance and he must obtain the authority to speak from someplace beyond his private self. The voice of Rusticello resolves this problem in the opening of the prologue:

And each one who shall read or hear this book must believe it fully, because all are most truthful things. For I make you know that since our Lord God fashioned Adam our first father & Eve with his hands until this moment never was Christian, Saracen, nor pagan nor Tartar nor Indian nor any man of any kind who saw & knew or inquired so much of the different parts of the world & of the great wonders so much as this said Master Marc Pol searched out and knows, nor had travelled through them. . . . And therefore he says to himself that it would be too great evil if he did not cause all the great wonders which he saw & which he heard for truth to be put in writing so that the other people who did not see them nor know may know them by this book. (1)

6. The book's earliest title was *Diuisament dou monde*. See Latham, *Travels of Marco Polo*, introd. 7.

Thus, while Marco's authority is indeed founded in his personal experience, that experience is in a way transpersonal as well. As the *first* man to see the whole world, he exists in the mythic-heroic sphere of first and founding gestures, *in illo tempore*. He is literally a living legend, and it is from that order of existence that he speaks, and because of that that the reader can "believe it fully." We are reminded of the traveler's mythic nature at several other points in the book as well: at the end of the section on Cathay, before we turn to India, Rusticello says:

Master Marc Pol stays there in Indie so long and went and came there so often and inquired and asked so much, that both by hearing and by sight he was able fully to learn and to see and knows so much of them, of their affairs and of their customs and of their trade, that there was scarcely a man who ever knew or saw so much of them, as he did, who would know better how to tell the truth about them. (157)

And again, in the epilogue of a fourteenth-century manuscript, the opening formula is repeated:

But I believe that our return was the pleasure of God, that the things which are in the world might be known. For, according as we have told at the beginning of the book in the first heading, there never was any man, neither Christian nor Saracen nor Tartar nor pagan, who has ever explored so much of the world as did Master Marc son of Master Nicolau Pol noble and great citizen of the city of Venice.

Thank   God   Amen.

Like *Wonders of the East*, and for some of the same reasons, this work is, as I have said before, a group effort. The "I" (variously rendered throughout any one manuscript as "I," "he," "one," "we," and "you") is not the authentic "I" of a private and personal self but an image created by Marco Polo, Rusticello, and a host of translators, redactors, and editors over a period of centuries. The image is that of First Traveler, and the position it takes in relation to the World is the result of a concensus among literate men as to what that position must be. There is a real variety among the texts, not in structure but in what fills the space between the setting out and the final account of the Tartar wars. The book came to be seen as a sort of encyclopedia, to which later knowledge (or ignorance) and fuller detail from other sources could be added at will, sometimes in the middle of a sentence.[7] What information the original manuscripts contained was frequently distorted and altered by translators and editors whose scant knowledge of the East did not equip them for their task.[8] But Polo's authority is stamped on every version, and when a mapmaker drew from him, he did not worry about how close his manuscript was to an "original"—or to the truth.[9] (This is of course a characteristic medieval approach to authorship: Moses, Aristotle, Albertus Magnus, any number of writers became posthumous fathers to work not their own, in an inversion of the equally characteristic practice of plagiarism. But it is interesting in light of Marco's unique claim to authority. Neither "ancient" nor ecclesiastic, he has become an umbrella figure on the basis merely of living in and moving around the physical world.)

The information contained in the manuscripts varies, but it is always handled in the same way, by a series of formulas and according to a system of priorities that give the book its ultimate integrity. The strict itinerary structure of the pilgrimage narrative

7. The following sentence from F, for instance, is expanded in the middle and at the end by VB (a fifteenth-century Venetian manuscript): "They have a very great quantity of Indie nuts very large [—as large as a man's head—] and good to eat fresh [but in the middle of the shell of the fresh nut it is full of a liquid of a taste like wine or syrup]" (167). Ramusio's text also expands the sentence, but differently, likening the milk to "clear fresh water, but better to the taste" (Yule, *Book of Ser Marco Polo*, III.x).

8. Compare the F and Ramusian texts on the subject of the Land of Darkness: "Still further north . . . there is a region which bears the name of DARKNESS, because neither sun nor moon nor stars appear, but it is always as dark as with us in the twilight" (F); "because for the most part of the winter months the sun appears not, and the air is dusky, as it is just before the dawn when you see and yet do not see" (R). See Yule, IV.xxi, n. I. The question of which more closely represents Marco's original, F (Yule's "Geographic Text") or the manuscript from which Ramusio compiled his Italian edition, is too complicated to go into here. In general, Yule and Cordier appear to consider both texts as including later additions and deformations, and Ramusio's as sometimes including Marco's own later revisions and corrections of his original. In his note to this particular passage, Yule is inclined to blame Rusticello for F's inaccuracy and credits Marco's revisions for the Ramusian text's correctness.

9. For instance: "Some geographers of the sixteenth century, following the old editions which carried the travellers south-east or south-west of Java to the land of Boeach (for Locac), introduced in their maps a continent in that situation. (See, e.g., the map of the world by P. Plancius in Linschoten.) And this has sometimes been adduced to prove an early knowledge of Australia" (Yule, III.vii, n. 3).

is not so important here. The route is relatively arbitrary, as there are no stations of the cross to be followed across Asia. Nor is there any reason for us to follow so closely in this traveler's footsteps: it is not vicarious experience he means to offer, but knowledge in more or less raw form.[10]

But while we do not follow Marco's exact itinerary, there is a route here (as opposed to the "concatenation" of *Wonders*) and it is based on Marco's experience—or on the rough map into which that experience has crystallized in his memory. We are explicitly kept in the dark about India in the earlier portion of the book, even though our route passes as close as Kashmir:

> We shall not go forward, because if we were to go forward twelve days marches further we should enter into Indie . . . and I do not wish to go in there at this point because on our return journey we shall tell you all the things of Indie in order in the third book. And so we will go back to our province towards Badascian, because by other road or in other directions we shall not be able to go. (49)

There is no geographically logical reason not to talk about India after discussing Kashmir. The obstacle is that Marco himself did not discover the two places in that order. In his later discussion of the kingdom of Mangi, which "the Great Kaan has divided into nine parts" (152), he tells us only about three of those parts (though we fully expected to hear about all nine):

> Of these three however we have told thus in order because Master Marc made his passage through them, for his way was directed hither. But of the other six also he heard and learned many things, and we should know well how to tell you of them; but because . . . he did not travel over them he would not have been able to tell so fully as about the others. (157)

---

10. Marco's most renowned critic, Leonardo Olschki, claims that the book "is not, as is commonly supposed, a book of travel and adventure, but a treatise of empirical geography; that is to say, it is both a guide book and a doctrinal work, fused into a literary combination so successful that it is impossible to tell the one from the other" (*Marco Polo's Asia*, 14.) At least the first half of this remark is an untenable oversimplification, and Olschki contradicts himself in a later chapter. The problem is one of terminology: Marco's book is not, indeed, what we *now* call a "book of travel," but it marks a crucial stage in the development of the modern genre. In its own time, it was generically too novel to be labeled, as its peculiar popular title, *Il milione*, suggests. The problem of genre in Marco's book is worth a longer discussion.

On the arrangement of his discussion of Cathay:

Now you may know that . . . Master Marc Pol himself, the great lord sends him as a messenger towards sunsetting. And he set out from Cambulac and went quite four months of days journeys toward sunsetting, and therefore we shall tell you all that he saw on that road, going and coming. (105)

This seems an odd sort of fidelity to an arbitrary order. Marco's experience was a temporal and contingent one, and the material of his book is laid out on a fixed and spatial grid. Why transfer the temporal order to what seems primarily a rendering of space, a verbal *mappa mundi*? The answer lies in the fact that Marco and Rusticello are consciously creating a book, not a map, a reading experience that exploits the linear and sequential path of the person who turns the pages, one after another, or of the person who listens to a story being told. Despite its encyclopedic breadth of topics, their book seems intended to be read straight through like a novel, rather than dipped into like a reference book (and the recent introduction of paper into Italy had made such private reading more common). More explicitly than Egeria, the authorial "I" is taking us on a journey (in which he frequently becomes "we"), a journey that has its own present and future tenses in addition to Egeria's simple and ultimately uninviting past.

"We shall now leave this district with out going any further . . . " "On our return journey we shall tell you all about India . . . " "If the traveler leaves Karakorum and Altai . . . " "Let us now continue our journey towards the East." "For this purpose the Great Khan leaves this palace and goes elsewhere. But before we follow him . . . " "So let us return to Zaiton and recommence our book from that point." "We told you earlier in the book about Hormuz and Kais and Kerman. Since we went out by another route, it is fitting that we should return to this point. But . . . we will not loiter here now." "But, now that we have embarked on this topic, we have had second thoughts about setting it down in writing . . ." Not only do we share with the authorial "I" a present-tense mental journey, complete with future possibilities and roads not chosen, but the author even allows us into the present tense of his dictation: the book itself, as well as the journey it creates, exists in time. "Now I will tell you" and "I have told you" occur on almost every page. "We have already told you," "we told you earlier about," and "now you have heard" are frequent. Particularly intimate are the spots where Marco changes direction in midparagraph. He begins to tell us about the Black Sea:

On the mouth of the entry of the Greater Sea on the side of the sunsetting there is a mountain which is called the Far. And after we had begun about the Greater Sea then we repented of it . . . , because many people know it clearly. And therefore we will leave it. (219)

Now since we have told you of these Tartars of the Sunrising then we will leave them for you and will turn again to tell about the great Turquie so as you will be able to hear clearly. But it is truth that we have told you in the book above all the facts of the great Turquie . . . and so we have nothing more to tell of it. And so we will leave it. (215)

Of course these passages sound like the sort of thing one might expect from a slavishly transcribed dictation. But, as noted earlier, Rusticello did not simply write down what Marco said. The work is thoroughly embellished with refining rhetorical touches and set pieces from chivalric romance. The opening and closing fanfares, already quoted, the fine speeches put in the mouths of Tartar "barons" during the account of their wars, Rusticello's occasional remarks of praise or wonder at the extent of Marco's travel or the breadth of his observation: all this betrays the scribe's editorial confidence and autonomy. That he did not choose to refine away these particular moments of hesitation suggests that they seemed appropriate to the work's intentions. Certainly they are not isolated from the effect of the whole.

There is something intricately artificial in all this. Despite the loud claims the text makes for the authenticity of its data and the plain veracity of its author, and despite Europe's serious need for information about the East and the Tartars, the experience it gives us is predominantly one of pleasure, and the pleasure is rooted in the work's overt manipulation of our imaginative faculties. We are to pretend we are on a journey. We are to pretend that we share in the identity of the narrator. We are finally and most exquisitely to pretend that our reading *is* a journey, that in some sense we are moving, embarking, loitering, passing on, as we sit still in our rooms turning the pages of a book.

Many refused to believe Marco Polo, and legend has it (according

to Ramusio, his sixteenth-century Venetian editor and biographer)
that at his deathbed friends begged him to retract his book. No
doubt this was partly the effect of his subject matter, much of
which is hard to credit even now (though most of it has been
verified by later travelers). But the work bears about it as well the
smell of fiction, for the first time in this previously documentary
literature. It will not be long now before Mandeville erupts onto
the scene, in a fictional work that ironically enough inherited
much of its credibility from its likeness to the slightly suspicious
book of Marco Polo.

It is not hard to see in this kind of transmission the rudiments of
what Bakhtin calls, idiosyncratically, the novel—in contradistinc-
tion to the epic. Egeria's transmission of the Holy Land was the
product of what Bakhtin would term "epic consciousness," in
which

> both the singer and the listener, immanent in the epic as a genre, are
> located in the same time and on the same evaluative (hierarchical) plane,
> but the represented world of the heroes stands on an utterly different and
> inaccessible time-and-value plane, separated by epic distance. To portray
> an event on the same time-and-value plane as oneself and one's contempo-
> raries (and an event that is therefore based on personal experience and
> thought) is to undertake a radical revolution, and to step out of the world
> of epic into the world of the novel. (*Dialogic Imagination*, 14)

Of course Bakhtin is tracing the lineage of this genre at a level
deeper than that of textural formalities. He is interested in the
whole project of consciousness into which the novel as we usually
think of it fits, and he thinks in terms of the *longue durée*. But
when speaking of literary origins, one is always speaking of shift
and expansion in a culture's imaginative relations with the world
of which literature speaks. Both the novel and the modern travel
book express a concern with personal, individual experience once
almost entirely absent in Western literature. The story of its growing status in our literature brings the histories of the two genres
closer together than critical tradition might indicate.[11]

11. Adams's chapter 3 ("The Truth-Lie Dichotomy") in *Travel Literature and the
Evolution of the Novel* documents a period in the histories of the two kinds, during
the late seventeenth and early eighteenth century, when the reading public sometimes had difficulty telling them apart.

Bakhtin would place the roots of this "radical revolution" far earlier than Marco Polo. Because for him the novelistic consciousness is the product of "polyglossia," the "cultural interanimation, interaction of ideologies and [especially] languages," he traces it as far back as Xenophon's *Cyropaedia*, in which the hero (Cyrus the Great) is "foreign and barbaric." "The world has opened up; one's own monolithic and closed world (the world of the epic) has been replaced by the great world of one's own plus 'the others'" (28–29).

Marco is certainly a latecomer to this consciousness produced by the interanimation of languages; most European countries have been bilingual (at least) for well over a millennium by his time, as well as in contact, however tentatively, with other cultures—Slavic and Islamic. But one might imagine that each new step toward the alien would be accompanied by a new flurry of novelistic activity, a sharper, deeper engagement with the contemporary world and the project of rendering it. Who could be more likely than such a traveler as Marco to reproduce, on a smaller scale, that great plunge into reverence for the present which first took place during the Hellenic confrontation with the otherness of Persia? Ctesias, often considered the first Western travel writer, fought in the same war that "opened up the world" to Xenophon, and Marco is his direct heir, another avatar of the First Traveler.

One of Bakhtin's criteria for the novel is the coexistence within a text of several metalanguages, the parodic or quasi-parodic use of voices from many genres to produce a single voice identified with none of them. In Marco's text we find at least three: the present tenses of the letter writer reflecting the time of writing ("we have already told you"); the narrative present tense that enacts the time of reading ("when the traveler leaves"); and the biblical, or textbook, present tense which, in Todorov's phrase, "institutes reality" and which has received its justification from Rusticello's valorizing of the traveler. The content of the East is transmitted in this last voice, in sentences that, like those of *Wonders*, declare the static and permanent existence of things.

This last and most purely discursive voice is what seems to separate Marco definitively from the genres of memoir, autobiography, and the novel. It functions to secure his claims to truth and operates by erasing the individual Marco of the "letter writer" (as well as the individual reader-"traveler" who "leaves," "embarks," "loiters," and so on). Marco remains admirably dense to the con-

notations of the things he chooses to transmit. He evaluates rarely
and does not speak (as Friar William had, or as Odoric of Pordenone
would a few years later) as a propagandist for the Western norm. He
is interested in neither shattering nor protecting familiar visions of
the East, as his depiction of the unicorn, quoted earlier, makes
clear. Where the evidence of his senses confirms "our stories," he
shows no disrespect for them, and where it does not he is scan-
dalized at having been misinformed.[12]

But for the most part Marco is not revising or replacing old
images but filling in blanks where even blanks have not been previously imagined. The frequent baldness of the style, despite occasional rhapsodic passages (to which we will return later), further
emphasizes the annunciative quality already noted in his sentence
structure, where little beyond existence is predicated. Detail is
repeatedly eschewed as tedious: "And I would well tell you how
[the ships] were made, but because it would be too long a matter I
will not mention it to you at this point." (19); "and you may know
that we do not tell you of all the cities of the kingdoms [of Mangi]
because it would be too long a matter to mention" (183).

Often satisfied with describing the parts of large territories by
repeating a formula in which only the proper nouns change, his
apparently fuller passages are really only finer articulations of the
major pattern ("x exists").[13] Marco has divided the East into countries and territories that do or do not owe allegiance to the Great
Kaan. These countries are usually further divided into cities and

12. "Moreover I wish to say and make you know that those who bring the little
dead men [pygmies], as is said, from Indie, it is a great lie and a great deception . . .
for I tell you that those which they say are men . . . are made so by hand on this
island" (166). After debunking the notion of the salamandar as a lizard with fleece,
and explaining that it is in fact a rock (asbestos), Marco snorts: "all the other things
that are said of it, that it is an animal, are lies and fables" (60).

13. Here is a particularly rigid and monotonous formula at work: "And you may
know that this Vugiu is one day's journey distant from Sugiu. And it is a very great
city and good and of great trade and of great industry. And because there is nothing
of novelty which does to mention we will leave it and will go and will tell you of
another city which is called Vughin. And this Vughin is also a great city and
important, the people of which they are idolaters and subject to the rule of the great
Kaan, and have money of notes. And there is great quantity of silk and and of many
sorts of other costly goods. And they are clever merchants and clever at handicraft.
Now we will leave this city and will tell you of another city also, named the town of
Ciangau. Now you may know that this city of Ciangau is very great and noble and
rich. They are idolaters and are subject to the great Kaan, and have money of notes,
and they live by trade and handicraft" (151).

stretches of countryside through which "the traveler" passes. The cities are divided into buildings and markets, people, and products, while the countryside is divided into fauna, wild flora, agriculture, and mineral deposits. Countryside is characterized as "fine" or "desolate," depending on its productivity, and cities as beautiful or splendid. If the city is big or the countryside "fine" he will go on to subdivide it, filling in more blanks:

Cobinan is a very great city. And the people of that country worship the abominable Mahomet. There is iron and steel and andanique enough, and many mirrors of the finest steel are made there very beautiful and large. And tutty is made there, which is not made elsewhere, which is very good for disease of the eyes. And with it spodium is made there also; which I saw made, and I will tell you how they are made. (39)

And again there is a beautiful plain in which there are cranes enough and pheasants and partridges enough and many other kinds of birds. . . . And there are found five kinds and manner of cranes in these regions, which I will describe to you. The one kind is all black like a raven with great wings and they are very large. The second kind is all white . . . [etc.]. (74)

The practical result of this tendency in the work has already been noted—the variations and distortions from manuscript to manuscript are limited almost entirely to the content of Marco's blanks and formulas, as if that content were somehow less sacrosanct than the syntax and the formulas that contain it. And why not? The differences between Boeach and Locac, southeast and southwest, one hundred *li* and one hundred miles, are of interest only to another merchant or to a prospective conqueror. Marco's book is formally addressed to *"all people* who wish to know"—not to specialists, not necessarily to those whose self-interest could be served by an exact knowledge of the East. Olschki calls its presentation of geographical data vague, conventional ("the various data . . . are nearly always generic, not specific, and are often blurred or arid"), and points out that even the commercial data it contains are nothing so systematic as the lists and instructions in Pegolotti's *Pratica della mercatura* (published fifty years after Marco's book; Olschki, *Marco Polo's Asia*, 131, 98).

The book is neither geography nor a merely mercantile itinerary. Neither is William of Rubruck's book, which is far more autobiographical and more finely detailed, and which suffered almost *no* textual distortions in the history of its dissemination. But William's book is specifically addressed to the missionary and military interests of the crusader king Louis IX. William is reporting, while Marco is excitedly establishing a matrix for existences.

The particular kind of entertainment the book offers is based on the reader's ability to believe that what he is hearing about and imagining is actual, but it does not matter too much *what* he is imagining. "Boeach" and "Locac" offer an identical pleasure, the pleasure of the exotic name. Real exotica are more titillating than the fabulous variety, and thus the book was more pleasurable to those who could believe it. Marco made it as believable as he could, in particular by means of its comprehensive scope and formulaic description, and as a result Europe altered its maps and its ideas of the *orbis terrarum* according to the book's new lattice. Later accounts of travel to the East would not be able to claim as their raison d'être the establishment of a palpable image of the East and would function as correctives, addenda, analyses, or memoirs. From Marco's time on, Europe had an East in its real geography— an East that it had yet to evaluate and respond to, but one through which it had ridden with eyes open, and soul asleep and dreaming.

So far we have been paying particular attention to the structural devices through which *Il milione* makes its claims to authority and historicity. Its successful and novel achievement of both qualities assured that its informing vision would become canonical as well as its data. The exuberant, even joyous, nature of that vision is separable from the scientific or journalistic truth value of the data that embody it, but was destined to control even scientific attempts to represent the East for centuries to come. It is time then to turn our attention to the purely imaginative and psychological satisfactions of Marco Polo's Elsewhere.

Marco's book is a tissue of compromises and cross-purposes in which the voices sometimes subvert each other's aims and strategies. His literary situation is a confusing one: he is producing a new kind of book about an old topic, based on an old mode of experience in a completely new world. Despite the originality of his practical orientation and attempted transparency, his book maintains the quality of wonder that had characterized the Western attitude toward the Orient, in one form or another, since before Ctesias. The definition of *wonder* has shifted a little, and its relative importance has dimmed, but the word appears twice in the first few sentences of Marco's prologue and frequently introduces a description.[14] More than that, it is a quality of Marco's perception implicit throughout the work in the relation of certain types of phenomena.

A wonder is more than simply something we do not have at home. The travel memoirs of the twentieth century are full of exotica, but the climate of the times discourages the perception of wonders except in the stubbornly naïve. (Erik von Daneken and John Lilly pander to what is left of our capacity in this area.) A wonder partakes of another Nature—it cannot be crossbred with our fauna or wholly imported to our shores. And there is something essentially positive about it. No matter how ugly this crocodile is, one is expected to enjoy the fact of its existence:

And the very great adders are bred in this province, and those great serpents which are so much beyond measure that all men who see them have great fear of them and must wonder at them. . . . And I will tell you how large and thick they are. For you may know for truth that there are some of them ten large paces long and some more and some less, which are quite as thick as a large butt, for they measure ten palms round; and these of this size are the largest. And they have two short legs in front near the head, which have no feet except that they have three claws, namely two small and one larger claw made sharp like a falcon's or a lion's. It has the head very large and the eyes such that they are larger than a large loaf of ours worth four dinars, all shining; the mouth is so large that it would well swallow a man or an ox at one time. It has very large and sharp teeth. And it is so very exceedingly hideous and great and fierce that there is no man nor woman nor beast in the world that does not fear to go near them, and has not dread of them. (119)

(Characteristically, this ferocious monster's flesh "is very good to eat and they eat it very gladly," and his gall "is much prized because great medicine is made of it" which cures cancer, rabies, and the pangs of childbirth—an extension into the purely phenomenal sphere of the *bonus* and *malus* significances of the old allegorical *monstra*.)

Although the physical description of the crocodile is almost ped-

14. Another popular early title of the book was *Ce liure des merueilles du monde*. See Yule, Appendix F, 2:534.

antically accurate and true to life, we have not so much been given an addition to our zoological knowledge as a tangible expression of the Other World. Unlike the fire-breathing serpents of *Wonders*, this monster has been verified by an eyewitness and its properties and powers do not exceed the bounds of easy belief. But like so many of the less practical tidbits in Marco's book, and contributing to a total effect that subverts the work's overtly familiarizing approach, it proclaims the fundamental difference of the world in which we are traveling.

This difference is presented at a much higher pitch of intensity in *Wonders* and founded on a much more obvious distinction in the sacramentalizing pilgrimage itineraries. And in fact Marco subdues his own sense of it in his book with his attention to what is or could be close kin to the normal and by the empiricism that continually pits the evidence of his senses against traditional fabulous lore. Strangeness is by no means a crucial criterion in his selection of data, as it had been for Arculf: towns that manufacture steel and plains full of pheasants are perfectly possible in Europe, and their presence in the East titillates more by their familiarity than by any alien qualities they may manifest.[15]

But the undertone of otherness is there, and in its freedom from the cruder qualities of the supernatural emphasized by *Wonders* and the Alexander romances, the book renders more clearly the fundamental components of the East's imaginative appeal. Supernature is only one of the Natures from which we can feel alienated and to which we can be drawn for relief from our own. What Marco cannot quite refrain from dwelling on, despite his urgent objectivity (and despite the paganism and "barbarism" that so appalled Friar William, John of Plano Carpini, and Odoric of Pordenone), is the splendor, the power, the fecundity of the East. It will be remembered that even Egeria, the zealously idealist pilgrim, was stirred into an *occupatio* by the physical splendor of the churches of Jerusalem on Easter—the most enthusiastic plunge into physical description in her whole letter. Marco too is prodded into a more emotive discourse when opportunities arise for him to treat

---

15. Marco pointedly leaves out a description of the strange powers and accomplishments of the Tibetan sorcerors: "They do . . . all by devil's art, which it is not good to tell in our book because the people would be too much surprised" (116).

of the Khan's splendor and the splendor of his chief cities and palaces.

In some ways the Khan *is* the East—certainly all of it but India and Japan is in his power and pays him tribute, and thus its wealth and productivity reflect directly on him:

Now I have told you the way and the reason why the great lord must have and has more treasure than any man of this world. . . . Moreover I will tell you a greater thing, that all the lords of the earth have not so great riches, treasures, and expenses as the great lord has alone. (96)

After a description of the Khan's winter hunting parties:

He stays there this term in the greatest enjoyment and in the greatest delight in the world, so that it is a wonder to tell, for there is not a man in the world who did not see it who could believe it, because it is much more, his grandeur and his business and his delight, than I should be able to tell you. (94)

After a description of the Khan's feasts:

And again I will tell you a thing which I had forgotten to relate, which seems a great wonder which is somewhat fit to relate in our book. For you may know that when the great Kaan makes feast and ceremony as I have said above, a great lion is brought before the great lord. And as soon as he sees him the lion throws himself down lying before him and makes signs [of] great humility, and seems to know him for lord. He is so tame that he stays thus before him with no chain and not tied at all, lying quietly at the king's feet like a dog; and it is indeed a thing which makes one wonder. (90)

The long section of the book which treats explicitly and almost exclusively of the Khan's magnificence is introduced in these words:

Kaan means to say in our language the great lord of lords, emperor, and this lord who now reigns indeed he really has this name . . . by right because everyone knows truly that this great Kaan is the most powerful man in people and in lands and in treasure that ever was in the world or that is now from the time of Adam our first father till this moment. . . .

And this I shall show you quite clearly in the course of this our second book . . . so that each will be sure that he is . . . the greatest lord that ever was born in the world or that now is, and in the following chapters I shall show you the reason how. (76)

The Khan has hereby been removed (with the same formula that transformed Marco himself in the prologue) from the sphere of the mundane. Not that he is made fabulous—the whole weight of Marco's account supports the notion of the actuality and palpability of his power, its present-tense and provable truth. But his valorization separates him from all the rest of "the lords of the earth" and reestablishes the old gulf between the Natures of the West and the East. It is not so much that the East is in all ways *better* than Europe ("Nevertheless," Marco remarks after one particular burst of enthusiasm, "there does exist I know not what uneasiness about the people of Cathay")[16], but that its possibilities are separate and alien from our own. It cannot ultimately be better because it is spiritually benighted, but in Marco's book it is confirmed as the location of all that an oppressively spiritualized culture dreams of most deeply and inchoately.

They do not grow on "berries 150 feet long," but gems are peculiarly plentiful:

And do not believe that the good diamonds come into our Christian countries but the greater part & the most noble diamonds they go and are carried only to the great Kaan and to the kings and barons of these different regions and realms, for they have the great treasures of the world and buy all the dear stones for themselves. For those which come to our countries, nothing comes but their leavings. (175)

Costliness is everywhere; even the peasants dress in embroidered silks and satins. It is a shiny world: it is not wealth simply as wealth that Marco so admires, but wealth as manifested in radiance and color.[17]

16. Marco's sentence appears in the Ramusian text and is included in note 7 to Yule, II.xi.

17. In Manuel Klamroff's 1953 edition of Marco Polo, the index shows a total of seventy-five listings under headings that designate various precious minerals. Aldous Huxley devotes a long section of his essay on visionary experience, *Heaven and Hell*, to the peculiar appeal of shiny and radiant materials, particularly in the Middle Ages (for which see 16–32). In this connection he quotes Socrates from the

Organic nature is hardly less splendid:

> There are in this kingdom many strange beasts different from all the others in the world. For I tell you that there are black lions without any other colour or mark. And there are also parrots of several kinds more beautiful than those which are brought to us this side of the sea, for there are some parrots all white as snow and they have the feet and the beak red, and again there are some parrots red and some white and green which are the most beautiful thing in the world to see, and green ones also. There are some again very small which are likewise very beautiful. There are also peacocks much more beautiful and larger and of another sort and size than ours. And also they have hens very different from ours and better than ours. And what shall I tell you about it? They have all things different from ours, and they are more beautful and better. For . . . they have no fruits like ours, nor any beasts nor any birds; and this comes to pass, they say, through the great heat which is the rule there. (180)

The climatic theory of cultural differences referred to in the last sentence had usually in the past been called on to explain the inferior natural and human forms of alien places.[18] Here it seems to explain the opposite. Not only is this paradise full of *more* beautiful birds and flowers than we have at home, but it is emphatically *full* of them. The lists of which Marco is so fond have the effect of stuffing our visual field, so that the beauties of the East appear to us only in the form of abundances. His method of description lends itself so naturally to the production of this effect

---

Phaedo: "In this other earth the colors are much purer and much more brilliant than they are down here. . . . The very mountains, the very stones have a richer gloss, a lovelier transparency and intensity of hue. The precious stones of this lower world, our highly prized cornelians, jaspers, emeralds and all the rest, are but the tiny fragments of these stones above. In the other earth there is no stone but is precious and exceeds in beauty every gem of ours." The Christian Celestial City, from the Apocalypse to the Middle English *Pearl*, is characteristically fashioned of gold and gems—as is Milton's Pandemonium.

18. See, for instance, the statement quoted in chapter 2 (p. 68) from *Airs, Waters, Places.* Old habits die hard. At the turn of our own century, Maj. Arthur Glyn Leonard had this to say about the Niger Delta, in *The Lower Niger and Its Tribes*: "The country may be described as one in which Nature is at her worst. From the slime and ooze of the soil up to the devitalizing heat and humidity of the atmosphere, it leaves its mark on the people in an enervating and demoralizing influence, which continues unbroken and perpetual, without any of those compensating or redeeming features that tend in the direction of vitality or recuperation" (quoted in Robert M. Wren, *Achebe's World*, 67).

that although he is rarely drawn to the description of savage or unpleasant places, he renders them with an equal sense of abundance:

And the men make fires like this to protect themselves and their animals from the fierce wild beasts of which there are so many throughout that country and throughout that land that it is a wonder. And it is because no people live there [Tibet, which "Mongu Kaan has destroyed by war"] that these wild beasts have so multiplied. . . . And with all this some lions come sometimes or some bears and some of the other wild beasts which do them harm; for there is very great plenty of them in the land. (115)

Inside the town dare live no sinful woman . . . , these are the women who do service to men for money, but I tell you they all live outside in the suburbs. And you may know that there are so great a multitude of them for the foreigners that no man could believe it, for I dare tell you in truth that there are quite twenty thousand, . . . and they all find a living. . . . Then you can see if there is great abundance of people in Cambulac since the worldly women there are as many as I have told. (95)

This is no country for old men. Marco gives us several accounts of tribes that practice willing cuckoldry to entertain foreign travelers and freely countenance adultery ("if the woman be willing") and polygamy. The Oriental potentates with their hundreds of wives seem to spawn sons like mackerel, and Marco relishes the statistics. After describing a tribe that values most highly as brides women who have been promiscuous before marriage, he says: "Now I have told you of this marriage [custom], which it does well to say the manner of it. And into that country the young gentlemen from sixteen years to 24 will do well to go" (115).[19]

The wonder of this East then does not lie in the isolated monstrosities of the fabulous literature, nor in that propensity for miracles characteristic of the Holy Land of pilgrimage accounts. In Marco's book it is an atmosphere, compounded of brightness, license, and plenitude, which is not supernatural but otherworldly

19. Olschki interprets Marco's commercial figures along these lines as well: "when he reports the amount of dues levied by customs officials of the Great Kaan in the ports of China, he certainly has no intention of instructing Italian merchants concerning the taxes the state would levy from them, as Pegolotti systematically does, but he makes use of these figures to illustrate the immense wealth that flowed into the imperial coffers from these parts" (*Marco Polo's Asia*, 99).

in its manifestations. Crocodiles, parrots, ruby mines, artificial hills of lapus lazuli, golden birds that sing, trained leopards, postal systems, polygamy: none of this is in the least impossible. It is unlikely, *unheimlich*, but credible. What makes it so *poignantly* unlikely, and wondrous, is that while it is not characteristic of Marco's Europe, it is characteristic of European dreams. Marco's factual celebration of the East is the bright shadow of the West's own poverty and political factionalism, its famines and depopulation, its spiceless cookery and rigid sexual morality. The qualities he discovers in the East characterize as well the imagined other worlds of "dream visions," chivalric romances, troubador love poetry, the backgrounds of medieval religious paintings, the mineral splendor of altar decorations, the growing (and controversial) sensuality of church music.[20]

But the undertone of envy and desire in Marco's account is curiously resigned. Roger Bacon's remark on the importance of geography does not suggest that places have changeable natures: "If [the longitude and latitude of every place] were known, man would be able to know the characteristics of all things in the world and their natures and qualities which they contract from the force of this location" (*Opus majus* 320). Europe is what it is; its latitude and climate are its destiny, and though we can bring home cinnamon and galingale, the Land of Spices will remain a synonym for desire.

Creation ex nihilo is humanly impossible. Despite Marco's valiantly clear-eyed effort to photograph the memory of his journey without prejudice or fabulation, to let us know, simply, "the things which are in the world," he has added another link to the long chain of visions which constitutes our Elsewhere. It is a new link, in its empirical basis and its novelistic awareness of the reader's experience, but it is a vision, not a photograph. The East as complement to the West will necessarily change as the West's self-image changes, but in Marco's hands it remains largely a complement,

20. In 1322, Pope John XXII issued a decree forbidding the use of discant in church services, in an attempt to stem the "intoxicating" development of polyphony: "[Certain disciples of the new school] truncate the melodies with hoquets, they deprave them with descants, sometimes even they stuff them with upper parts (*triplis et motetis*) made out of secular songs. . . . Their voices are incessantly running to and fro, intoxicating the ear, not soothing it. . . . As a consequence of all this, devotion, the true end of worship, is little thought of, and wantonness, which ought to be eschewed, increases" (Buck and Wooldridge, *Oxford History of Music*, 1:295).

dependent for its significance and its conceivability on the nature of the West. The being Marco has given it, by means of his bald declarations and copious lists, is the body of the West's desire. Friar John's *Historia Mongolorum* is a more complete and accurate account of the Mongols; Friar William is a much better writer; and Odoric's account (twenty years later than Marco's) reflects more faithfully the conscious European attitude toward the politically and spiritually "barbarous" Oriental states. But Marco's is the book that lived and entered into history, because in him the real and reachable Orient and the country of the heart's desire were inseparably, if unevenly, joined.

William of Rubruck

Friar William of Rubruck's account of his missionary journey to the Mongols, undertaken in the service of Louis IX during the Seventh Crusade, slipped almost immediately into relative obscurity (although not before Roger Bacon had pillaged it for his *Opus majus*). Only five medieval manuscripts are known. This obscurity is a fact worthy of note, since, despite its improvisatory quality (the letter, to Louis IX, was written on demand and in a hurry), it has been hailed by modern commentators as a beautiful and intelligent piece of writing. Olschki, for instance, calls it "one of the most original and interesting masterpieces in the whole of medieval Latin literature" (*Marco Polo's Asia*, 69). Yule remarks that "it has few superiors in the whole Library of Travel" (*Book of Ser Marco Polo*, 1:105). Rockhill speaks of "the equity of Friar William's claim to the highest recognition" (*Journey of William of Rubruck*, Preface, ix). It is a serious, scrupulous, and useful document as well and, written in 1255, reached Europe only eight years later than the very first Western account of the Mongol's East— Friar John of Plano Carpini's *Historia Mongolorum*.[21] As such its potential appeal should have been immense, especially since it is a piece of travel writing proper, as opposed to Friar John's textbook cultural history.

21. An English translation of this work, along with several other, shorter accounts of missionary visits to Mongol princes during the period, is available in Dawson's *Mission to Asia*.

As a reporter on Mongol affairs, however, Friar John scooped Friar William. John's account was a primary source for the most authoritative encyclopedia of the later Middle Ages, Vincent of Beauvais's *Speculum historiale*, which was finished in 1253 (the year of William's departure for the East). Friar John's book is less useful to modern historians, though with chapter headings like "How to Wage War against the Tartars" it might well have seemed more useful to a contemporary audience. At any rate because of its format we pass over it in favor of Friar William's letter: only one (the last) of its nine chapters is devoted to the journey itself, and Friar John (like Herodotos before him) considers himself and his journey only as source materials for a history. Friar William's letter is not only more appropriate to our concerns, it is also the high water mark of literary excellence among the travel accounts of the Middle Ages. Claude and René Kappler, in the introduction to their annotated French translation, are so impressed as to liken some of its effects to those of Bocaccio, Chaucer, "and even the Shakespeare of certain comic scenes, or Rabelais" (*Voyage dans l'Empire Mongol*, 62).

The work is Friar William's account not of a place or of a culture, but of an event: it begins at the beginning of his journey and ends at the end of it, with only a few additional paragraphs apologizing for the writer's lack of skill and, by way of summary, suggesting the ease with which Turkey could be conquered. It contains no romantic fables and few stories of battles, and has no points to prove. Its few generalizations are drawn from fully depicted experience. It makes no claims for itself or its author as anything special—in its matter-of-fact modesty and lack of rhetorical excitement it sounds eerily modern.

But the most revolutionary aspect of this text is its personality. In William we have finally found a traveler-author who speaks in his own voice, from his own real position in the practical world. He neither submerges nor exalts himself, is neither invisible nor polemical. And his full presence in the account of the journey allows us something Marco's text cannot: a sense of what it would be like to travel in the East. As well as remembering what he saw, Friar William remembers what he felt when he saw it and seems to find that equally worthy of record. No generic formulas adulterate or distance the transmission of his experience, and his lack of rhetorical repetition and redundancy, together with his fondness for gratuitous detail, combine to produce the mild suspense of real life, in which no two moments are quite the same.

As Rockhill notes in his translation for the Hakluyt Society, "none of the MSS presents any variations of importance, the different readings in them being clearly attributable in nearly every case to negligent copying" (xlii). This is not a text like Marco's to which one would be tempted to add. Its primary tense is the closed narrative past, as opposed to Marco's infinitely expandable descriptive present. And it records not "the things which are in the world," but the things William saw, when and as he saw them, in an order integral to the shape and purpose of the whole. William's letter has, in short, a plot and a character.[22] Although he was not free to invent either of them, he was free to make their functions active in his account, which after all is justified by neither. His *duty* was to describe the physical and political geography of the East. The method was up to him.

After Marco's almost erotic struggle with empiricism, and the weirdly statistical dream vision that issued from it, William's disinterested naturalism comes like a slap in the face. The friar saw little to love in the filth and barbarism of the Mongol *ordas*, and he shows us the grimy underside of the incandescent East in such detail that empathy compels belief:

The great lords have villages in the south from which millet and flour are brought to them for the winter; the poor provide for themselves by trading sheep and skins; and the slaves fill their bellies with dirty water and are content with this. They also catch mice, of which many kinds abound there; mice with long tails they do not eat but give to their birds; they eat dormice and all kinds of mice with short tails. (v.1)

They never wash their clothes, for they say that that makes God angry and that it would thunder if they hung them out to dry; they even even beat those who do wash them and take them away from them. They are extraordinarily afraid of thunder. (VII.1)

Scatatai was sitting on his couch holding a guitar in his hand, and his wife was beside him; really I believe she had cut off her nose between the eyes

---

22. Several characters, in fact. William delights in the accumulation of detail that makes for a literary character, and his portrait of the Armenian "monk" Sergius, with his polished fingernails, fatal medicines, and lunatic notions of diplomacy (he promises Mangu the pope as his vassal) is only the best of many.

so that she might be more flat-nosed, for she had no nose there at all and she had smeared the spot with black ointment, and also her eyebrows, which to us looked hideous. (x.3)

The meat they gave us was not sufficient and we found nothing which could be bought for money.

Furthermore, whenever we sat under our carts to get some shade, for the heat was great at that time, these men intruded upon us in such a churlish manner that they trampled on us in their wish to see all our things. If they were seized with a desire of relieving nature they did not go away from us so far as one can toss a bean; indeed they performed their filthiness by the side of us, chatting to each other; and many other things they did which were above measure trying. (xiii.4–5)

Of the twenty or thirty horses we always had the worst since we were foreigners, for they took the better horses before us; me they always provided with a strong horse, as I was very heavy. But as to whether it went at a steady pace or not, this was a matter about which I dared not enquire, nor did I even dare to complain if it proved a bad mount, but each one had to put up with his luck. This was the cause of one of our most difficult trials, for many a time the horses grew tired before we came across inhabitants; then we had to strike and lash them, even to put our clothes on to other pack animals, to change our horses for pack horses, and sometimes the two of us had to ride on one. (xxi.6)

This is not the kind of thing that excites wonder or desire. It satisfies curiosity, answers questions that never occurred to Marco, such as How did you get there? What was it like? Were you afraid? Marco's East, though actual, is not visitable, as its atmosphere is to be found only in the sum of its parts; its allure is an abstraction, structured by the generalized scarcities of Home. But reading William one can imagine an East made up, just like reality, of moments and footsteps. His technique offers a deeper verisimilitude than Egeria's or Arculf's or Marco's because the essential ingredient of our actual experience is subjectivity. "There are five different kinds of cranes" is a fact we can only believe or disbelieve. "That morning the tips of my toes froze so I could no longer go bare-foot" (xxviii.11) is a fact embedded in the sensual and psychological density of the life that is taking place even as we read. In William's letter, both the act of reading and the actions about which we read participate in the corporeality that separates life from dream, rapture from theology, cold feet from the cold.

The plot rendered in all these tiny brush strokes is one of humiliation and self-discovery. This plot is neither an intrusion into the business at hand nor an impertinence, as William was a sort of guinea pig missionary: what happened to him could happen to any who followed after him, and knowledge of the particulars of his failure could help to ensure future success. ("It does not seem to me expedient that any other Friar should again go to the Tartars as I went and as the Friars Preachers are going; but if the Lord Pope . . . would send a bishop with marks of honor . . . "; Epilogue, 5). A missionary journey for many reasons offers fertile ground for the development of the novelistic potential of travel writing. It is to begin with a spiritual journey, already equipped with a climax (or anticlimax) and invested with allegorical significance, particularly for a member of one of the wandering orders. As a journey with a more specific goal than the gathering of information, it demands a more dynamic engagement from the traveler, who becomes an agent as well as an observer. The business of saving souls is by definition a matter of contact with concrete individuals, and this kind of journey thus necessitates active involvement with persons rather than peoples. And the traveler bears a personal responsibility in carrying out his journey, opening up the dynamic of success or failure. After his last, unsatisfactory visit with Mangu Khan, William says with regret, "If I had had the power of working miracles like Moses, he might have humbled himself" (xxxiv.7).

A pilgrimage is of course a spiritual journey as well, but it is a repetition, a reenactment, and the pilgrim's involvement with the profane and actual world through which he travels is not only unimportant but sinful. He only seems to be in Palestine; to the extent that he is a pilgrim, he is in the Holy Land, whose nature is fixed and known. The kind of spiritual change a pilgrimage may enforce is in no way subversive and is understood in advance. It is so little dependent on the experience of difference offered by travel that it could be and, in the later Middle Ages, often was performed by proxy, or by wandering an equivalent distance in a maze.[23] All

23. For pilgrmage by proxy, see Sumption, *Pilgrimage,* 295–302. On the subject of unicursal mosaic mazes on cathedral floors (often called "chemins de Jerusalem"), in which the sinner might perform an alternative pilgrimage, see W. H. Matthews, *Mazes and Labyrinths,* 54–70. (The final degradation appears to have been the wall

the miles in a pilgrimage are equal to each other and are valued at the same rate of exchange as any other ascetic or penitential gesture.

But each mile of William's journey is part of a progress toward something only his specific journey can provide and the moral value of which can be understood in secular terms as well. After many months of cold, hunger, humiliation, and disillusionment, William and his interpreter ("Homo Dei") finally reach the Great Khan's court at Karakorum. They are now at the source of Mongol power and influence, where their evangelizing can do the most good. It is Epiphany, and an Armenian monk who follows the court has told William that he will baptize Mangu "on the day of the feast." But he will not allow William to be present, and the friar is by this time wise to the fabulous nature of the stories of Christian Mongol princes and to the lies and misunderstandings of the Nestorian Christians at their courts. That night, "some of the Nestorians . . . wanted to assure me that [Mangu] had been baptized; I said to them that I would never believe it nor tell anyone else, seeing I had not witnessed it" (xxix.16). The glowing hopes with which William had started out have been extinguished, replaced with a clear and almost cynical apprehension of the dispiriting truth:

The monk told me that the Chan only believes in the Christians; however, he wishes them all [idolators and Saracens as well] to come and pray for him. But he was lying, for he does not believe in any of them as you will hear later, yet they all follow his court like flies honey, and he gives to them all, and they all think they enjoy his special favor and they all prophesy good fortune to him. (xxix.15)

It has been a day that called on all of William's spiritual resources and that could have led to despair. But it is not over yet:

We came to our cold and empty house. They were providing us with bedding and coverlets, even bringing us material for fire, and giving meat of one thin little ram for the three of us, food for six days, and daily they gave us a bowl full of millet and a quart of millet ale a day, and lending us a

---

labyrinth, on which "of course, the journey would be even less arduous, being performed by the index finger"; Matthews, 67.)

cauldron and tripod for cooking our meat; which cooked, we were cooking the millet in the meat broth. This was our food; and it would have been enough, if they had let us eat in peace. But so many are famished, for whom food is not provided, who as soon as they used to see us prepare food would push in upon us, whom it behooved us to eat with. Here I experienced what great martyrdom it is to give largesse in poverty. (XXIX.17; translation mine)[24]

This paragraph is one of some structural complexity and provides a useful sample for biopsy. Several time lines are woven together in it. First, the narrative time of the story ("We came to our cold and empty house"), complete with self-consciousness effectiveness in rendering the last action of a deeply disappointing Epiphany. Then the imperfect flashback to earlier provisons made for the travelers by their Mongol hosts, properly subordinated to the perfect tense of the suspended narrative line, which is devoted to William's experience of disillusionment. With the continuation of the habitual past, the skimpy hospitality of the Mongols is extended outward from the shock of that night, giving it a context and turning the final moments of Epiphany into the initial moments of a subsequent physical ordeal. We are told about the problem of the starving beggars in the same generalizing tense, so we have to apply it ourselves to the time of the narrative, strengthening the connection between the events of that evening and privations still to come. The paragraph ends with a return to the narrative, this time in the perfect tense of summary, in a sentence that characterizes and gives significance to the content of all the preceding predicates: we have been told about this evening and the ordeal of which it is a part because as a whole the experience gives body to an important spiritual initiation. As a Franciscan, Friar William has already vowed to "give largesse in poverty" and has

24. "Venimus ad domum nostram frigidam et vacuam. Lectiscrinia providebant et coopertoria, afferebant etiam nobis materiam ignis et dabant carnem unius arietis parvi et macilenti tribus nobis, cibum pro sex diebus, et cotidie scutellam plenam de milio et unam quartam in die de cervisia de milio, et mutuabant caldariam et tripodem ad coquendam carnem nostram; qua cocta, milium coquebamus in brodio carnium. Iste erat cibus noster, et bene suffecisset nobis si permisissent nos comedere in pace. Sed tot sunt famelici, quibus non providetur de cibo, qui quam cito videbant nos parare cibum, ingerebant se super nos, quos oportebat comedere nobiscum. Ibi expertus sum quantum martirium sit largiri in paupertate" (van den Wyngaert edition).

probably made a practice of it for years past. The journey he is on, however, has offered him the ultimate and definitive opportunity for the practice and in so doing has deepened both his experience of it and his capacity for it.[25]

William's timing is all important here. Only with the bitter events of this Epiphany in mind can we fully appreciate the impact of his hunger or the self-surprising magnanimity of his sharing. And only his perception of the ordeal as a spiritual opportunity can fuse the events of the day and evening into an organic whole, more shapely than the arbitrary record of an itinerary, more significant than the schematization of a map. William is alive to the idea that informs autobiography and the modern realistic novel: that private experience is significant and readable—not as the fulfillment of gnomic or biblical "truths," but as contingent and particular behavior in a world of moral challenge.

In the friar's first sentence (after the obligatory greeting to the king) lies the essential difference between his account and Marco's: "It is written of the Wise Man in Ecclesiasticus: 'He shall pass into strange countries, he shall try good and evil in all things.' This have I fulfilled, my Lord King, but would that it were as a wise man and not as a fool; for many perform the same actions as a wise man, not however in a wise manner but rather foolishly; and I fear I am to be numbered among these" (Prologue, 2).

Although the self-doubt (which goes on for several sentences) is conventional in addressing the aristocracy, it seems appropriate to offer this as a contrast to Marco Polo's (or Rusticello's) invocation, also addressed, though not exclusively, to aristocrats: "Lords Emperors, and Kings, Dukes, and Marquesses, Counts, Knights, and Burgesses, and all people who are pleased and wish to know the different generations of men and the diversities of the different regions and lands of the world, . . . take then this book and have it read (1).

This is conventional too: Benedetto has pointed out that the

---

25. The business of charting personal change is apparent on a more Rabelasian front as well. William reports of his first taste of *cosmos*, the Mongol drink made of fermented mare's milk, "as I drank it I sweated all over from fright and the novelty of it" (IX.4). By the time he is given wine at Baachu's encampment in Persia on the way home, "I would have preferred to have [cosmos], if he had given it to me. The wine was new and special, but cosmos is a more satisfying drink for a hungry man" (XXXVII.23).

sentence was in fact taken from one of Rusticello's own Arthurian romances.[26] The two conventions lead in opposite directions—suggestively, in light of the twin foci of travel writing, the journey and the journey's setting. However much Marco eschews the fabulation of romance, he has retained its otherworldliness and its emphasis on the imaginative pleasure of an Other World. William, as much as is seemly in a document intended to be of practical use, offers instead the experience of a man in search of wisdom and unsure of whether he has found it: he is not the First Traveler of Marco's myth, but he is in some ways Europe's first modern traveler.

William's dogged realism and the sense of personal adventure conveyed by his narrative were not of his time and would not appear again in the corpus for a couple of centuries. After sinking into oblivion, his book was to be resuscitated at last by Hakluyt and Purchas in their collections of voyage literature.[27] The book does not look at all out of place among the Renaissance "relations" that largely comprise those collections. When nonritual contact with alien lands was renewed and multiplied in the Renaissance, there was ample occasion at last for the generation of pure narrative within the confines of the travel account (as will be argued in detail in later chapters). William's book is not simply a sport: it is the adumbration of a literary result to be expected from circumstances such as those in which, and about which, he wrote.

Only with the thirteenth century's penetration into the secular East beyond the Holy Land could the literary struggle toward the establishment of the modern genre of travel writing finally, formally begin. The troubled point of view of the pilgrim toward the task of recording and assessing sublunary topography and merely human beings cannot interfere where there is neither sacred territory nor religious experience to focus on. Pilgrimage bequeaths to secular travel writing the idea of travel as a significant action, and the hope of transformation. The romances of Arthur and Alexander provide a background of fictional experience against which to mea-

26. See Latham, *Travels of Marco Polo*, 17.

27. William has been almost a naturalized citizen of British literature, receiving most of his medieval dissemination through Roger Bacon's inclusion of long passages from his letter in the *Opus majus*; rediscovered, printed, and translated by the two great British editors of travel literature; and surviving in manuscript form mostly in British libraries.

sure the actual. But Marco Polo and Friar William have begun to play with an experience that calls for new conventions and challenges the powers of language with an unprecedented object—the secular journey through the real world. And however little else they have in common, they harmonized the two chief tones of travel writing—the journey and the journey's setting—more effectively than anyone had before them. Place would continue to dominate persona for some time to come (though within a century Mandeville would have created a traveling persona of unforgettable charm). But in Marco Polo's and Friar William's accounts we find what we cannot quite find earlier: structures that follow space through time—emphatically the *traveler's* time, not the time of the scriptural past or the unnarratable, unvisitable present of *Wonders*.

4

"That othere half"
Mandeville Naturalizes the East

With *Mandeville's Travels*, the developing genre of travel literature in the West reaches a complicated and long-sustained climax. The book's popularity has been greater than that of any other prose work of the Middle Ages, and its practical effects farther reaching.[1] To investigate the reach and nature of its artistic effects, it will be necessary first to stand back and take the long view of the tributaries that feed it and the genre for which it helped carve a new bed.

Although his most important modern critic, Josephine Waters Bennett, calls Mandeville's book a "travel romance," that is precisely the term I hope to avoid in sketching Mandeville's literary context. The capacity to conceive and construct romance out of the materials of history is an accomplishment for which medieval writers had long been sitting on their laurels. Mandeville was up to something more novel. In a sense crucially qualified by the nature and degree of his readers' imaginative receptivity, he was writing realistic prose fiction—for the first time since Petronius. Fiction was not of course entirely foreign to prose in the fourteenth century. Prose romances such as the thirteenth-century French *Lancelot* had kept alive the possibility of fictional meaning for secular

---

1. Josephine Waters Bennett lists about 250 surviving manuscripts in Appendix 1 of *The Rediscovery of Sir John Mandeville*. The book was first printed in 1470, one of the earliest of all printed books. According to George Sarton (in "The Scientific Literature Transmitted through the Incunabula"), Mandeville is the eighth most popular author on Arnold Kleb's list of the incunabula; none of the leading seven is a medieval prose writer.

prose narrative, but in the safe confines of material too unremit-tingly marvelous ever to be mistaken for actuality. (According to Auerbach's scathing dictum, "the courtly romance is not reality shaped and set forth by art, but an escape into fable and fairy tale"; *Mimesis*, 138). But Mandeville's realism was a challenge to an ancient dichotomy between the "fables" of poets and the "truth" of science and history which was still seen as nearly identical with the rhetorical opposition of verse and prose. From the beginning, the question of his creation's epistemological status has confused its most perceptive readers. The controversy over the "truth" of Mandeville's document suggests that in it may be found one seed of the crisis over historicity and significance which signaled the birth trauma of the modern novel.

The generally acknowledged complicity of romance in the gen-esis of the novel is a peculiarity perhaps insufficiently appreciated as peculiar. To begin with, romance is a genre characterized by its material, while the novel is characterized by its technique. And to whatever extent the novel *could* be said to have a generic material, it lies at the furthest extreme from that of romance: where romance wanders among marvels in distant or otherworldly places, the novels of "the Great Tradition" tend to play themselves out in the intimate and familiar settings of bedrooms, kitchens, and parlors. (Under the influence of this tradition, Hawthorne called "romances" those of his novels set in the past or in Europe.) Ultimately, though, we recognize a novel more by its delivery than by its setting. Its earliest protagonists *are* in fact wanderers, and many of them wander far from home. Robinson Crusoe and his island are the stuff of romance, but *Robinson Crusoe* is emphatically not. The palpability of its presentation works against the marvelous elements in it, and out of nameless, exotic flora Crusoe constructs a bedroom, a kitchen, a parlor—in exhaustive, gratuitous detail.

Concern with the details of the phenomenal world once belonged most properly to the prose of history and "natural phi-losophy." But an aerial view of the novel's prehistory in medieval narrative and prose will disclose a vast, slow shift in consciousness which redefined the mutual boundaries of history, geography, and romance and thus helped set the stage for *Robinson Crusoe*. *Man-deville's Travels* was an important enabling factor in this process, but its precocious realism is not historically inexplicable. By Mandeville's time the fabulous and romantic Matter of the East had already begun to intersect with the more or less documentary forms of chronicle and *itinerarium*. The Crusades had domesticated the Levant, bringing it closer to the sphere of the mundane and merely natural (and at the same time pushing back the threshold of the "fabulous" East so far that, in the end, men like Columbus could begin to think of sailing *west* to reach it). That foothold in the mundane essential even to "magical realism" was at last available to a man who wanted to write about Elsewhere.

The demystification of the actual East begins as early as Fulcher of Chartres's eyewitness account of the First Crusade, the *Historia Hierosolymitana* (finished c. 1127). After describing an eclipse of great beauty, Fulcher expostulates over God's power to create wonders and says:

Consider, I pray, and reflect how in our time God has transformed the Occident into the Orient.

For we who were Occidentals have now become Orientals. He who was a Roman or a Frank has in this land been made into a Galilean or a Palestinean. . . . We have already forgotten the places of our birth; already these are unknown to many of us or not mentioned any more. . . . Indeed it is written 'the lion and the ox shall eat straw together' [Isa. 62:25]. He who was born a stranger is now as one born here; he who was born an alien has become a native. (III.xxxvii).[2]

Fulcher at least finds this conflation of Occident and Orient a matter for wonder. The process of demystification has gone even further by the time of the Fourth Crusade, when Villehardouin can speak this matter-of-factly of Constantinople's Hagia Sofia (traditionally a catalyst for expressions of solemn awe and wonder): "And then [Dietrich] went back with a great party of the emperor Henry's men; and found that the castle was pulled down, and he closed up and fortified the church Sainte Sophye, which building is high and fine, and held it to use for the war" (*La conquête de Constantinople*, 2:271).[3]

2. All quotations from Fulcher will be cited, by volume and chapter numbers, from Frances Rita Ryan's translation, *A History of the Expedition to Jerusalem*. Ryan's translation is based on Heinrich Hagenmeyer's definitive text, *Fulcheri Carnotensis historia Hierosolymitana* (1913).

3. "Et cil s'en rala a grant partie de la gent l'empereor Henri; et trova que li chastiaus ere abutez et ferma et horda le moutier Sainte Sophye, qui mult ere halz et biels, et retint iqui endroit la guerre."

The opening up of China by missionaries and merchants in the thirteenth century and the annexing of Palestine by European powers during the period of the Crusades had enlarged the *oikumene* of Europe and allowed for significant overlap of this world and the Other World of the imagination. Mandeville's terms for West and East are "on this half" and "in that half." Halves of what? Of one physical, spherical whole in which the laws of nature operate unilaterally and where if one sails far enough one ends up back at home:

And therfore hath it befallen many tymes of o thing that I have herd cownted whan I was 30ng, how a worthi man departed somtyme from oure contrees for to go serche the world, And so he passed ynde and the yles be3onde ynde . . . And so longe he wente be see & lond & so enviround the world be many seisons, that he fond an yle where he herde speke his own langage, callynge on oxen in the plowgh such wordes as men speken to bestes in his own contree, Where of he hadde gret mervayle. (xxi, 122)[4]

It may not be too farfetched to see reflected in this little tale the peregrinations of fiction itself, from the wanderings of Odysseus across what Joseph Campbell calls "the Threshold of the Known" to the wanderings of Leopold Bloom among the transformed streets of his hometown, "where of he hadde gret mervayle."[5] For eventually the Threshold of the Known was pushed past even far Cathay, to the Caribbean, to Roanoke, to New Jersey, and the

4. This and all further quotations are indicated by chapter and page number, and are taken from the Early English Text Society edition of Hamelius (1919). This is a documentary edition of MS Cotton Titus Cxvi. Although the Cotton manuscript is not the version Hakluyt disseminated so importantly in the first edition of his *Voyages*, and in fact did not reach print until 1725, I have chosen it as my chief text of the *Travels* because it is closer to the French original than the once prominent "Defective Version," and I am as much interested in the author's conscious artistry as in the wider influence of the work in its many abridged versions. References to Hamelius's notes will be cited by volume and page number of the EETS edition.

5. The terms of Joseph Campbell's Jungian analysis of what he calls the "monomyth" of the heroic journey (in *The Hero with a Thousand Faces*) can be applied with some usefulness to accounts of actual travel to the East and to the New World, although Campbell is talking about myths, folktales, and dreams. The connection lies in the fact that the travelers whose accounts we are looking at had themselves a mythic understanding of their activity: they were on pilgrimage to the World Navel, or, in going farther East or sailing to the New World, they were leaving the *oikumene* behind them and entering "a dream landscape of curiously fluid and ambiguous forms."

Earthly Paradise filled up with farms and cabins and post offices and, in the end, with shopping malls.

By the time of Mandeville (in the Cotton text, the *Travels* is dated 1356 by its author), travel to the once sacred or fabulous places of the East had dropped off sharply: the Crusades were over, and the relatively gregarious Mongol Empire had been overthrown in China and was being absorbed by hostile Saracen Turks closer to home.[6] But the chronicles of crusaders and travel accounts of missionaries had familiarized both the Near and Far Easts for Europe's reading public and themselves had grown even a little stale.

It was the perfect moment for a literary hoax (though Mandeville made something more than that). With actual contact slowed to a trickle, "news" of the East was out of the question and the Matter was going stagnant again. The forms in which the Matter was contained were widely familiar and, because they were infrequently used, had rigidified in their conventions. And with so few Eastern travelers around, verifiability was not a pressing restriction on the writer's art.

The "hoax" worked because it imitated something recognizable. There is evidence that at least some people believed in the *Travels* for a long time. Ralegh, Frobisher, and (apparently) Columbus all read it earnestly—Frobisher even brought it with him to Baffin's Bay in 1576. Mercator and Ortelius cite Mandeville as an *auctoritas* in their world atlases. Hakluyt included it in the first edition of his *Principall Voyages* (from which he excluded the probably authentic *Relation* of David Ingram for lack of "credibility").[7]

Since we now know that Mandeville's credibility was founded neither in personal experience nor for the most part in the transmission of accurate facts, it must be a literary credibility, a sort of intertextual verisimilitude.[8] Mandeville must be received as truth

6. Shortly after the fall of Acre in 1291, the Persian khan Oljaitu converted to Islam. The Mongols in Persia, Russia, and Turkestan were quickly absorbed into the Moslem cultures around them, and relations with the West broke down. A Christian mission remained in China, but fell with the fall of the Mongols there: the last Western missionary, John of Marignolli, left China in 1347, and the Christians were expelled in 1369 by Chinese nationalists.

7. Hakluyt's successor, Samuel Purchas, admits that he "smell[s] a Friars (Lyars) hand in this," but hints that it was Odoric—the real traveler from whom Mandeville adapted much of the second half of his book—who later "stuffed" it full of "Fables" (Purchas, *Purchas His Pilgrimes*, 11:363–64). For the story of Ingram see Adams, *Travelers and Travel Liars*, 133–34.

8. The credit for first bringing to light the extent of Mandeville's plagiarisms belongs to two nineteenth-century scholars: Albert Bovenschen, whose dissertation

(where he is so received) because he sounds like truth. A close look at the *Travels*, then, will be in part a close look at its genre in little, as the genre had come to be understood by the time of its first great parody (since Lucian). That the *Travels is* in part a parody, however, cannot be forgotten: it discards and subverts and extends the possibilities of many of its inherited characteristics. And the spirit that shapes it is almost wholly new.[9]

We have already taken note of most of the main currents feeding the *Travels'* stream: the eyewitness pilgrimage narratives, the Alexander romances and their spin-offs, the mercantile and missionary accounts of India and Cathay. But there are other, newer sorts of texts around by 1356 which also convey the reader to places I have been calling Elsewhere. Accounts of the Holy Land best termed guidebooks (foreshadowing the degradation of eighteenth-century Grand Tour accounts into nineteenth-century Baedekers) are a flourishing subliterary genre, and of course the Crusades have been thoroughly chronicled. Neither kind of book contributed much directly in the way of style or topics to the *Travels*, but both form part of its literary context and helped shape Mandeville's opportunity.

The guidebooks are the sadly degenerated offspring of Egeria's letter to her Venerable Sisters—not quite a return to the itineraries of late antiquity, but lifeless and depersonalized. Some features of the style of a representative fourteenth-century account are identical with some of Egeria's. Almost all the places described are "places where" some scriptural (or, by this time, apocryphal) event took place; miraculous features are qualified by "it is said"; transitions from one description to another announce distances: "Thence you shall go forty miles to Gaza." But in place of Egeria's

---

"Die Quellen fur die Reisebschreibung des Johann von Mandeville" was published in Berlin in 1888, and Sir George Warner, who edited the Egerton manuscript for the Roxburghe Club in 1889. It is difficult to believe that some of this was not noticed far earlier, as the *Travels* was often bound in manuscripts together with some of its sources. (See Bennett, *Rediscovery of Sir John Mandeville*, Appendix 1.)

9. Iain Higgins (currently working at Harvard University on a dissertation about *Mandeville's Travels*) has suggested that I qualify my use of the word *parody* in connection with the *Travels*, since current usage restricts its meaning to a kind of stylistic joke. The word in its older, etymological, sense suggests a text that stands alongside other texts in critical or ironic imitation of them, and it is in that sense that the *Travels* is parodic. Higgins's wide-ranging and sensitive study of the *Travels* did not reach my attention until this book was in press; it will be a valuable addition to Mandeville scholarship.

experienced pauses for prayers and readings at the holy places, we are confronted with the formulas "and there is an indulgence for seven years and seven Lenten seasons" and "there is absolution from pain and guilt." The work is completely nonnarrative in structure and, most importantly, voiceless. No particular person administers or receives the absolutions and indulgences. No one judges among the marvels, hikes up the mountains, chats with a bishop: no one even writes the book—at least half of it is plagiarized from a thirteenth-century guidebook and seamlessly so. In the following extract, section 40 is plagiarized and section 41 is new:

(40) Thence you come to the doors, and in the midst of the choir is the place called the Centre of the World, where our Lord Jesus Christ laid his finger, saying, 'This is the centre of the world.' And there is an indulgence for seven years and seven Lenten seasons.

It should also be known that at the great altar is an indulgence for seven years and seven Lenten seasons, and at all the altars constructed within the church.

(41) Thence you come to a pillar near the chamber of the holy sepulchre, above which it is said that the following miracle took place. A certain Saracen entered the Church of the Holy Sepulchre, and looking round saw the aforesaid image painted above the pillar. Then he tore out the eyes of the image, and straightway his own eyes fell out on the ground (Bernard, "Guidebook to Palestine," 8–9)[10]

But although the structure of the work is nonnarrative, it is full of stories: some from Scripture, some from the Apocrypha, some from martyrologies, some from legend. Egeria and Arculf retold stories as well, but for the most part far more briefly. Of the mountain Agrispecula, for instance, Egeria says: "This is the mountain on which Balac, son of Beor, put the soothsayer Balaam to curse the children of Israel and God, as it is written, was unwilling to permit that" (XII.10). Egeria's micronarratives are reminders of stories told in full in the Scriptures and function chiefly to identify the places she describes. In the fourteenth-century guidebook they are amplified in both length and number, and drawn from almost every

10. Section 40, according to Bernard, is one of many in the work stolen from the thirteenth-century account of Phillipus Brusserius Savonensis.

possible source. Like the epic simile, they function far beyond the limits of their apparent task:

(66) As you go down Mt. Sion is the place where the Apostles, as they bore the body of the Blessed Virgin to burial in the valley of Jehoshaphat, laid down the bier. And the Jews who lived in the village hard by collected at the spot, that they might carry off the body to burn it. Then the chief priest of the Jews, more bold and imprudent than the rest, laid his hand on the bier, whereupon his hands were withered. Then he besought blessed Peter to pray for him, and to restore his hands to him. To whom blessed Peter said, 'If thou believest that this is the mother of Christ, and art willing to be baptized, thou shalt be made whole.' And he believed, and was restored to his former health. And there is an indulgence for seven years and for seven Lenten seasons.

(78) Then you come to a declivity of Mount Olivet, two furlongs eastward, to Bethphage, which is, being interpreted, the House of Figs. There our Lord sent two of his disciples, viz., Peter and Phillip, for the ass and her colt on Palm Sunday, saying, 'Go into the village over against you, and straightway ye shall find an ass tied, and a colt with her; and they, having gone, brought the ass and the colt, and they set Him thereon.' [Matt. 21:2, 7] And He was led upon the ass from that place to Jerusalem with hymns and praises, and was received with honour by the children of the Hebrews bearing palm branches. And there is an indulgence for seven years and seven Lenten seasons. ("Guidebook to Palestine, " 13–14, 16)

About two-thirds of the length of each of the two representative sections quoted above is given over to anecdote, narrated at much greater length than the needs of identification would require. The stories are not new or otherwise difficult of access: their charm is the unadorned charm of narrativity itself. They compensate for the guidebook's lack of structural narrativity—a necessary absence in an *itinerarium* without an itinerant.

Not all the guidebook's narrative excurses qualify as full stories, but the urge toward amplification is evident everywhere, even in the briefest of notices: "(107) Also near the church, it is said, was the palace of King Herod; and near there was the house of Judas the traitor, *where he lived with his wife and children*" (11, emphasis mine). This development from Egeria's mere identifications to a framework literally "stuffed" with tales has a musical analogy in the thirteenth century's development of the motet from the *clausula*: the brief phrase of the *clausula* acquired a full and usually secular text in its ornamental upper part, which resulted ultimately in a new and self-contained musical form, the motet.[11]

Such hypertrophy of an ornament is surely a sign of exhaustion in the host form, as is the extensive plagiarism among the later accounts of the Holy Land. But why *not* plagiarize? With the closing of the Crusades there was little new information to bring back, at least under the traditional heads, and the pilgrimage routes were almost as old and established as the Gospels that had inspired them. The guidebook is the detritus of a tradition a millennium old, and in a literary culture bound by a rhetoric of set topoi, figures, and arguments, the notion of plagiarism is almost beside the point. Tradition dictates not just the loci to be described, and their relative importance, but even their characterizing details. Of Mt. Olivet: "and the stone which He had under His feet still retains their impression, and it is visible to this day" ("Guidebook to Palestine," 15); "Within this [chapel] may be seen the mark of Christ's left foot, which He imprinted on the stone when He ascended into heaven" (Poloner, *Description of the Holy Land*, 9); "Know that on Mt. Olivet Jesus Christ went up to heaven on the day of the Ascension, where the form of his right foot appears yet in a stone" ("City of Jerusalem," 40).

What there was to be seen, even the order in which it ought to be

---

11. Pope John XXII's encyclical of 1322 (quoted in chap. 3, n. 20) forbidding the increasingly florid ornamentation of liturgical music, and particularly outraged at the "stuffing" (*inculcare*) that introduced secular texts into the performance of the organa, was effectively an attempt to halt the development of polyphony. And yet the fourteenth century saw the creation not only of the earliest extant polyphonic mass (the "Tournai mass") but also the initial development of the "parody mass," in which all the voice parts were borrowed from another, secular, text. These musical instances of the simultaneous presence of two or more nonconsonant "voices" and/or texts in one extended musical work are nicely analogous to Bakhtin's ideas of "polyglossia" and parody as essential generic features of the novel. Musical and purely verbal "polyglossias" seem parallel in instinct and related as well to the institution of the farce, originally a comic/parodic interlude between acts of a liturgical drama (in fact, the term *farcing* was synonomous as a musical—and culinary—term with *stuffing*). That the structure of Mandeville's book can be illuminated by these terms, in its weaving together of the anecdotes and the very words of such disparate texts as Marco Polo's, Wilhem von Boldensil's, Odoric of Pordenone's, and Vincent of Beauvais's encyclopedias will soon be clear. A feeling for the spirit of polyphony is useful for a full appreciation of Mandeville's art, and a combined analysis of the terms *polyphony* and *polyglossia* might even unearth some suggestive common denominator in the literary and muscial developments of the later Middle Ages.

seen, had been so extensively codified that an autobiographical account could offer only the addition of the author's own personality. Necessary as this may seem from a literary viewpoint, it was of course problematical from the devotional angle. Hundreds of years had passed since the times of tentative and scanty travel in which Egeria's and Arculf's personalizations of their accounts were justified. It still happened now and again—for instance in Ludolph von Suchem's account, almost exactly contemporaneous with Mandeville's, and to some extent in that of his traveling companion, Wilhelm von Boldensil, from whom Mandeville plagiarized parts of his work. But the guidebooks were the rule, a rule that called out to be broken with the flamboyant magnificence Mandeville expended on his task.

One of the few original conceptual features of the *itineraria* of the later Middle Ages is found in their occasional reference to the scriptural future and to the present as marking the fulfillment of old prophecies. This is even more notable, naturally enough, in the Crusade chronicles: on the arrival of the army of the First Crusade at Nicaea, Fulcher says:

What then shall I say? The islands of the seas and all the kingdoms of the earth were so moved that one believed the prophecy of David fulfilled who said in his Psalm "All the nations whom thou has made shall come and worship before Thee, O Lord" [Ps. 85:9], and what those who arrived later deservedly said "We shall worship in the place where His feet have stood" [Ps. 131:7]. Of this journey moreover we read much more in the prophets which it would be tedious to repeat. (*History of the Expedition*, I.xlix)

How like and yet unlike Egeria's instructions to her Venerable Sisters to read further in Numbers about the place she has mentioned, as she is too pressed for time to describe it herself. The peculiar relationship of text and Scripture, by way of a geographical *materia* that is itself a figure or a sign, remains the same, but present time as well as present space seem now to participate in the reality to be transcribed.

Time and its events provide the backbone of the Crusade chronicle, and the form is for that reason important to the development of a fully narrative genre of travel writing. But to the extent that public reality is more important in the chronicle than private experience, and topography only significant from a military perspective, it is at most tangentially related to the still spatially oriented, descriptive, and (potentially) subjective genre on which we are focused. Traveling with an army into occupied territory certainly insulates the eyewitness chronicler from immersion in the alien: still, in its reintroduction of the first-person narrative to the mise-en-scène of the Eastern world, the form in its rhetorical aspect demands some commentary here.

Justifying a first-person narration in the chronicle form is no trouble—most of the chronicles were written by real movers and shakers whose experience was indeed history. But this history was taking place on ground until now the province of the pilgrimage narratives and biblical commentaries, in which description and identification of the Holy Places were a matter of course. Under the influence of this literary heritage, the chroniclers bring together again the separated functions of autobiography and geographical description, or at least make them visible between the covers of a single book. This fortuitous intersection may have helped pave the way for the resurgence of autobiographical matter in the pilgrimage accounts, and certainly it nourished the art of prose narrative. (At the end of the fourteenth century, Philippe de Mézières produced the weird hybrid *Le songe du vieil pèlerin*, a fictional, allegorical, autobiographical prose *itinerarium* propagandizing for a new crusade. As a prose fiction set in historical time and geographical space for serious moral purposes, it deserves at least a mention in the history of the novel. But as allegory and propaganda, its fictionality is too blatant and its structure too anti-mimetic to provide a really new experience for the imaginations of its first readers.)

As I have said, the result of the domestication of the East by the crusaders and their chroniclers was to push back its border, toward India and China. The fabulous place is still there, and it is still Elsewhere. At home in Palestine for twenty years, Fulcher, during a lull in the crusading action of which his chronicle has become a running commentary, undertakes to summarize the flora, fauna, and ethnography of his new country. He takes almost all of his data from Pliny's third-century epitomizer, Solinus, and it is mostly about the animals of Egypt and India: "The very little that I have said I have excerpted as far as possible from that most sagacious investigator and skillful writer Solinus. What Alexander the Great

likewise found in India and saw there I shall relate later on"
(III.xlix).

This borrowing suggests that what has come to be called the
"marvels material" is so intimately a part of any account of the
East that it finds its way perfunctorily into even a work written in
a nondescriptive, historical genre, by the magnetic virtue of the
setting. It is on every level a digression from the business at hand
as it appears in Fulcher, and as such testifies to an overwhelming
impulse of confused literary decorum. Fulcher is one of the very
first Crusade chroniclers, and as I have said, the literary heritage on
which he must draw includes not only previous chronicles of other
historical events, but the existing literature on the East. But the
displacement of his attention from the part of the East in which he
lives into other parts of which he is conscious of having no authority to speak is a telling gesture. Coming as it does toward the end of
a relentlessly autobiographical eyewitness account, it is a particularly clear sign of the link between the ideas "marvels" and "Elsewhere." Busy in the work of sacking and fortifying cities, he has
seen no marvels here in Palestine. If, as he puts it, the Occident has
become the Orient, then the imperative Orient of the mind's geography must lie farther to the East, and to the South. Since he is
writing about the East, he must include the marvels material, but
since the East has become Home, that material must belong elsewhere.[12]

That this tortuous logic directs his pen instead of the urge to

---

12. Olschki observes that Marco Polo tends to push the most extravagant of his
descriptions of Oriental splendor into Japan, the Utter East that he has not himself
visited: "It is only beyond the boundaries of Cathay that he mentions gold for the
first time—in order to evoke the riches of Japan, where he had never set foot"
(*Marco Polo's Asia*, 60). Something, obviously, has changed by the time Montaigne
can say: "Wee neede not goe to cull out miracles and chuse strange difficulties: me
seemeth, that amongst those thing we ordinarily see, there are such incomprehensible rarities, as they exceed all difficulties of miracles" (*Essayses*, 2:509). It is this
sentiment that most clearly divides the modern novel from the travel narratives in
which it incubated. And it is perhaps something more than a felicitous figure for
this development in the scope of literary attention that, as the Renaissance drew
near, the marvels crept closer to Home. In his article "The Basilisk" (in *Mythical
and Fabulous Creatures*), Laurence Breiner notes "the general shift of the basilisk
into a domestic *European* monster," and certainly the crown of necromancy was
shifting from Chaldea to Britain during this period.

De draconibus Indiæ & Aethiopiæ.

DRaco maximus est serpentum, habetᶫ dentes acutos & ferratos:uim tamen maiorem habet in cauda quàm dentibus, nec habet tantum de ueneno sicut alij serpentes. Si quem cauda ligauerit, occidit, nec elephas est utus est corporis sui magnitudine. Nam circa semitas delitescens per quas elephanti gradiuntur, crura cauda sua alligat & innodat, suffocatos'que perimit. Gignitur in India & Aethiopia. Vnde Plinius:Generat Aethiopia dracones Indicis pares,uicenum cubitorum. Solent autem ad quatuordecim aut quindecim mutuo se cōplecti, & erectis capitibus uelificare per mare & flumina ad ꝓabula *Dracones uicenū cubitorū.*

Fig. 5. "On the dragons of India and Ethiopia." Chapter heading from book 6 (on Asia) of Münster's *Cosmographiae universalis.* Basel, 1554. Courtesy of the John Carter Brown Library at Brown University.

describe what flora and fauna he has actually become familiar with is also suggestive. The title of the chapter on animals is "The Different Kinds of Beasts and Serpents in the Land of the Saracens" (see fig. 5 for a later equation of marvelous serpents with the East). India, Ethiopia, and Scythia do not really qualify as Saracen lands, and he has not even visited them. The duty of the travel writer, which for a moment he has become, must then be, at least in Fulcher's eyes, to reiterate the existence of Nature's "fringe elements," to reassure the homebound that Nature is indeed more healthy at the center and more exciting on the edges.

In "Geography, Phenomenology, and the Study of Human Nature," Yi-fu Tuan speaks of the importance of the binary opposition "home-journey" to the continued felt identity of the term "home": "Home has no meaning apart from the journey which takes one outside of home" (188). That this opposition has been unsettled in Fulcher's colonial experience is clear from the slightly pensive extract, quoted earlier in this chapter, on God's miraculous transformation of Occidentals into Orientals. This later reinstatement of the characteristically bizarre Elsewhere may function in part to steady the writer's own nerves.

The Lord of Joinville inserts a similarly parenthetical account of the lands farther East in his hagiographical *Vie de Sainte Louis* (finished c. 1207), a chronicle of the Seventh Crusade, during which Joinville acted as a special adviser (and close friend) to the king. Envoys sent to the khan to negotiate an alliance against the Saracens have returned with bad news, and Joinville takes the opportunity to report other "news" they have brought back, chiefly ethnographical and historical, about the Tartars, Prester John, and Gog and Magog. Outside of a passage on the cult of the Assassins, it is the only such reporting in the book; the rest focuses entirely on the deeds of Louis, the events of the Crusade, and Joinville's personal relationship with the king.

The *Vie de Sainte Louis* is a beautiful book and difficult to pass over without a little further comment. In it is advanced to the highest degree since perhaps Augustine's *Confessions* the technique Richardson was to call "writing to the moment" and which was to prove so central to the technique of the sentimental novel. In the following extract, the passage of narrative time is so minutely detailed as almost to replicate the real duration of the incident recounted, and this reverence for the minutiae of time is essential to the concerns of the novel:

(431)While the king heard grace, I went to an open window which was in an embrasure next to the head of the king's bed. And I passed my arms through the bars of the window. And I thought that if the king went into France that I would go to the prince of Antioch, who thought of me as a father and who had sent to ask for me, until such time as another expedition came to the country by which the prisoners might be delivered, according to the counsel that the lord of Boulaincourt had given me.

(432) While I stood there, the king came and leaned on my shoulders, and held my head in his two hands. And I thought that this was my lord Phelippe d'Anemos, who had irritated me enough already that day because of the counsel I had given. And I said thus: "Leave me in peace, my lord Phelippe." Unfortunately, as I turned my head the hand of the king fell across my face and I knew that this was the king by an emerald that he had on his finger. And he said to me: Keep quite still. Because I want to ask how you could be so bold, that you who are a young man dare advise me to remain, against all the great men and the sages of France who advised me to go.

(433) --Sir, I said, even if I had the cowardice in my heart, still I would not for anything advise you to do it. --Are you saying, said he, that I would be doing wrong if I went away? --So help me God, sir, said I, yes. And he said to me: "If I remain, will you remain?" And I told him yes, "if I can, either

at my own or at someone else's [expense]." --Then rest easy, said he. Because you are in my good graces for what you have advised me. But don't say it to anyone all this week. (*La vie de Sainte Louis*, pars. 431–33)

There is nothing like this in Mandeville; indeed, European prose will wait long for another such detail as the king's hand sliding down his vassal's face until Joinville recognizes the emerald ring. But the amplification of detail to render an object or event both credible and accessible is a technique Mandeville will put to important use, as will be seen later in this chapter. Its appearance in an account of distant travel marks a crucial shift in the nature of the genre's attention to its subjects. Wonder is brief; sympathy is ample.

The chronicles display a number of novelistic features: in particular the use of suspense and the depiction of character over time (as opposed to the iconographic *effictio* prevalent in romance and more detached historical writing). But their major contribution to travel writing itself, as it then stood, conditioned by the status of its most typical subject matter, the Near East, lay in their focus on present time. For Egeria and her descendants, events were over, sealed into places, and already recorded in Scripture. Fulcher's events are fulfillments of scriptural hints and prophecies, and many of his "places" are in the process of becoming sacred almost as he speaks. (Even Joinville's essentially biographical "chronicle" is *hagiographical*, intent on rendering its crusader-king as a saint, an agent of divine history.) The Crusades are seen as a chapter in eschatological history, taking place on the same soil as the history recounted in the Bible. With this perception, their chroniclers can and do speak of events in the Holy Land, at last, in the present tense. It remains for the *curiositas* of the later Middle Ages to secularize this present tense, to detach it from the eschatological frame so that it can carry the events of a private man's excursion across the "Threshold of the Known."

Mandeville and Fiction

In his *Manual of English Prose Literature* (1872), William Minto grandly called Mandeville the "father of English prose." M. C. Seymour, Mandeville's most recent editor, is convinced that he was French, but convinced of little else—he refers to him in the notes as "Mandeville," inside quotation marks. Robert Burton denounced him (in the same breath as Marco Polo) as a "Liar"; recently, Donald Howard and Christian Zacher have published elegant close readings that implicitly issue him a poetic license to "call the sun a rush candle if it pleases him."[13] But Mandeville was neither simply a liar nor simply a poet, and if it is true enough that he fathered English prose, it is also true that his book was written originally in French.[14] Even looked at in the light of its genre and its time, the book is singular and, beneath its dazzle, baffling. But the standoffs between its critics are perhaps unnecessary; at least in part they stem from incomplete consideration of the issues and conventions of its literary and "scientific" genealogy, as they were understood to function in Mandeville's own era.

The world owes the rediscovery of *Mandeville's Travels* as a work of art primarily to three people: Josephine Waters Bennett, Donald Howard, and Christian Zacher.[15] They have performed an important imaginative task in realizing and publicly re-presenting the beauty and delicacy of the book. But they have perhaps leapt too quickly over old-fashioned problems of authorial intention and audience reception and in the process misrepresented some of its beauty. In his letter to Can Grande, Dante, Mandeville's near contemporary, reiterates the old list of points to consider in interpreting a work of literature; "form" and "purpose" are two of them.[16] Neither can be understood rightly from the vantage point of a

13. See Donald R. Howard, "The World of *Mandeville's Travels*" (1971); idem, *Writers and Pilgrims: Medieval Pilgrimage Narratives and Their Posterity* (1980); Christian K. Zacher, *Curiosity and Pilgrimage: The Literature of Discovery in Fourteenth-Century England* (1976), chap. 6.

14. The controversial point is whether the author did indeed, as the English texts claim, English the book himself. Hamelius finds gross errors in the translation from the French that would be hard to account for if the author had done his own translation. On the other hand, Bennett says "enough manuscripts survive to provide ample evidence that the original version was written in the French of Gower and the English court in the mid-fifteenth [sic] century, and that it was written, in all probability, in England, since the best texts are written in English hands and are still preserved in English libraries" (*Rediscovery of Sir John Mandeville*, 176). Howard follows her, citing "the greater subtlety of the English diction" ("World of *Mandeville's Travels*," 4n).

15. Sir Malcolm Letts preceded them in 1949 with his *Sir John Mandeville: The Man and His Book*. But his treatment of the book is a recapitulation of the most amiable of old attitudes and assumptions, and contributed little to its newly elevated status.

16. "Sex igitur sunt quae in principio cuiusque doctrinalis operis inquirenda sunt, videlicet subiectum, agens, forma, finis, libri titulus, et genus philosophiae" (Toynbee, *Letters of Dante*, x6.119–22).

literary culture in which the words *science* and *art* refer to activities opposed in both method and language.

Bennett argues that the *Travels* has been received from the very beginning as a work of what we now call art:

> He is free to mix truth with fantasy because he can trust his readers to distinguish between them. He is free to decorate the borders of his moral earnestness with delicate (and indelicate) grotesques without fear that those for whom he is writing will be unable to distinguish between the text and the decoration. The decoration is intended to amuse, just as the impish monsters and absurd postures in the borders of the fourteenth century missals and psalters were intended to amuse, without detracting from the seriousness of the text they illuminated. (*Rediscovery of Mandeville*, 78)[17]

A presupposition lurks here with which one must agree—that we have no business discussing the *Travels* as an object constructed to stimulate imaginative pleasures if it could not have so stimulated its original readers. But a number of more careless assumptions lurk with it about that readership and about the nature of "truth" in the fourteenth century

It is true that Dante mixed "truth" with fantasy for a receptive audience at about the same time. According to Curtius, the long tradition of Homeric and Virgilian allegoresis allowed him to do so with impunity—though even so, there were complaints.[18] But Dante, like Homer and Virgil, wrote in verse, which gave his audience a necessary rhetorical cue. Mandeville wrote in the vernacular prose of a scientific popularizer, and there are no borders or margins in such discourse to make the separation obvious between "moral earnestness" and "delicate grotesque." Nor was the level of geographic and ethnographic knowledge high enough in the fourteenth century to permit even the most sophisticated reader to

17. Cf. Letts: "For most contemporary readers the book had to rest on its own foundations, and as the marvels which Mandeville set down as sober facts can be capped and even outrivalled by other writers—the author of Prester John's letter, for instance—the reading public of the fourteenth and fifteenth centuries probably swallowed their Mandeville whole" (*Sir John Mandeville*, 34).

18. See Curtius, *European Literature and the Latin Middle Ages*, chap. 12. In this chapter Curtius quotes from the preface of the *Tractatus de reprobatione monarchie composite a Dante* of Guido Vernani: "In the preface Dante is described as a poetizing visionary and verbose sophist, whose delusive pictures lead the reader away from the truths of salvation ('conducit fraudulenter ad interitum salutiferae veritatis')" (221).

dismiss the Acephali (still being "earnestly" reported by Ralegh two and a half centuries later), while attaching his belief to the historical but almost equally bizarre "Old Man of the Mountains."

Mandeville himself knew when he wrote, as we know now, that he was in many instances lying, plagiarizing, fictionizing. But he was making use of a form devised to transmit facts and never previously used with any antifactual intent. It is also important to remember that many of his "delicate grotesques" had claimed the status of fact for at least two millennia and would continue to do so well into the eighteenth century.

A fact and its linguistic representation are clearly separable entities in a culture long possessed of experimental science. Nor is *descriptio* any longer the only method of representing facts: facts are now displayed in the forms of graphs, charts, statistical columns, photographs, their significance discernible without much linguistic mediation to anyone familiar with the conceptual systems that provide their contexts. Before the advent of museums and the taxonomic organization of such sciences as botany, zoology, ethnology, and geology, men were dependent for their knowledge of the visible world on the prose descriptions of select eyewitnesses and their epitomizers. (Astronomy presents an obvious exception: a significant portion of the night sky is visible to anyone.) A fact and the words in which it was encapsulated were much more clearly identical than they are now: for all practical purposes a change in wording was a change in fact, a mistranslation could alter the world. What Margaret Hodgen, in *Early Anthropology*, sees as a stubborn, paralytic resistance to new knowledge could be seen more generously as a linguistic conservatism motivated by the need literally to conserve what data were already available.[19] Iconographic representation (the characteristic method) simplifies and restricts knowledge. It also preserves it, or at least preserves a fuller spectrum of possibility than would otherwise be visible. In the form of the conventional unicorn, memory of the rhinoceros was preserved in western Europe for thousands of years. The manticore memorialized the man-eating tiger, the Gymnosophists the habits and habitat of the Yogis.[20]

19. See chap. 2, p. 74, for quotation from Hodgen on this point.
20. According to Friedman, "even the improbable-sounding Hippopodes may have had a basis in fact. A tribe exists today in the Zambesi valley on the border of Southern Rhodesia among whose members 'lobster-claw syndrome' has become an established characteristic. This condition, which is hereditary, possibly via a single

The presence in the *Travels* of the formulaic marvels material suggests neither a scorn for facts nor a mere delight in the picturesque. The material is not our clue to the fictive nature of the *Travels*, nor was it likely to have been separated out by the men of that time. Subsequent redactions, epitomes, and chapbook descendants of the original isolate parts of its material on the basis of subject matter, devotional or sensational appeal, but not according to truth value.[21]

The facts and data of the Middle Ages were not just wrong, they were literary or at least linguistic objects, attributable in that aspect to the specific authors who first promulgated them. Thus Fulcher carefully quotes Solinus even to describe the one animal he *is* likely to have seen, the crocodile (III.xlix). In the twentieth century we are continually trying to alter and refine our descriptions of facts, while at the same time trying to stabilize literary texts in "definitive" editions. The description of a fact has no acknowledged literary value and becomes disposable at a moment's notice. The description of a fantasy, once canonized as literature, becomes immutable.

It is therefore a task requiring some care from us to avoid anachronism in imagining the "form" and "purpose" of a literary work of the fourteenth century which sets out to describe "sum partie of thinges that there ben." Knowledge was scarce, reverenced, and largely inseparable from the particular texts that transmitted it. At the same time, texts themselves were fluid: plagiarized, misquoted, mistranslated, interpolated upon, bowdlerized, epitomized, transformed, and transformable at every stage of their complex dissemination. When new knowledge did arrive it was easily enough corrupted into older images, particularly in the process of

---

mutated gene, results in feet that are divided into two giant toes instead of five smaller ones—'ostrich feet,' as they are described by neighboring tribes. The remoteness of the region and a considerable amount of inbreeding have encouraged the trait" (*Monstrous Races in Medieval Art and Thought*, 24).

21. See C. W. R. D. Moseley, "The Metamorphosis of Sir John Mandeville," for a full account of the *Travels'* rich and various *Nachleben*. According to Moseley, subsequent "bastard versions" in both prose and verse tended to flatten "the subtleties and curiosities of [Mandeville's] description" (14), concentrating on the *Travels'* information rather than on Mandeville's arrangement or delivery of it; his readers, he concludes, "used it as a storehouse of *exempla* as well as for entertainment and instruction" (10). Although some redactions turned the *Travels* into a "Wonderbook," real "wonders" were also retained or added, such as descriptions of the khan's court or, in the "Metrical Version," of Rome.

translation. Marco Polo's information about the short days and long nights of the Russian winter had regressed into the year-round "Land of Perpetual Darkness" by the time of the "Geographic Text."[22] The authors of the encyclopedias and cosmographies that perpetuated the scientific misinformation of the Middle Ages were shoring fragments against a ruin: in their manic comprehensiveness can be seen an attempt to halt the endless fluctuation and circulation of verbal data-ions by cramming them all together in a small container. Without articulated taxonomies this attempt was bound to fail: proximity does not necessitate bonding.

Mandeville's book can be seen as part of this same serious struggle and the learned plagiarist as confronted by the same debilitating array of disconnected data that inspired the encyclopedists. Mandeville did not invent a taxonomy; instead, he shaped a fiction. His building blocks were those peculiar entities impossible for us to define either simply as data or simply as passages from other works. For him they were above all building blocks; his aim and his contribution were (at last) to build something with them. What he built was true because coherent; like any good building, it was used and it lasted.

Unlike most good buildings, though, it was subversive. Its coherence lent authority to the misinformation included in it, and its prose assertiveness disturbed, for some, the conventional credibility of prose. (Not that travel accounts had not always strained credulity: the anxious, even florid, claim to veracity and reliability is a conventional feature of any premodern, first-person narrative of travel and is parodied in the very title of Lucian's *A True Story*.) But most subversive of all is Mandeville's aesthetic attitude toward fact: he is a hedonist of knowledge. Unable to test the truth of his materials, he settled for arranging them, as if they were in fact just so many words, as if "everything possible to be believ'd is an image of truth," as if beauty were truth, truth beauty—Keats never wrote a geography.

22. See my chap. 3, n. 8. The process of scribal transmission can of course create new marvels as well, in the "curiously fluid and ambiguous" context of accounts of the East. Paul Gibb gives an example of a scribally created bird-centaur in his introduction to *Wonders of the East*: "Loose punctuation, together with the curiously inverted *ut aves leni voce*, 'with a soft voice like birds,' seems to have caused *ut aves* to be reinterpreted as part of the preceding clause in line 17:3, resulting in the untenable corruption *longis cruribus ut aves*, 'with long legs like birds'—a most unusual way of describing Centaurs" (23).

Although Mandeville's prologue has a familiar feel to it, many of the conventions and topoi we might expect are absent from it or subverted. There is no address to the reader and no dedication. There is no *occupatio* in which the traveler claims only a humble style and an incapacity for the task ahead. There is only the most deliciously ambiguous of truth claims, and the long sentences that promise to explain why the writer should write, or the reader read, yet another account of "the lond of promyssioun" drift to an end without delivering.

But it elaborately amplifies a topos hinted at in the first chapters of Fulcher's *History of the Expedition to Jerusalem*, in Burchard of Mt. Sion's splendid thirteenth-century *Descriptio*, and in Ludolph von Suchem's *Itinerarium* (c. 1350):[23] the contrast between the decadent West, where lawlessness and faithlessness are rampant, and the sacredness of the Holy Land, which the West has allowed to fall into the hands of the infidels. Ludolph and Mandeville both refer to the Holy Land as "the Promised Land"—Mandeville in his very first sentence. Desire to possess, or repossess, has become a new face of the West's desire for the East and a breach opened for an earthly utopianism to replace the old quandary of the pilgrim who found in Jerusalem only the shadow of his celestial goal.

That lond he [Jesus] chees before all other londes as the beste & most worthi lond & the most vertuouse lond of all the world. . . . Wherefore every gode cristene man that is of powere & hath whereof scholde peynen him with all his strengthe for to conquere oure right heritage and chacen out all misbeleevynge men. . . . But now pryde couetyse and enuye han so emflawmed the hertes of lordes of the world that thei are more besy for to disherite here neyghbores more than for to chalenge or to conquere here right heritage before seyd. (Prologue, 1–3)

This sort of thing is very earnest in Fulcher and the others, but in Mandeville a little less so, since we find him later employed by "misbeleevynge men" as a mercenary (xxIV, 144), and putting an eloquent speech of moral wisdom and rebuke into the mouth of the Saracen "soudan" (xvI, 88–90).

23. See Fulcher, *History of the Expedition to Jerusalem*, I.i-v; Burchard of Mt. Sion, *Description of the Holy Land*, 1–3; and Ludolph von Suchem, *Description of the Holy Land*, 3.

There are two conventional reasons for writing an account of the Holy Land: because men want to hear about it who cannot go there ("possessed by a desire to picture to their minds those things which they are not able to behold with their eyes"; Burchard, *Description of the Holy Land*, 4), and because the author is an eyewitness ("I have dwelt in those parts for an unbroken space of five years"; Ludolph, *Description and the Way Thither*, 1). Two long, unfinished sentences in Mandeville's prologue hint at these topics but do not deliver. The dependent clauses become so enthusiastic and thus so long that they end at last without result clauses:

For als moche as the londe be3onde the see that is to sey the holy londe that men callen the lond of promyssioun or of beheste passynge all othere londes it is the most worthi lond most excellent and lady and souereyn of all othere londes & is blessed & halewed of the precyous body & blood of oure lord jhesu crist; jn the whiche land it lykede him to take flesch & blood of the virgyne marie to envyrone that holy lond with his blessede feet; And there he wolde of his blessedness enoumbre him in the seyd blessed & gloriouse virgine marie & become man & worche many myracles and preche and teche the feyth & the lawe of crystene men vnto his children. (Prologue, 1)

And for als moche as it is longe tyme passed that ther was no generall passage ne vyage ouer the see and many men desiren for to here speke of the holy lond and han there of gret solace & comforte, I John Maundevylle knyght all be it I be not worthi that was born in Englond, in the town of seynt Albones & passed the see in the 3eer of oure lord jhesu crist Mill ccc & xxij. in the day of seynt Michell & hiderto haue ben longe tyme ouer the see & haue seyn & gon thorgh many dyuerse londs & many prouynces & kyngdomes & jles And haue passed thorghout Turkye Ermonye the lityll & the grete [the sentence continues without grammatical resolution for several more lines]. (Prologue, 3)

It could be that Mandeville cannot handle so complex a syntax as he initiates in these two sentences and, intoxicated with his *amplificationes*, forgets about the claims of grammar and sense. If so, it is his last spate of such weakness. On the other hand, these highly conventional rhetorical moments are perfect opportunities for a quasi-parodic abandonment of sense. The reader should know what sentiments and justifications lurk in the wings.

It is even easier to put these deliriously collapsed sentences down to artfulness when we encounter the coy and suggestive truth claim that concludes the prologue:

And ȝee schull vndirstonde that I haue put this boke out of latyn in to frensch and translated it aȝen out of frensch in to Englyssch that euery man of my nacioun may vnderstonde it. But lordes & knyghtes and othere noble & worthi men that conne not latyn but lityll & han ben beȝonde the see knowen & vnderstonden ȝif I seye trouth or non. And ȝif I err in deuising for forȝetynge or ell that their mowe redresse it & amende it. For thynges passed out of longe tyme from a mannes mynde or from his syght turnen sone in to forȝetynge because that mynde of man ne may not be comprehended ne with holden for the freeltee of mankynde. (4)

It is true that some of the more suggestive touches in the English version may be the results of mistranslation or interpolation by the Englisher (although Mandeville may have been the Englisher himself). In good medieval fashion, *Mandeville's Travels* (like the far earlier *Wonders of the East* or the more recent *Travels* of Marco Polo) is the product of more than one consciousness, and a certain amount of unconsciousness as well. But in general drift, the French and English versions agree: in place of the anxious vow to tell the truth, the whole truth, and nothing but the truth, Mandeville leaves it up to the traveled among his readers to gauge his veracity. This is cagey in two ways: first, it begs the question of whether or not he has been the eyewitness his "I John Maundevylle" sentence implies he was—his work can contain nothing but "facts" and remain "untrue" by virtue of its fictional narrative frame. Second, in the very first chapter he comes out with a lie that a traveled reader would probably recognize as such: describing the famous golden statue of Justinian that stood before the Hagia Sofia, he falsely claims that the "round appell of gold in his hond" has fallen out (and when replaced will not remain) because "this appull betokeneth the lordschipe that he hadde ouer all the world that is round"—which lordship has been broken.[24]

The imagined traveled reader thus knows early on "ȝif I seye

24. "The cross on the orb was blown down in 1317. Boldensele and Bondelmonti (*Liber insularum Archipelagi*, ed. 1824, p. 122) saw the apple in its place. John of Hildesheim . . . also describes the statue as holding its orb and threatening the Saracens in the East with its right hand" (Hamelius, *Mandeville's Travels*, 2:25).

trouthe or non." At this point the traveled reader is confronted with a new twist to the reading experience, the aesthetically justified "lie." The lie does a number of things for the book that mere truth could not accomplish. It allows Mandeville to emphasize the presence of the "fallen West" as a starting point in both space and time—this is of enormous structural importance in a work that takes us eventually to the gates of the Earthly Paradise in the farthest East, takes us back to an *unfallen* place and time as it takes us to the cardinal point geographically opposed to England in the extreme West. And it ties this theme of the fallen world to his theme of the round world. The "round appell of gold . . . betokeneth the lordschipe that he hadde ouer all the world that is round." Both the hope and the pessimism of the writer are bound together in this image of the fallen golden orb, to bear fruit in the peculiarly passionate chapter on "the roundness of the erthe" and all that that implies.

But how about the untraveled reader, who may also "conne not latyn but lityll" and therefore be unable to compare Mandeville with his sources and contemporaries? This more likely reader has had a marvel thrust upon him that is perhaps even more striking as "fact" than as pure symbol. Fortuitous congruences of matter and significance had (and still have) a hold over the Christian imagination, anchored as it is by the Incarnation and nurtured on allegoresis. For this reader, Mandeville is not the artist, God is. Mandeville merely reports His artistry. While Mandeville was writing in an age without extended prose fiction, it was also an age that saw symbolic meaning everywhere—in letters, comets, stones, and maps, in the number of the fixed stars and the quills of the porcupine. In an Age of Faith, the symbolic nature of Christ's life on earth allowed for a conception of life in which reality need not be restructured by the literary artist for significant pattern to inhere in it. Even such a random event as the hooting of an owl in the night could carry symbolic overtones of a restricted kind. The history of the earth itself was seen as a fiction created by God, and, as we have seen in chapter 2, the geography of the earth was a physical figure of spiritual realities. In this atmosphere, even the naïve reader who accepted the book as "factual" could have and would have seen beyond concrete detail. If life was allegorical, then so was a record of it. We are looking back to a vanishing point where not only fact and text, but fact and fiction partake more of each other's natures than they are now felt to do. But by consciously constructing the "facts" himself, Mandeville is taking a step in our direction.

Of course, in between these two readers, the traveled and the naïve, there must have been a skeptical third who recognized the anatomy of marvel formation and suspected the traveler's traditional impulse to overshape his rendering of the exotic. The skeptical third was to inherit the earth; in his eyes, all the language strategies with which the medieval traveler converted the Unknown into the knowable were fictions in the meanest sense.[25] But Mandeville does not write for him: "And tho that han ben in tho contrees and in the gret Canes household knowen wel that I seye soth And therfore I will not spare for hem that knowe not ne beleue not but that thei seen for to tell зоu a partie of him and of his estate" (xxiv, 145). To Mandeville the skeptical reader is a Doubting Thomas whose failure of imagination makes him dismissable. He wants belief, but this may include the special kind Coleridge called suspension of disbelief: "And whoso that wole may leve [believe] me зif he will, And whoso will not may leue also" (xxiv, 145).

Mandeville's fictionality is not to be gauged by the truth value of his inherited data: he is not a liar whose charm has cozened a later age into dubbing him a poet. In undermining the reader's desire and ability to simply believe or disbelieve his account, he is creating an imaginative freedom for his reader and himself, and directing our attention toward a realm in which faith—the active form of belief—is required of us, and contemplation matters more than the acquisition of knowledge. At the root of fiction is a magical gift, like the shield of invisibility or the shoes of flight: we are released by this mode of discourse from having to deal responsibly

25. Next to Odoric of Pordenone's name in the index to the eighteenth-century *Astley's Voyages* the editor has written "A great Liar." The eighteenth century in England was the inheritor of the Royal Society's "correspondence instructions" to travelers, and the voluminous travel literature it produced has erected a monolithic norm of "objectivity" behind which it is difficult to see how serious and authentic the reports of earlier travelers might be. The combined amplitude and impersonality of the eighteenth-century observer's style and its serene assumption that objectivity is possible in the situation of the traveler abroad have reached their own climax in the emergence of the modern "foreign correspondent." The temptation to believe in the self-supposed transparency of such reportage can be overcome by reading an article or two from a Chinese newspaper's coverage of the day's events in Washington.

with new knowledge. We can view and consider data that we need not integrate into our survivalist map of the actual. There are of course facts in every fiction; historians piece together pictures of the daily lives of past peoples from their poems and novels, no doubt fairly accurately. But when fiction functions as itself it is precisely to allow us a sabbatical from the hunting and gathering of information. The most obvious device for signaling our freedom to us is the introduction of the impossible, the presence of the unreal—the magic ring, the flying horse, the one-eyed giant. Travel writing, then, hovers at the brink of the fictional abyss. In the days before travel was common and photographs offered conclusive documentation, travel writing presented its readers with an inherently problematic experience. A marvel in any other context signals the freedom I have been talking about. But here it may provoke the attempt to alter radically one's map of the actual and possible. In fact it did, as Augustine's struggle with the monstrous races gives evidence.

The customary claim to veracity with which medieval travel narratives open (or close, or both) is a response to this problem—a problem inherent not only in the material but in the formulas through which much of it was characteristically transmitted. The much later *Pilgrim's Progress* opens with the defensive epigraph (taken from Hosea), "I have used similitudes." The Bible's use of similitudes, as Curtius clearly outlines, occasioned a whole literary apologetics among medieval churchmen, for similitudes are figures, and figures are *"mendacia poetarum."*[26] The Bible, it was decided, uses similitudes to hide its wisdom from the vulgar. The travel writer has no such motive; in fact his use of similitudes has precisely the opposite intention—to convey his knowledge to the vulgar. The defensiveness of Bunyan's loud announcement indicates a still vivid sense in his readership that figures are lies and lead away from, not toward, the truth.

How much more vivid must have been Mandeville's sense of mendacity, an author who was not writing an obvious allegory and who was using a traditonally documentary form. The absence of an unambiguous truth claim in his prologue, then, is a matter of real importance in our assessment of his literary intention, and his

---

26. See Curtius, *European Literature and the Latin Middle Ages,* chap. 12, especially sec. 3.

intention a matter of inspired illumination concerning the nature and potential of his chosen genre. He has taken the doubt with which the reader may greet the figural encoding of the alien and exotic and transformed it into the potential experience of free imaginative contemplation. And the total object that he gives us for that contemplation is a redeemed world, a world he insists is round and human, where God is present "in alle places" and worshiped in most of them.

Mandeville and Travel Writing

So far I have been dealing chiefly with Mandeville's relation to the development of fiction. That an analysis of this most glorious of all premodern travel works should entail a discussion of fiction is significant, but it is time now to look at the work under the rubric of travel writing per se. Although we will uncover a structure that has significance of the sort that the structures of fiction do, the flesh of the *Travels* is the same stuff of which Odoric, Burchard, Ludolph, and William made their *itineraria*—often quite literally the same.

William of Boldensil provides much of the flesh of part 1, the account of the Holy Land. Odoric of Pordenone, who journeyed as a missionary to the khan between 1316 and 1330, is the primary source for part 2, the excursion into the Utter East.[27] Marvelous information from Vincent of Beauvais's *Speculum historiale* and *Speculum naturale* is scattered strategically throughout, as are motifs from legend and romance belonging more or less to the public domain. If Mandeville had done nothing but combine William's and Odoric's accounts into one journey, he would still have made a notable breach in the consciousness of his age. The journey to Palestine was always formally motivated by the central religious purpose of pilgrimage (the Crusades, called "general passages," were considered large-scale pilgrimages). The journey far-

---

27. A scholarly translation of Odoric is available, with copious notes and a Latin and an Old Italian text appended, in volume 2 of Sir Henry Yule's compendium *Cathay and the Way Thither*. Quotations from Odoric will be taken from this edition, cited by chapter number. There is no English translation of William of Boldensil. The most recent printed edition is that of C. L. Grotefend, "Itinerarium Guilielmi de Boldensele," in *Zeitschrift des Historischen Vereins für Niedersachsen* (1852).

ther East was of two types, mercantile or missionary, and as we have seen in the last chapter these purposes provided characteristic organizing criteria for the writer as well. Mandeville-the-narrator emerges from his conflation of these subgenres as a pure wanderer, and travel as an activity in and of itself. Thus, if we are naming fathers, we can call Mandeville not only the "father of English prose" but the father of modern travel writing.[28] It is a felicity of history that the first such traveler did all (or most) of his travel in his head and that the first such account was essentially a fiction. The form and attitude of this fiction were so prophetic of those of later "true stories" that, as late as 1866, Sir Henry Yule (no mean traveler himself) was making use of Mandeville to corroborate or explicate details in Odoric.

Mandeville starts us at Home and takes us back there at the end; the first chapter is called "To teche you the weye out of Englond," and in the last he tells us "now I am comen home mawgree myself to reste for gowtes Artetykes that me distreynen, that deffynen the ende of my labor aʒenst my will god knoweth" (xxxv, 210). Thus the Other World is drawn into some contiguity with this one, and though there is no overt description of home (such as begins Bruce Chatwin's *In Patagonia* or ends Robert Byron's *The Road to Oxiana*), there is a marvelously covert inclusion, in a late chapter on the Vale Perilous, of Tacitus's description of Britain. The multiple ironies of Mandeville's plagiarism of a depiction of his own people, as seen through the eyes of a more civilized foreigner of antiquity, inserted at the proverbially wildest margin of the earth, belong to the history of fiction in the way they complicate the relation of prose statement to meaning. But the coming to consciousness of travel writing as a vehicle for irony is also a notable event in itself.

Donald Howard has already commented on the irony that structures and flavors the *Travels*, and says about the link between travel and irony: "If his book is ironic, it is because travel itself is

28. As Percy Adams rightly pointed out in a note on the manuscript of this book, "every father has a grandfather." But for the purpose of identifying junctures in the *longue durée*, it is convenient to characterize as a father one who not only broke radically with his genre's stance and structure as they prevailed before him, but who, in so doing, redefined for others that genre's potential. No writer really fathers (or mothers) anything but his own book, but Mandeville is more than just an example of a new trend. His name came to signify "traveler" (as well as "liar") for European culture.

ironic: things are other than what we expect at home, and the contrast turns us back upon ourselves" ("World of *Mandeville's Travels*," 10). He also notes in passing that Mandeville "grasped this instructive feature of traveling better than previous authors" and speculates that this is because "he saw from afar, through a world of books." But if "travel itself is ironic," why should the untraveled Mandeville be the first to notice it? And to what extent do the pilgrimage and missionary accounts betray any sense of expectations surprised? (William of Rubruck does in fact convey that sense: his eye was keen and his disillusionment deep. But his tone is anomalous within the genre up to this point.) The continued and central presence of the marvels material in accounts of the Far East, and the mutual repetitiveness of the pilgrimage accounts, argues that travel as an experience may have been a quite different thing for Mandeville's predecessors from what it is for Naipaul, Rabin, Chatwin, Theroux, and their confederates. We have observed moments of change in the painfully slow opening up of perception in Western travelers over the millennium between Egeria and Mandeville, but the breaches have been small and induced by the kinds of cataclysmic historical events that require readjustment in even the most rigid dynamic of perception. It is as if the mentality of the West rejected the possibility of real surprise in the experience of travel, and it may be that that rejection was designed to protect an archetypal *imago mundi* of the sort described in chapter 2 and revealed so clearly in medieval world maps. The desire for a world that contains both text and border, Home and Elsewhere, mundane and sacred territory, and that contains them as somehow polar and unmixed, opposed and absolute, is a desire served admirably by the imperturbable repetitions of Pliny and Solinus and the ethnographic bareness that preceded Mandeville.[29]

29. For all its smug "objectivity," the eighteenth century, at least in England, showed signs of a similar stasis in the *imago mundi* preserved by its travel literature. The Grand Tour (primary object of this literature) became so codified, and the writer so fearful of egotism, that it became possible once again to plagiarize seamlessly. (See Adams, *Travelers and Travel Liars*, especially chap. 8, "Peculiar Plagiarisms.") The link between the genre and its essential subject matter is tight enough that it comes to seem part of the travel writer's task to preserve certain root images or necessary fictions, as much as to extend the horizon or intimacy of our knowledge. Annotation of the beloved world image of the English eighteenth century is outside the scope of this book: some of its outline can be gleaned from Charles L. Batten, Jr.'s *Pleasurable Instruction: Form and Convention in Eighteenth-Century Travel Literature*.

It may also be that the world's love-hate relationship with the *Travels* stems from the irony with which it subverts the image of that desire. Perhaps Mandeville was hailed as a liar because his ultimately round and human world was too mixed and contingent to satisfy the requirements of the ancient dream, and perhaps he was loved and believed because it was getting to be time for one of those brief periods of wakefulness in which history prods itself into continuing.

The chapters themselves may seem, to modern eyes, to have been constructed "dream-wise." This is partly the result of the book's category-shattering scope: it is not the record of a journey (except intermittently), nor is it the strict verbal map Burchard had produced, nor is it focused by a purely spiritual or purely mercantile interest in one specific territory. It is determined to be encyclopedic, but nothing like the modern encyclopedia's formal set of subheadings has yet been generated, and what has is insufficient to the task at hand. The bonds between the pieces of data conveyed in any one chapter are usually eidetic, contributing enormously to our overall sense of being presented with an "image of truth"—an image that, qua image, is more amenable to interpretation than simple belief.

Chapter 5, untitled in the Cotton manuscript, seems at first glance a mere grabbag of information in which the reader's consciousness is asked to skip not only from topic to topic, but from mode to mode—from fable to history to flat topographical description—without transitions. And yet there is clearly something like the "concatenation" we saw in *Wonders* at work here, and something more. The chapter begins with the tale of a fallen city, "Cathaillye"—"lost thorgh folye of a ȝonge man." When this young man's paramour died, he climbed down into her marble tomb and "lay be hire," from which union was begotten a hideous adder "the whiche als swithe fleigh aboute the cytee & the contree & sone after the cytee sank down." Besides rearranging the motifs of the previous chapter's tale (of a serpent-woman under Diana's curse who can only be freed of her monstrous form by the kiss of a knight), this story leads us on to a number of other linked images.

"In the castell of amoure lyth the body of Seynt Hyllarie & men kepen it right worschipfully." "In Cipre is the manere of lordes & all othere men all to eten on the erthe, for thei make dyches in the erthe all aboute in the hall depe to the knee and thei do paue hem." "And there is the welle of the whiche holy writte spekth offe &

seythe: FONS ORTORUM & PUTEUS AQUARUM VIUENCIUM, that is to seye the welle of gardyns and the dych of lyuinge watres. In this cytee of Thire seyde the womman to oure lord: BEATUS VENTER QUI TE PORTUIT & UBERA QUE SUCCISTI, that is to seye: Blessed be the body that the baar & the pappes that thou sowkedest. And there oure lord for3af the womman of Chananee hire synnes." Then, in connection with the "port Jaff," we hear about Noah's Flood, and the rock where "Andromade a gret Geaunt was bounden & put in prisoun before Noes flode." Then by the river of Belon (at the site of an ancient glassworks sometimes mentioned by pilgrims on account of its glassy sand) we have the bottomless sea of "gravel schynynge brighte" which, like the "dych of lyuynge watres" or "the pappes that thou sowkedest," "be neuere so meche taken awey there of on the day at morwe it is as full a3en as euere it was." Finally we are reminded of the story of the "tresoun of Delida" and Sampson's entombment of himself, "his paramour," and the Philistines in their "gret halle whan thei were at mete." We are led out of this chapter by way of a "wylderness and desert" where "all weys men fynden god jnnes & all that hem nedeth of vytaylle" (v, 16–20).

Although other images are scattered throughout which bear superficial connections to one or another of these cited above, the major cluster is tomb/ditch/pit/well/breast/flood: earth and water, body and spirit, fecundity and carnality and necrophilia. Paradox is the major arrangement: the sea of gravel, the desert full of "vytaylles," impregnation of a dead body, entombment in the dining hall, the saint's body kept "ryght worschipfully" in the "castell of amoure."[30]

The East remains a kind of mantra in Mandeville's hands, or a setting for dreams. But this chapter does not dream *about* the East as a simple object of wish-fulfillment fantasy, as Marco Polo's chapters do. These "dream thoughts" are about the body, which is made of earth and eats in tombs, and the spirit, which drinks from a well of living waters, and this world, in which the Word was

---

30. Saint Hilarion, for whose life our primary source is Saint Jerome, was a desert-dwelling ascetic who lived on fifteen figs a day for years. Inconveniently popular, especially with women, he was driven from place to place around the Mediterranean in search of solitude. His miracles included stopping a tidal wave, bringing rain to the desert, and making a barren woman fruitful (by supernatural means). In short, his *vita* displays the same themes as Mandeville's chapter, arranged in similar paradoxes.

made flesh, in which women give birth to both beasts and gods, and the desert is full of "vytaylles" (for those who know where to look). The East remains a convenient screen for imaginative projection, as it was for earlier pilgrims and merchants of our acquaintance. But even this isolated chapter suggests that what is being projected is not so much a starved or hidden aspect of a culture's personality as it is a whole self. The issues that unify the concatenations are not necessarily galvanized by concentration on the East, Elsewhere, the Other World—they unify the *Vita nuova*, the *Roman de la rose*, the *Canterbury Tales*, the great poems and fictions of the later Middle Ages.

This is not to suggest that the overt charm of Mandeville's opus is not what it has always seemed to be. It is a book of marvels, it is a book about Elsewhere, its atmosphere is both grotesque and otherworldly. Overtly, it is a fitting culmination to a tradition reaching back to the *Odyssey* (and lingering into our time in Alexandra David-Neel's *Magic and Mystery in Tibet*).[31] And without this tradition (and the scarcity of data that underlies it) Mandeville would not have had the freedom to put his pieces together "dreamwise," nor to exploit in us the freedom of fictional contemplation. It is a moment of deeper change I am charting here, a change of attitude and understanding, clothed in the conventions and formulas and even the very words of what came before it. Mandeville is not averse to supplying his readers with a khan every bit as splendid as Marco's or Odoric's, and he is more willing than Marco to supply marvelous beasts and plants, more willing than Odoric to supply monsters. As usual, the farther we penetrate into the East, the weirder it gets, and the comparisons and similes used to help us visualize what we hear about have the usual alienating effect. Every ripple on the surface of this stream is familiar; it is the current that has shifted.

31. As Tibet has remained artificially unreachable into modern times, books about it are written under conditions that in some ways simulate those of the travel writers of antiquity and the Middle Ages. David-Neel, a relatively cool-minded Western scholar of Buddhism, went to Tibet to obtain precisely the sorts of information Hodgen berates the medieval writers for not seeking and not receiving. But the title of her book, *Magic and Mystery in Tibet*, is a clue to the kind of information it contains—in large part what Hodgen calls "the abnormal, the monstrous, the trivial." The proportion of lascivious anecdote is as high as in Marco's treatment of Tibetan mores, and her fascination with necromancy as intense as Odoric's, if less horrified. (And like Marco, Odoric, and Mandeville, she is a lot of fun to read.)

Some attention to the ways in which Mandeville fiddles with Odoric's account of the Far East, even when he is most clearly following it, will be revealing in the latter regard. Many of these instances have been pointed out before, by stern editors and admiring critics, usually as evidence of mendacity or broadmindedness in the author (which they are). Perhaps most problematic for current critics is Mandeville's inclusion of almost the whole gamut of the Plinian monstrous races at precisely that point in Odoric's account of "the gret yle that is clept DONDUN" where the friar disdains to report marvels that no one could believe. As this seems an obstacle to the prevailing desire to see Mandeville as enlightened beyond his era and a believer in natural law as geographically universal, Bennett says: "It is highly improbable that he believed at all in the unnatural marvels which he retold from Odoric and Solinus and the *Letter of Prester John*" (*Rediscovery of Mandeville*, 36). Moseley goes even further, into flat-out untruth: "Comparison of *Mandeville's Travels* with its sources shows that the author deliberately edited so as to *reduce* the incidence of 'wonders'" ("Metamorphosis of Mandeville," 6). Hamelius, in his notes to chapter 23, refers at this juncture to Mandeville's "licentious imagination" (*Mandeville's Travels*, 2: 110).

But Mandeville's context is at every point denser, richer, more constraining than has been possible in previous, less nearly metaphysical works. He may or may not believe in the monstrosities (or he may have an apprehension of them conforming to their previously discussed status as part fact/part text). What matters more is that they operate in the service of some truths unfolding beneath the surface of their chapter. This is the chapter of the Cornucopia, the prelude to the long, conventionally superlative treatment of the khan—a locus for the theme of plenitude since Marco Polo's initial swoon.[32]

32. The cornucopia is a feature equally of literal and imaginative journey tales—it represents an expectation of the psyche. In his study of the paradises and hells of both folk and "serious" literature, *The Other World*, Howard Patch documents the motif of abundances as essential to the imagination of paradise—abundances of trees, of birds, of colors, of gems, of food, and often of women. (Marco Polo's claim that twenty-thousand prostitutes were living on the outskirts of one of the khan's cities for the convenience "of the foreigners" is a good instance of the last.)

Since Joseph Campbell is ultimately interested in the progress and liberation of the individual human psyche, he concentrates on cornucopian events at the climax of the Hero's journey, rather than on places. In this connection he quotes from the *Jataka* a description of the state of the universe after the Buddha reaches enlighten-

The diversity and plenitude of human forms and customs manifested in the list of mostly monstrous races are followed immediately by a discussion of "Mancy": "And it is the beste lond & on the fairest that may ben in all the world, and the most delectable & and the most plentifous of all godes that is in power of man. . . . And there is more plentee of peple there than in ony other partie of ynde. . . . In that contree is no nedy man ne non that goth beggynge" (XXIII, 135). And so on. Then we come to the idols (stripped of Odoric's gleeful hooting at the way they receive only the smoke of sacrifices while the worshipers get the meat), the abbey where the monks feed "Apes, Marmozettes Babewynes & many other dyuerse bestes," and, at the gateway of "the gret Chans" domain, the "PIGMEYES."

Mandeville in this chapter compresses into smaller compass and neater geographical organization a particularly meandering and xenophobic stretch of Odoric's text, as well as adding from other sources the account of the Plinian races.[33] His most obvious amplifications and changes are in the direction of tolerance and understanding: he omits to tell us, as Odoric did not, that DONDUN means "unclean" or that the cannibalistic funeral rite of its people is "foul," and he leaves out the anecdote of Odoric's berating them over it. In place of Odoric's dogmatic conversation with the monks who feed apes, about whether or not the apes are reincarnated men, Mandeville questions, with far more humanity, the justice of feeding animals instead of the poor: "And their answerde me & seyde that thei hadde no pore man among hem in that contree" (XXIII, 137). From one sentence in Odoric—"But these pygmies have rational souls like ourselves" ("habent autem animam rationalem sicut nos"; 316)—he develops a whole cultural being for the pygmies, and one that includes an irony so pungent in relation to

---

ment under the Bo tree: "Throughout the ten thousand worlds the flowering trees bloomed; the fruit trees were weighed down by the burden of their fruit; trunk-lotuses bloomed on the trunks of trees; branch-lotuses on the branches of trees; vine-lotuses on the vines; hanging lotuses in the sky; and stalk-lotuses burst through the rocks and came up by sevens" (192).

Mandeville, like Marco before him, scatters the cornucopian largesse all across his East—here a "land of Feminye," there a "welle of 30uthe"—but as in Marco's book, the khan is its magnetic center. The New World voyagers were perhaps even more obsessed with this image: the cornucopia has become the symbol of the first specifically American holiday, and even before they landed, sailors could smell it in the shore breeze off Roanoke.

33. See Odoric, *Travels*, chaps. 26–35.

Odoric that one must wonder if Mandeville's text is at open war with its source: "This lityll folk nouther labouren in londes ne in vynes but thei han grete men amonges hem of our stature that tylen the lond & labouren amonges the vynes for hem. And of tho men of oure stature han thei als grete skorn & wonder as we wolde haue among us of geauntes 3if thei weren amonges us" (XXIII, 138).[34] Touché!

But Mandeville's understanding goes beyond the rejection of Odoric's offensive xenophobia. He has explained idol worship in a previous chapter, and the difference between idols and *simulacra*: "For symulacres ben ymages made after lykness of men or wommen or of the sonne or of the mone or of ony best or of ony kyndely thing, & ydoles is an ymage made of lewed will of man that man may not fynden among kyndely thinges" (XIX, 109). He (or else a scribal interpolator) has also told us what a monster is: "a thing difformed a3en kynde bothe of man or of best" (VII, 30). Here we find idols and monsters in the same chapter, a chapter suffused with a spirit of toleration and organized around the theme of plenitude. Mandeville's examples of idols given in the earlier chapter include "an ymage that hath jiii hedes" and one that is "of an ox the on parte & the other halfondell of a man." Among the monsters in chapter 23 we find "folk that han non hedes" and "folk that han hors feet." (See fig. 6 for an illustration of monsters worshiping an idol.) He has been kind toward the idol worshipers, and kind toward Pliny and Solinus, and made an astonishing identification of our emotions with those of the pygmies. Is it too much to claim for this characteristically ironic and generous sensibility that he has sensed a strain of idol worship in the West's tenacious attachment to its geographically displaced monsters, and forgiven it in the same breath with Odoric's "idolators" (who become, in Man-

34. The predictable fact that manuscripts of Mandeville and Odoric were often bound together supports the possibility of their being read in this relation accurately. So too does Mandeville's most whimsical bit of play with Odoric's text, completely lost on anyone not familiar with Odoric: in the episode of the Vale Perilous, a personal anecdote stolen from Odoric, Mandeville mentions that his company for this adventure included two "worthi men Frere Menoures, that weren of lombardye that seyden that 3if ony mon wolde entren, thei wolde gon in with us" (XXXII, 188). Odoric was a Minorite friar from Lombardy who traveled with a colleague. But in Odoric's self-serving version, "I hesitated not to go in that I might see once for all what the matter was" ("Et quamquam in illa sic omnes moriantur, tamen volui intrare ut viderem finaliter quid hoc esset"; *Cathay*, 2:332).

Fig. 6. Monsters worshiping an idol (or "simulacrum"). From a German printed edition of *Mandeville's Travels*. Strasbourg, 1507. By permission of the New York Public Library.

deville's words, "gode religious men after here feyth & lawe"; XXIII, 137)?

At any rate, the monsters were a part of his "data," part of the total but till now fragmented image of the world he had set out to make coherent and redemptively significant. He has included them in such a place that certain of his readers' braces must relax. If there are monsters, then the idols that resemble them are no worse than the benign *simulacra*. If there are not, then our belief in them is little better than the "ymages" of the gently tolerated idolators. And whether God's creation or our own, they form part of the plenitude of this "fairest . . . & most delectable" of lands. "And whoso that wole may leve me ʒif he woll, And whoso will not may leve also."

One notable aspect of the pageant of monsters in Mandeville is its iconographic mode of presentation—notable in that this is *not* usually Mandeville's way. Perhaps he has fooled Moseley into believing that he edited "so as to reduce the incidence of monsters" by his more characteristic amplitude. Scorning as he does, with effects already discussed, the conventional strategies of inducing belief in his readers (truth claims, refusal to report what will be too hard to credit, reliance on the *auctoritas* of his sources), he is forced to rely on a kind of proto-verisimilitude. One of his many techniques (among which might be numbered his growing presence as an actor on the scene, in the second and more incredible part of the book) is the amplification of his inherited iconographic images. The sheer length of his treatment of the pygmies, as compared to Odoric's, makes them more vivid and thus "realer" to the imagination. Of course this method extends and emphasizes the marvels, but it also rationalizes them and "naturalizes" them. Odoric's pygmies are conveyed in the usual fashion: in five sentences, five disconnected features of their physical nature, habitat, and custom are listed, and then we are off to another topic. Mandeville, while exaggerating one marvelous aspect—Odoric's pygmies procreate at age five, Mandeville's "whan they ben half ȝere of age"—invents another marvelous aspect to rationalize the first: "thei lyuen not but .vi ȝeer or .vij at the moste." Mandeville's pygmies are not only more detailed, their details complement and make sense of one another. In the world of nature as it operates in England, life span and body size are logically related. So they must be in "the lond of PIGMANS."[35]

It is a feature of the iconographic mode that its selectivity of detail can make a marvel out of anything unfamiliar.[36] It is also the case that a detailed enough description, provided there be usefully interrelated categories in which to anchor the details, can

35. Mandeville's sense of humor was basically sneaky. Although at first glance his amplification of Odoric has the effect of rationalizing the marvel, he has in part remarvelized the PIGMANS in the same breath. Now that they live only to the age of six or seven, their giving birth at six months is proportionately just as strange as Odoric's pigmies giving birth at five years old.

36. The Lilliputians' report on the contents of Gulliver's pockets is an instructive inversion of the traveler's perspective. It parodies the results to be expected from the Royal Society's "correspondence instructions" to the travelers of the new scientific age by producing, via the new method, the same old marvel material—out of a pocket watch: "And we conjecture it is either some unknown Animal, or the God he worships" (Swift, *Gulliver's Travels*, 18).

demystify a marvel, unfold the data hidden within. Mandeville's unusually long descriptions are part of a literary step forward toward the establishment of a scientifically usable fund of information. The other major steps—development of the "scientific method" and taxonomies—were the task of natural philosophy. Slow refinements in the rhetorical conventions of travel literature were to prove useful to the philosophers in their task.

But so far as he is concerned, Mandeville's method is a literary device in the service of imaginative, not philosophical, truth. Another of his devices for establishing verisimilitude is to claim that he has *not* been somewhere, *not* seen something with his own eyes, and cannot necessarily vouch for the truth of other men's reports. This device is put to particularly poignant use at the end of part 2, when after transforming Odoric's final story, of a perilous valley fraught with devils (Mandeville calls it "on of the entrees of helle"), geographical logic leads him to "paradys terrestre . . . towardes the EST at the begynnynge of the erthe" (xxxiv, 202).

Odoric's narrative ends with the Vale Perilous, from which he "came forth scathless" because he was "a baptized and holy man" (*Cathay*, 262–66). His account is almost criminally self-congratulatory; it is tempting to see behind Mandeville's inclusion of a complementary sacred place, unvisited because "I was not worthi," an intentional corrective. But there are a number of broader considerations. Mandeville has aimed for an unprecedented totality in his coverage of the lands beyond, and to leave out the Earthly Paradise would be to place a black hole on the *mappa mundi*. On the other hand, he is writing in a cultural climate that considers *curiositas* a sin and the limiting of intellectual greed a matter of moral propriety.[37] There is an angel at the gate of paradise with a sword of flame: what better place to be brought up short? The traditional mode of presentation for paradises is what Patch calls the "negative description": it is appropriate to the increasingly narrative method of the *Travels* at this point that "paradys terrestre" be present as a place not visited.[38]

But present it must be, as a redemptive complement to the "entree of helle," as the ironically located birthplace of the human race (the point furthest from what we now call Home), as the

37. See Zacher, *Curiosity and Pilgrimage*, chap. 2.
38. See Patch, *Other World*, 12–13.

primitive and original place in which Mandeville's backward journey through historical time (elegantly traced by Donald Howard) can find a fitting climax.[39]

And as Christian Zacher points out, "for Mandeville the moon-driven traveler, the earthly paradise—which 'toucheth nygh to the cercle of the mone, there as the mone maketh hire torn' . . . —has turned out to be his true destination" (*Curiosity and Pilgrimage*, 151). Mandeville has earlier pinned his predilection for travel on his national origin and its climatic influence: "For in our contrey wee ben in the seuenthe clymat that is of the mone. And the mone is of lyghtly mevynge & the mone is planete of weye. And for that skyll it 3eueth vs will of kynde for to meve lyghtly & for to go dyuerse weyes & to sechen strange thinges & other dyuersities of the world, For the mone envyrouneth the erthe more hastyly than ony other planete" (XIX, 108). How right and lovely that his destination should be paradise, like that of the pilgrims before him, and like theirs one he cannot enter. And how true to what appears to be an essential paradox of travel—that "you can't get there from here" (or, as Joyce puts it in *Ulysses*, "the longest way round is the shortest way home").

Elsewhere has been moving steadily East for some time, as Home has expanded its borders. It was Mandeville's last move to place it ultimately out of man's reach, beyond the "derke Regyoun" (descended from Marco's Russian "Land of Darkness") on the "highest place of erthe" and "enclosed all aboute with a wall." The Elsewhere of sub- or supernature, into which the West

39. "The second half of the book, from chapter 16 on, is a voyage into the Orient, but it is integrated with the first part in a remarkable way and differs from other members of its genre precisely because it is cast in the form of a quasi- or anti-pilgrimage through a state of nature. We pass beyond the land of Prester John to a shrine one may not enter: 'Paradise Terrestre, where that Adam our foremost father and Eve were put that dwelled there but little while, and that is towards the east at the beginning of the earth' (33). The pilgrimage to Jerusalem was a journey backward in time: one saw the relics of New and Old Testament times, what the Middle Ages would have called the Age of Grace and the Age of Law (that is, the law of Moses). Mandeville keeps this reverse order: in the second part we learn that Noah's ship is on Mt. Ararat; that each of Noah's sons inhabited one of the three continents, Asia, Africa, Europe; that the round earth was wasted by Noah's flood; that there is a lake in Ceylon where Adam and Eve wept a hundred years. In this world of the distant past lies the dispersal of individuals, peoples, and languages; at the root of all, the expulsion from Paradise. We pass through the leavings of the *first* age of the world, the age before the law of Moses, the Age of Nature" (Howard, *Writers and Pilgrims*, 272).

had so long projected the other halves of its divided self, is *not* accessible to the earthly traveler, and Mandeville has rendered the places and peoples that once belonged to it as "part of nature, part of us." He has rolled all that truly Otherworldly sweetness up into one ball and perched it at "the begynnynge of the erthe," beyond a veil of darkness, at the place where time began for us, and all our woe—at the place and moment of our birth.

It is precisely at this point that he reminds us of the "roundeness of the erthe, of the whiche I haue towched to ȝou of before." The inaccessible paradys terrestre is really only temporally "at the begynnynge of the erthe." For "that is not that EST that we clepe oure EST on this half, where the sonne riseth to us, for whanne the sonne is EST in tho partyes toward paradys terrestre, it is thanne mydnyght in oure parties on this half for the roundeness of the erthe."

It is in his avoidance of the absolute and its closure that Mandeville is perhaps most new. His paradise is many things, including—figuratively—his destination. But it is not the end, nor even the end of the book. Geography, shapeless and real, must here part company with the shapely hierarchy of the theological map. The center of a spherical world cannot be found on its surface, and the edge cannot be found at all. Mandeville has used his geography symbolically, as did the makers of the *mappae mundi* and the biblical commentaries. But his method is an inversion of theirs: they imagined a geography expressive of preordained ideas. He shaped ideas out of the geography of the real.

Mandeville the artist was indeed "ahead of his time," ahead, as good artists are, of any time. The climate and conditions of his moment permitted him his emotional and intellectual lucidity; the quasi-scientific, quasi-imaginative status of his genre permitted his balancing act with two kinds of truth. But as the later history of his book reveals, he was soon to be romanticized and literalized, as the intellectual realms that coalesced in the *Travels* began to draw apart. Columbus may have been both his best and worst reader, who sailed West over "the roundeness of the erthe" to reach, not America, but that high place from which "the iiij flodes" flow. And all our woe.

Adam and Eve and the Tree of Knowledge. A frontispiece to part 1 of Theodore de Bry's *Great Voyages*. Frankfurt, 1590. Courtesy of the John Carter Brown Library at Brown University.

PART TWO

THE WEST

5

"The end of the East"
Columbus Discovers Paradise

From this point on our account of premodern travel writing will concentrate on texts that belong at least as clearly to other kinds of literature and are directed to primary audiences whose role in relation to the places described was far more active than that of the curious armchair traveler (or armchair pilgrim). Travel writing is more than usually dependent for its form and posture on the experience that motivates it. In turning to Columbus we will seem to be turning away from the prototypes of the genre; Columbus's travels were royal commissions, and his accounts were a mixture of official report and propaganda. From the point of view of history, his travel was not private and his experience not personal—was not, in short, what we now call "travel."

But if exploration and conquest are not forms of travel, then neither are pilgrimage, crusade, nor the pointed wanderings of merchant and missionary. Travel as we have come to understand the term—or as it is used in bookstores and the *New York Times's* "Travel" section—is a form of behavior that could come into its own only after the world had been mapped, for "travel" consists largely in the collision between inherited and experienced knowledge. Frances Trollope traveled to America. Columbus discovered it, Cabeza de Vaca explored it, Ralegh tried to colonize it. The explicit pursuit of geographical experience itself is a self-referential goal, and all urgent devotional and practical motives must atrophy before it is possible. The travel accounts we have looked at so far resemble their modern offspring chiefly in that, whatever the trav-

eler-author's ulterior motives, the texts bespeak that conflict
between mythic expectation and mundane fact which has become
one of the generic foci of travel writing.

The journals, letters, histories, and tracts we will be looking at
next played a large part in the developments of ethnography,
anthropology, and European colonialism, and they helped to establish the basis for a "justified" Christian imperialism. They are
guilty texts, and sometimes difficult to speak of with the relative
detachment of a literary critic. Nor do I want to detach the literary
aspects of any text from its political and historical consequences:
my hope is that in isolating and characterizing those features of
rhetorical tradition and improvisation that constitute the "literary
aspects" of such works, we may shed some light on the part they
play, *as* literature, in history itself. My chief goal is not the
exposure of the by now plentifully exposed underbellies of colonialism and its servant anthropology, but an understanding of the
rhetorical means by which their earliest texts communicated—
and helped to control—a suddenly larger world.[1]

Travel literature was involved in the development of many new
kinds of writing: if it is implicated in the origins of anthropology, it
is also implicated in the origins of the modern novel, the renewal
of heroic romance, and the foundations of scientific geography.
That such various discourses are so mutually entangled in the
corpus of Renaissance travel literature is a fact of real importance
to the histories of all of them, but perhaps most of all to the history
of literature. No text is an island, least of all the texts of a period
and a culture that tried to annex all the islands in the world. Perhaps even the novels of Jane Austen can be seen more clearly in a
history of literature that has absorbed the relation of her genre to
the prose of imperial conquest and empirical science.

Renaissance travel literature did not spring into being with the
first letter of Columbus from the New World, although that letter
heralded great changes. Other, quieter kinds of travel writing preceded and followed the voyage literature with which the rest of
this book is concerned. After Mandeville had presented Europe

---

1. For some recent critiques and rhetorical analyses of anthropology and ethnography per se, see James Boon, *Other Tribes, Other Scribes* (1982); Anthony
Pagden, *The Fall of Natural Man* (1982); Johannes Fabius, *Time and the Other*
(1983); and James Clifford and George E. Marcus, eds., *Writing Culture: The Poetics
and Politics of Ethnography* (1986).

with a (fictional) model for the private, secular travel account, Petrarch, Aeneas Silvius, Montaigne, and others followed suit, in works that recorded their experience of Europe's more familiar topography. And with the long history of pilgrimage accounts behind them, such later pilgrims to the Levant as Piero Tafur, Felix Fabri, and Bertrandon de la Brocquière could more nearly approach both the motives for travel and the rhetorical posture we find in modern accounts of the Near East.[2] What the traveler-writer needs is a backlog of earlier writing: "Monsieur de Montaigne found three things lacking in his travels . . . the third [was], that before making the trip he had not looked into the books that might have informed him about the rare and remarkable things in each place, or that he did not have a Münster or some other such book in his coffers" (*Travel Journal*, 28). For as it becomes a self-contained literary genre, travel writing becomes more and more impressionistic. Its interest has come to lie largely in the sensibility of the particular writer, less and less in its capacity or obligation to inform.

One could then turn aside here and finish with Montaigne and Coryate, whose records of travel to Italy and to the East rest on the requisite piles of earlier books, despite Montaigne's rueful desire to have read more of them than he had. These writers were conscious belles-lettrists. But the task of articulating the natural law of modern travel literature cannot properly begin until its many origins are accounted for. And by its nature, travel writing has as many origins as it has matters: each matter bespeaks a separate concern or fulfills a different requirement of the imagination, and the historical conditions of their development vary widely. The matter of the New World was perhaps the last major topic to be absorbed by the West. As Edmundo O'Gorman so lucidly argues, once the idea of one new continent, entirely divided from the contiguous land masses of Europe, Africa, and Asia, had been digested by the West, Australia and Antarctica were slighter challenges to the imagination.[3] If Columbus, Las Casas, and Ralegh were not travelers, they were nevertheless among the originators of New World description

2. English translations of travel accounts by all these authors are easily accessible, except for that of Bertrandon de la Brocquière, which is only available now in English (slightly abridged) in Thomas Wright's recently reprinted anthology *Early Travels in Palestine*. This anthology also contains the texts of Arculf and (modernized) of Mandeville.

3. See Edmundo O'Gorman, *The Invention of America*, especially parts 2 and 4.

and narration, and on their texts rests the pile of later literature. At the end of their lineage, Bruce Chatwin traveled to Patagonia to find a piece of dragon skin in the nuclear-free zone of the latter end of the world, where, as Joyce promised and Chatwin proved yet one more time, "there be terrible queer creatures."

The particular focus of this chapter is on the formal contribution of narrativity made to the developing genre by the writings of Columbus. Its notable intrusion into a kind previously dominated by *descriptio* was given entrance by the novel presence of the Hero in the scene to be described. At one stroke, Columbus gives the tradition two elements crucial to the modern genre: character and plot.

This development depended on historical circumstances and was certainly not accomplished by Columbus alone. It was a long and somewhat paradoxical process. For until the world was thoroughly mapped and "discovered," the foreground of a travel account was no place for the confrontation of individual sensibility and the alien that informs most modern travel writing. Europe had need of information from its earlier travelers. Although as we have seen, its curiosity was directed by desires and and expectations counterproductive in most cases to the discovery and transmission of hard data, nevertheless it was something *like* data that had to take center stage. The voyage of discovery and exploration is thus at once inimical to the modern poetics of travel writing and its historically essential minesweeper.

In the simplest usage of the word, it was history that pared down the task of travel writing until its dimensions were suitable to the impressionistic memoir of private experience. Everyone knows Columbus as a crucial enabling agent of history. But his landfall at San Salvador is part of universal history, as the Norse landfall at Greenland is not, because he wrote about it, to the right people (and in the right language), and because the printing press rapidly disseminated what he wrote. And so Columbus intersects both the political history that enlarged and demythologized the world of the traveler and the literary history of the travel account. The same set of texts illustrates both intersections—indeed, constitutes them. As a result, literary history *is* political history here, and discussion of rhetoric and imagery will entail some discussion of the political realities they responded to and helped effect.

Columbus did not simply bump into a new continent and leave

it for the expansionist Iberian nations to colonize, nor was the discovery of America a simple enlargement of European territory. In his journals and letters, Columbus interpreted what he found, as Marco Polo interpreted China. His interpretation was a dream very like Marco's and Mandeville's dreams, both of which he had read, but in his case a dream from which the pressures of circumstance would at last awaken Europe. As his interpretation was dismantled, so were the assumptions underpinning it. The farther apart the mythic and practical aspects of the *novus mundus* came to appear, the harder it became to look at any alien place through the obscuring terms of dream and nightmare. Daily contact with "the end of the East," which turned out to be the West, began to demystify the notions of the East which had so long kept a stranglehold on European consciousness, even of itself.

Columbus's interpretation of his Caribbean discoveries was an inheritance from the past we have examined in previous chapters. But the rhetorical mold into which he poured the old images and terms was something new. In other hands it would one day transmit a humbler and more reliable image: in chapter 6 we will examine a text (Ralegh's *Discoverie of Guiana*) much freer of fantasy. Meanwhile, it is time to take a look at how fantasy and the formal constituents of romance conspired to engender the genre's new capacities. Treatment of the mise-en-scène established in the *Letter to Sanchez* will lead naturally to the heroic function of the writer in that *scène*. These topics are prerequisites to discussion of the narrativity of the *Journal*.

The *Letter to Sanchez*

Columbus had to render Elsewhere in words, and so the nature of his linguistic task puts him in the same company with his more strictly literary successors. But, as with Mandeville, we are looking back to a vanishing point at which the beautiful and the useful coincide, at which the linguistic and the phenomenal become effectively one. In the grand sentence of López de Gómara's near-contemporary *Historia general de las Indias*, the discovery of the Indies was "the greatest event since the creation of the world, save the incarnation and death of Him who made it." Seen in this light, the first *Letter* and *Journal* of Columbus belong to the class of works we are concerned with as the Gospels do to the genre of biography. Their historical importance, of which their author was confusedly aware, overshadows their literary functions and overburdens what rhetorical resources past travel literature had to offer him. They are holotypes.

Columbus devotes several pages of his *Journal* of the first voyage to a storm encountered on the return to Spain (Feb. 14, 1493), his anguish at the thought that "our Lord willed that he should perish there," and his hope "that God would bring him in safety, so that such news, as he was bearing to the Sovereigns, should not be lost." Finally, in the midst of the physical chaos of the storm, he writes an account of his discoveries on parchment, "earnestly begging whomsoever might find it to carry it to the Sovereigns," rolls it in a waxed cloth, ties it, and seals it in a wooden cask which he throws overboard.[4] He has spent nine years trying to find a sponsor for his quest and clearly feels that if the ship goes down, his "Indies" go down with it. He was probably correct, in the short run. The words he threw overboard *were*, for the moment, the fact of the Indies, worth a million times their weight in gold (or their volume in Indian blood).

Such weight could never again rest on the narration of a journey.

In searching for methods of making sense to his readers, Columbus stepped beyond the bounds established for him by Polo and Mandeville. In his *Letter* and *Journal* we see yet another example of old and disparate genres being twisted together to make a new rope. From a literary-historical point of view it will be more useful to investigate the presence and effects in Columbus's writings of those inherited elements than to speculate about his specific influence on later literature. (The *Journal*, for instance, could not have had any widespread immediate influence, as it remained unpublished until 1825.)

After Columbus, the characteristic genre of New World explorers in the Renaissance became, as during the Crusades, the chronicle. Voyages of "discovery" early on became voyages of conquest, and the news was of war (called "pacification" even then),

---

4. All quotations in English from the *Journal* of Columbus are cited by date of entry from *The Journal of Christopher Columbus*, trans. Cecil Jane. Jane's translation is dependent on the text established by Cesare de Lollis and Julian Paz in volume I of the thirteen-volume *Raccolta di documenti e studi pubblicati dalla R. Commissione Columbiana*.

not of places or visits. Nor did most of the eyewitness chronicles have anything to equal the literary excellences of Joinville or Villehardouin (except perhaps in Bernal Díaz del Castillo's *True History of the Discovery and Conquest of Mexico*, written in enraged response to the lacunae in Gomara's homebound account of the same events). The *cartas-relaciones* were official briefs. But Columbus, a public figure like the conquistadores, was also a reader, and he engaged himself in the act of making literature. Whether or not he became a model for other writers, his representations of the New World have for us a significance in themselves, as the work of a writer with Pliny, Polo, the *Letter of Prester John*, and Mandeville behind him and the radically New (at last) in front of him.

How did the literature of the past contribute to the vision, encapsulated in Columbus's works, of "a new heaven and a new earth," of an Earthly Paradise at the mouth of the Orinoco shaped "like a woman's nipple"—and to what extent do the cynical and bloodthirsty accounts of succeeding explorers record a catastrophic rejection of the notions behind his rhetoric? Although the latter issue might seem to belong more properly to the historian's sphere, we are dealing with an upheaval in the heart of a culture's imaginative possessions that can only be known through texts—texts that have not as yet received the literary and philological attention they require.

Columbus scholarship is so fraught with controversy that parody of it seems to have become a category of the imaginative literature about the Discovery.[5] Since the classic account represented in Washington Irving's biography began to crumble in the later part of the nineteenth century, historians have taken up ever more extreme and ingenious positions on the issue of what Columbus believed his project and accomplishment to be. Henry Vignaud's massive researches were an attempt to prove that Columbus was searching not for Asia, but for a New World in fact; Cecil Jane's thesis was that he was really looking for Australia—he annotated his books *after* the discovery to create the impression that he had

---

5. E. g. Walter Hugh McDougall, *The Un-Authorized History of Columbus, Composed in Good Faith by Walt McD.; Containing No Maps, References or Facts* . . . (1892); John Brougham, *Columbus el Filibustero!! A New and Audaciously Original Historico-Plagiaristic, Ante-National, Pre-Patriotic, and Omni-Local Confusion of Circumstances, Running through Two Acts and Four Centuries* (185–?).

been seeking what he came to believe he had found. Edmundo O'Gorman claims, through a somewhat tortuous semantic argument, that although Columbus sailed to America he did not discover it (*invenire*) because he never realized its nature as a land mass distinct from the known *orbis terrarum*. The evidence for all these arguments (and more) is textual and linguistic, but the terms and figures of those texts have changed their meanings over time. As Wilcomb Washburn complains in his survey of the controversy, "Would that the historical profession had members willing to compile the word lists which form the grist of the philologist's mill" ("Meaning of 'Discovery' in the 15th and 16th Centuries," 15).

That complaint was issued in 1962, and few Americans have risen to the challenge since, although Virgil I. Milani's monograph, "The Written Language of Christopher Columbus," at least lays to rest Jane's image of an unread and nearly illiterate Discoverer.[6] To analyze Columbus's account of his experience, one must take up a position on what that experience was. But a literary analysis need only consider the texts themselves—along with their textual ancestors and progeny. Given Columbus's *explicit* intentions and interpretations, how do his written accounts represent them, or in other words what are his ideas of the decorum attaching to his overt literary task? His terminology is all we have, and all his contemporaries had, to understand and respond to. What kinds of rhetorical structure, what matrix of topoi did that terminology appear to him to dictate?

Because the *Journal* of the first voyage is only available to us as edited and frequently epitomized by Las Casas, it is safest to begin with the earliest extant edition of Columbus's *Letter to Sanchez,* written in Spanish on board the *Niña,* "off the Azores," and translated into Latin by Alexander de Cosco—the *Epistola de insulis nuper inventis,* as it is known in the card catalogs.[7] It was through de Cosco's "semi-barbarous" Latin that the letter received its

6. See note 27 to this chapter.
7. (Rome: S. Plannck, after April 29th, 1493.) Ten prose editions (eight of them in de Cosco's Latin), and three more in Guiliano Dati's Italian verse, are listed under the year 1493 in John Alden's bibliography, *European Americana: A Chronological Guide to Works Printed in Europe Relating to the Americas, 1493–1776.* (It was Van Wyck Brooks who called de Cosco's Latin "barbarous," in a note to his English translation. He was right. I have relied on de Cosco's text anyway, as it was by far the most common version in print during Columbus's lifetime.) As there are many

widest dissemination. In this version, Columbus states unequivocally: "On the thirty-third day after having left Cadiz I arrived in the sea of India." Other versions read "the Indies," rather than "sea of India." All versions agree in identifying these *insulas nuper inventis* (or *repertis*) as a part, and *that* part, of the known *orbis terrarum*. A few lines later, Columbus is even more explicit: "I found it [Cuba, which he has named Juanna] so large, with no ascertained end, that I believed it to be not an island but the continental province of Chatai [Cathay]."

Whether or not Columbus is lying, accommodating himself to the desire of his sponsors that he find lands associated with great wealth, is not of particular interest here. The thesis that the document must make appropriately manifest is that the writer has arrived by a new route at a remote part of the Old World, last rendered from direct experience by Marco Polo and unthreatening to the broad outline of traditional geography. At the same time, he states that the particular islands he has visited (among the 12,700 Marco reports are to be found in the Sea of India) have not been seen before by men of the Christian West: "For although men have written or spoken of these islands, all was conjecture and circumlocution: no one claims to have seen them. Hence it seemed nearer to fable." His job then is to corroborate and to flesh out the hearsay reports of his predecessor, and where necessary to correct inaccuracies. What had seemed like fable must be made to seem real. The detail of all this is recorded in the *Journal*: the *Letter* is an outline (eight quarto pages long). Its narrativity is minimal and intermittent, functioning mainly as an implicit truth claim. "I understood in the meantime from certain Indians I had taken in that place that this province was an island, and so I followed the coast eastwards for 322 *milaria* to where it ended." This sentence contains pieces of data that could have been delivered as straight description: "Juanna is an island, at least 322 *milaria* long." The first-person narrative statement of these facts is more convincing and imaginatively accessible, referring as it does to the firsthand experience that authorizes the speaker, and so the letter begins in this mode. Once the palpable existence of these Indies is thus

---

modern editions of the *Letter* available, as well as many editions from the fifteenth and sixteenth centuries, all with slightly different pagination, I have not cited page numbers here. In any edition the letter is only a few pages long.

established, Columbus turns to a kind of rambling topographical *effictio*, and this is the manner of most of the rest of the letter:

And the said Juanna and other islands in the same place appear very fertile. It is surrounded with many very safe and sheltered harbors, incomparable to any others I have seen. Many great and healthful rivers flow through it and the mountains there are many and very high. All these islands are very beautiful and distinguished by various shapes, accessible, full of a great diversity of trees touching the stars, which I believe are never bare of leaves. For I saw them as flourishing and adorned as they usually are in Spain in the month of May; some blossoming, some bearing fruit, some in other states thrived according to their nature. The nightingale chattered, and other sparrows, various and innumerable, in the month of November where I myself went strolling among them. There are moreover in the said island of Johanna seven or eight kinds of palm which in height and beauty, just as with all the rest of the trees, herbs and fruits, easily excell ours. And there are wonderful pines and fields and very vast meadows, various birds, a kind of honey, and various metals, excepting iron. In that island, moreover, which I called Española above, there are great and beautiful mountains, vast woodlands and plains very fruitful and very fit for planting and grazing and for putting up buildings. The convenience of the harbors and the excellence of the many rivers contributing to the health of men in this island exceed belief, except for him who has seen. The many trees, pastures and fruits of this island differ from those of Juanna. Further, this Española abounds with spices, with gold and with metals.

What we are given here is a classical *locus amoenus*—complete with strolling poet—modified slightly to make it answerable to economic as well as sensuous imaginations.[8] Even those modifica-

8. In the first chapter of his *Medieval Dream-Poetry*, A. C. Spearing provides a generic description of the heavenly topos (and its sources in the Eden of Genesis, the heavenly paradise of the Apocalypse, the *hortus conclusus* of the Song of Songs, and the pastoral landscapes of Homer, Theocritus, and Virgil). "It is typically set in bright southern sunlight (perhaps augmented by or transformed into the jewelled brilliance of the Apocalypse), but it also provides shade against the sun, and is therefore furnished with a tree or trees, often fruit-trees. The trees will be in a flowery meadow, which will provide fragrance as well as bright colours, and there will probably be birds singing in them (though in some cases the place of birds is taken by human or angelic song). In the meadow there is almost invariably a spring or brook, often rising from a fountain, and there will usually be a breeze, both features being necessities for comfort in a hot country. It is perhaps somewhat surprising that this Mediterranean ideal should have been taken over so readily into the literature of northern Europe, where water and breezes might be thought com-

tions resonate with established legends: the vegetable fertility and abundance are found in the Land of Cockaigne, the gold is from the Garden of the Hesperides and Solomon's Ophir, the spices (nonexistent in Haiti) had always given the "fabulous East" a voluptuous as well as commercial appeal. Although Columbus was quite explicitly anxious for his credibility (especially in the *Journal*, where he uses up his superlatives early on and is pressed into ever more hysterical pleas for belief), he cannot resist the temptation to utilize the bird's-eye *descriptio*, which rolls all sweetness up into one ball. Dr. Chanca's letter to the *cabildo* of Seville, written during the second voyage, exhibits an alternative and usually less seductive approach. He sees up close, for instance, the houses of the natives around the first Spanish settlement at La Navidad: "As for those who live on the shore, it is marvelous how barbarously they build, for the houses situated there were so covered with green or damp that it is astonishing how they exist." Even his perceptions of beauty are specific and discrete:

At a distance of three leagues there appeared a waterfall as broad as an ox, which discharged itself from so great a distance that many wagers were laid on the ships, since some said that it was white rocks and others that it was water. *When we came nearer to it, the truth was apparent,* and it was the loveliest thing in the world to see from what a height it fell and from how small a space so great a waterfall originated. (emphasis mine)[9]

But Dr. Chanca's letter is an idle document compared with Columbus's: Columbus has to convey the meaning and significance of his islands to the royal couple upon whose whim their further exploration wholly depended. Naturally he will want to convey the deepest significance consonant with the facts. Whether strategically or spontaneously, deceptively or sincerely, he has called on

---

moner and less desirable. But taken over it is, spreading gradually north-west as far as Scotland, where in the early sixteenth century Douglas is still describing a supposedly Scottish scene which includes grapes and olives" (17–18). Like Douglas with his Scottish grapes and olives, Columbus tends to provide his Caribbean islands with features that belong to the topos rather than to the place—e.g., nightingales, spices, perfect peace and harmony.

9. The quotations in this paragraph are taken from Cecil Jane, *Select Documents Illustrating the Four Voyages of Columbus,* 1:52 and 26. Jane prints the original Spanish of all these documents, taken from Navarrete's *Colección de los viages y descubrimientos,* on facing pages.

a constellation of tropes that will eventually lead him to his declaration, during the third voyage, that "these lands" are those "in which I am assured in my heart that the earthly paradise is."[10]

This letter is an attempt to *place* the discovered lands as much as to describe them. In Columbus's uses of the terms *Indies, insula, terra firma, orbis terrarum,* and *novus mundus,* historians seek clues as to his pragmatic geographical sense of where he was, where he was heading, the relation he conceived of this land to the known world. Part of the trouble Washburn hoped would be solved by compiling word lists is that, in a culture possessed only of theoretical knowledge (and that controversial) of the geographical world picture, such terms had necessarily floating significations.[11] It may be possible to discover the precise meanings of Columbus's idiosyncratic usages, but I doubt it. The overwhelming effect of the description in the *Letter* is that of imaginative and psychological placement. We are in the Golden Age, in Eden (which it turns out is "distant from the equator 26 degrees"). The people have gold but "no iron or steel or weapons." They "always go naked, just as they were brought into the world," and they give "with marvelous love." And unlike Europe in another way, "in all these islands, I saw no great diversity in the appearance of the people or in their manners and language, but they all understood one another, which is a very convenient thing."[12]

10. "Estas tierras que hagora nuevamente e descubierto, en que tengo assentado en el ánima que allí es el paraýso terrenal" (Jane, *Select Documents,* 47). Columbus makes the identification on his first voyage as well, but more indirectly. See note 31.

11. "The Indies" as a plural form, for instance, stemmed from the later inclusion of Ethiopia in the concept " India," which, in turn, stemmed from confusion over the exact location of the mythical Christian kingdom of "Prester John." It was known to be an "Indian" kingdom, but as contact with India proper dropped off, and greater efforts were made to penetrate Africa, rumors of Coptic Christians in Ethiopia invited its identification with the related concepts "Prester John" and "India." See Francis M. Roger, *The Quest for Eastern Christians: Travels and Rumor in the Age of Discovery* and, for a passionate interpretation of this pluralization, the first chapter of Christopher Miller, *Blank Darkness,* esp. 23–29. Opinionated but well-informed discussions of the range of meanings covered by the terms *orbis terrarum, insula,* and *terra firma* can be found in Edmundo O'Gorman, *Invention of America.* In general these terms are so infected by the mythical and quasi-theological nature of the geographical "science" they served that it seems wrongheaded to attempt translations across the centuries, as though Columbus had "geographical" notions of the sort we could recognize and simply lacked a clear scientific terminology with which to express them.

12. The Spanish edition has *singular* instead of *perutilis.*

Compare the observations of Dr. Chanca, written two years later:

The decoration of men and women among them is to paint themselves, some with black, others with white and red, becoming such sights that to see them is good reason for laughter. Their heads are shaved in places and in places have tufts of tangled hair of such shapes that it cannot be described. In conclusion, whatever there in our Spain they might wish to do to the head of a madman, here the best of them would regard it as a great honor. (Jane, *Select Documents*, 1:64)

They eat all the snakes and lizards and spiders and all the worms which are found in the ground. So it seems to me that their degradation is greater than that of any beast in the world. (1:70)

It is certain that for an unarmed people they can do great damage. (1: 60–62)

Obviously the two writers have very different personalities. I quote from Dr. Chanca mainly to emphasize the degree to which Columbus has shaped his materials. The Noble Savage is not yet the popular figure he will become (although Mandeville had produced a few, and the naked, meditative gymnosophists of the Alexander romances had always been tendered an ambivalent respect). But Columbus helped to popularize him by linking the American "Indians," whose heathenism was circumstantial and therefore not culpable, to Old Testament figures of innocence—prelapsarian Adam and Eve in their unselfconscious nakedness, the pre-Babel population in its linguistic unity.[13]

This is a new development of the old tradition of the simile and analogy, which converted the features of an alien territory into more or less grotesque collages of the familiar. Similes created composite monsters in *Wonders*, Oriental Christians in the works of Marco Polo and William of Rubruck; through his use of analogy, Mandeville populated the East with industrious dwarfs as rational as Europeans, and pious cannibals whose liturgy, like ours, includes the eating of human flesh. Columbus's motive is perhaps the same at a very deep level: to banish the presence of the utterly

---

13. For a clear exposition of the kinds of *infidelium* recognized in the period, and their respective degrees of culpability, see Pagden, *Fall of Natural Man*, 37–38.

alien, to translate the Other into a distortion of oneself—in a word, to domesticate. But the method is different. Columbus does not use similes very often and in fact reverses the domesticating function of the analogy twice: the harbors of Juanna are "incomparable to others I have seen," and there are "very high mountains, to which the island Tenerife is not comparable."[14] The explicit linkages of simile and analogy give place in the *Letter* to implicit metaphor. The conventional imagery of the *locus amoenus*, the prelapsarian conditions and qualities he emphasizes in his picture of Indian *mores*: such rhetorical and topical features of the *Letter*'s prose bespeak the buried vehicles of Paradise and Eden. The equations are always covert in the first *Letter*, but become quite explicit, even apparently literal, in the third (written, it should be remembered, in the period of his declining favor and influence).

To speak of metaphor without some qualification would be anachronistic in this context. There is a world of difference between the conceit of Donne's apostrophe to his mistress, "Oh my America, my new found land," and Columbus's identification of Haiti in his letter to the pope of 1502: "This island is Tarsis, is Cythia, is Ophir and Ophaz and Cipango, and we have named it Española" ("Esta isla es Tarsis, es Cethia, es Ofir y Ophaz é Cipanga, y nos la habemos llamado Española"; Navarrete, 2:280). For Columbus, both terms of the metaphor belong to the same species of reality. It is only since the conquest of geographical science over legend that we have come to perceive a category distinction between such places as Ophir and Haiti. And yet, as I have hoped to show in the preceding chapters, there is enough of a distinction available to Columbus's understanding that we can use the term *metaphor* for lack of a better one. "Ophir" is that which has been spoken of and longed for, while "Española" is that which has been seen and discovered (*inventus*). Columbus's sentence to the pope could perhaps be described as the fraction form of a whole number, a form that refers to the same thing as does a simple integer, but expresses a relationship along the way. Ophir (or Ophaz, etc.) is the denominator, Española the numerator. The relation between the two names is still important, to Columbus; geog-

14. This last clause does not appear in the Latin version; for the Spanish Barcelona edition, see the facsimile in *A New and Fresh English Translation . . .* , ed. Morison.

raphy still lies in the embrace of scriptural history and *fabulae poetarum.*

In the covert metaphorical structure of the first *Letter,* the vehicle half hidden among the details of description is compounded of a great variety of legendary motifs. I have mentioned some of them already, including some from the biblical East. Here also are details from the Land of Prester John, Saint Brendan's Isle (still appearing on maps well into the sixteenth century), the Fortunate Isles, the Purgatory of Saint Patrick, the Ganges of the Alexander romances.[15] The typical rhetorical strategies for conveying those locations of romance are resorted to continually: the negative list, the trope of multiplication, the insistence that only seeing is believing, the impossibility of full enumeration. There are no storms, no weapons, no monsters, no enemies, no cities. There are "innumerable" islands, "incomparable" harbors, islands "of a thousand shapes," birds, herbs, and trees "of a thousand kinds." There is "countless gold" and an "innumerable population." The harbors of the sea are "such as you could not believe without seeing them." The islands are "all more richly supplied than I know or could tell."

These figures constitute the "inexpressibility topos" of what some call "travel romance." They are familiar from *Wonders of the East,* Marco Polo, and the second half of Mandeville, and significantly absent from the accounts of the early pilgrims and the crusaders. The pilgrims and crusaders had no need of the inexpressibility topos: to the extent that the East of their matter was sacred it was already inscribed in a Book. Their *descriptio* was in a sense redundant, that of the "romancers" helplessly evasive. Both strategies (dependency and evasion) fend off an essential problem of travel writing: the traveler's medium is language, and the language he uses has evolved as an envelope specific to its region and culture. It has no words for what is alien—at least, no words that do not contain and express their roots in the state of alienation (as in the abstractions "heathen," "barbarian," "*outre-mer,*" "*unheimlich,*" Mandeville's "that other half," our own "Far East," or any of

---

15. For a thorough sampling of figures and images characteristic of those literary and fabulous locales, see "Earthly Paradises" in George Boas, *Essays on Primitivism and Related Ideas in the Middle Ages.*

the cuisine-linked names given by early Greek traders to distant peoples: Icthyophagi, Anthropophagi, and so on).

Columbus is not constant in his literary loyalties. This is, after all, Cuba or Haiti, and though his general style pays homage to Ophir and Eden, the fact of the difference is important, and sometimes unsettling for the reader. In the romance tradition he gives us naked, unarmed Edenites (see fig. 7). In an attempt to convey the density of actual experience (this is not a dream but a dream *come true*), he describes in some detail their clothes and weapons.[16] And in line with his declared purpose of describing from experience places previously rendered only out of conjecture, he pointedly disappoints the romance expectation of monstrous beings: "In these islands I have so far found no human monstrosities, as many expected." He goes on, however, to list reported exceptions to the paradisal negative: the man-eaters, the Amazonian women of "Matremonia" who consort with them once a year, the men with tails, the island of the hairless.

The relation between the sober and romantic assertions is one of factual inconsistency. The *Letter* tries to offer its readers a cake they can both eat and have. Columbus tells us by his mixture of styles that these islands are in themselves an oxymoron: a fabulous reality. No one fabulous name, no one mundane detail is particularly important. He compacts the glories of all legendary Eastern lands and chooses somewhat arbitrarily from the wealth of narrative detail and observation in his *Journal* the grit of data that will make the romance convincing. The letter is all style and innuendo. This seems perfectly appropriate to the kind of placement its author is trying to accomplish. The Land of the Heart's Desire is to be put on the map, but it must retain its "inexpressible" splendor and solace while it becomes familiar, Christian, and commercial. "It is a desirable land and, once seen, is never to be relinquished."

The application of the romance aesthetic to a situation out of real life was destined for trouble; from the back seat of the twentieth century it is easy to see how poorly desire and possession

16. E. g., "The inhabitants of both sexes always go naked, just as their mothers bore them, except some women, who cover their pudenda with some leafy frond or a cotton skirt which they provide for themselves. . . . They carry nevertheless for arms reeds burnt by the sun, in the roots of which they fasten a shaft of dry wood filed to a sharp point." (Morison dismisses the clothing of the women with this incredible remark: "But what is a breechclout among friends? The women were doubtless kind, and the mariners duly grateful"; *Admiral of the Ocean Sea*, 543.)

Fig. 7. Naked "Indians"; From one of the first editions of Columbus's *Letter*. Basel, 1493. Courtesy of the John Carter Brown Library at Brown University.

mixed. Within fifty years Las Casas's great howl of anguish went up in that most grotesque of all international bestsellers, the *Brevisima relación de la destruycion de las Indias Occidentales*:

Upon these lambes so meeke, so qualified and endewed of their maker and creator, as hath been said, entred the Spanish incontinent as they knewe them, as wolves, as lions, and as tigres most cruel of long time famished: and have not done in those quarters these 40 yeres be past, neither yet doe at this present, ought els save teare them in peeces, kill them, martyre them, afflict them, torment them, and destroy them by straunge sortes of cruelties never neither seene, nor reade, nor hearde of the like . . . so farre foorth that of above three Millions of soules that were in the Ile of Hispaniola, and that we have seene, there are not nowe two hundreth natives of the countrey. (A1v-A2r).[17]

How could something like this happen in Paradise? The answer to that question lies partly in the practical drawbacks of the aesthetic that labeled it Paradise in the first place. A crucial psychological function of romance as a genre is neatly epitomized in the trick performed by the Grail in the French prose *Lancelot*: "The Holy Grail entered through the great door, and at once the palace was filled with fragrance as though all the spices of the earth had been spilled abroad. It circled the hall along the great tables and each place was furnished in its wake with the food its occupants desired" (*Quest of the Holy Grail*, 44).[18] This is the genre of crav-

17. This and subsequent quotations from the *Brevisima relación* are taken from the Readex Microprint facsimile of the 1583 English translation.
18. Certain elements of the romance style, though not all, were so wedded to the matter of the East that Columbus's literary investigations would inevitably have infected his grid of perception. Even his letter from the Italian humanist Toscanelli on the subject of Western exploration manages to locate places in the Indies which can only be reached by the *aventur* that structures the plots of romance: "I have also marked down many places [on an accompanying chart] among the Indies, which may be reached by the occurrence of some casual event, such as contrary winds, or unlooked for accident of that sort." Toscanelli renders the coincidence of West and East in terms curiously reminiscent of the Grail's capacity to satisfy each separate palate at once: "Let it not create wonder that a westerly region is assigned for the country of spices, which have always been understood to grow in the East, for those who sail West will find those lands in the West, and those who travel East will find the same places in the East." It would seem that the romance style is as automatic in this context to the renowned physician and astronomer as it is to the sailor and chartmaker to whom he will send the letter. (These quotations are drawn from Van Wyck Brooks's translation, included in his *Journal of the First Voyage to America*, 237. The original Italian can be found in a diplomatic edition printed in Appendix D

ing satisfied, and often enough (even in the unusually spiritualized *Lancelot*) both craving and satisfaction are represented psycho-somatically: the Grail dispenses not grace or salvation, but each man's favorite dinner. Las Casas picks up this motif in his representation of the Spanish predators as "long time famished" and of the indigenous Caribbeans, so often depicted as cannibals, as their food.

Columbus's factual inconsistencies and misrepresentations are the jarring (to us) result of his mixture of the two generically opposed modes of romance and realism. The gold and spices of the *Letter* were not in fact products of the islands themselves; all Columbus really found there of commercial value was gum mastic, as can be much more clearly gleaned from the *Journal*. The gold and spices are part of a literary landscape generated over several centuries by the specific needs and scarcities of the actual landscape of Home. They are two items on a conventional list of paradisal abundances. Unfortunately for the Taino Indians, Europe was suffering a severe shortage of monetary metals at this time, and most European nations were possessed of gold coinages by the middle of the fourteenth century. And as Columbus's literal reading of Mandeville helped inspire his search for a "real" terrestrial paradise, so the Spanish conquistadores' literal readings of Columbus led them in search of real gold.

We have seen (in chap. 2) that the *twimann*, that feature of "travel romance" most directly related to the fate of the Indians, had traditionally been granted the two-dimensional status of the ornamental grotesque. Even in the writing of theologians he was conceived to be a marginal arabesque of God-the-Artist. (Part of Mandeville's startling originality had been to flesh him out and join him to the human family: in this gesture Mandeville most clearly broke with the romance mode in which his work is still stubbornly placed by critics.) It is no accident that romance of all sorts, from *Wonders of the East* to *The Faerie Queene*, is crowded with sub- and superhuman figures. Romance, in its unequal ratio of self-presence to other-presence especially, is the adventure of the ego in a world of total freedom and fulfillment. The superhuman power of the romance hero amidst the supermundane abundances

---

of Henry Vignaud, *Toscanelli and Columbus: The Letter and the Chart of Toscanelli*.)

of his territory can brook no sustained competition from beings whose reality is equal to his own—not even from his lover. Romance satisfies by allowing us to identify with a character whose being is denser and fuller than that of the figures around him, and whose power and riches are so much a part of his nature that he cannot escape them. Galahad, Amadís, and Gawaine cannot maintain the anonymity of humble status (reduced being) for more than a moment. Romance, whatever else and more it may be in the hands of a great artist, is a vehicle for infantile fantasies of singularity: the infant at the breast was, as the hero is, the sole inhabitant of a universe of plenty.

Columbus did not eat his Taino captives, but his treatment of them, both in the pages of the *Letter* and as a colonial administrator of the islands, recapitulates this important psychological feature of romance. No such fantasy is safe when imagined as fact or enacted in reality. Reality resists; the blissful infant can become the tiger "long time famished," and the spiral of frustrated greed and desperate resistance widens. Even literary romance has difficulty with closure. It is a characteristically long form, and its most self-conscious authors seem unable to end it without rupture: Gottfried's ends in a double suicide, Malory's in patricide and military defeat, Camoens's in dark prophecies of war to come. Spenser's does not end at all. In the unauthored plot of history, there is nothing to bring an end to greed but the loss of power or the destruction of its object. Resistance began in deadly earnest almost as soon as Columbus sailed back to Spain. The garrison he had erected on Haiti—La Navidad—was demolished and its soldiers killed, before his return the following autumn, by islanders outraged at the rapes and thefts of the Spanish left to gather gold. A few months later Columbus was to order the first beheadings. Before too long, the Tainos were extinct.

Lovely as the sensibility appears of the intrepid admiral who strolls among the "nightingales" in his hard-won paradise and has more to say to his sovereigns about trees and flowers than about the materials of commerce, there is something eerie, too, about the *Letter*'s romance. Its writer so resolutely refuses to see the human consequences of his act or the nature of his reception by the Tainos:

They are unacquainted with any idolatry, in fact they believe firmly that all power, all might, and in short all good [!] is in the sky, and that thence with these ships and sailors I have descended. And in this spirit I was received everywhere, after they had banished their fear. Not that they are slow or ignorant; rather they are highly acute people who navigate that sea without end, and give account of everything marvelously. But they had never seen people clothed nor ships of this sort.

He goes on to marvel at the persistence of the belief in his divinity, even among the captives he "took by force . . . in order that they might learn Castilian," and exults that "they were the first to announce this wherever I went, and the others went running from house to house and to the neighboring towns with loud cries of 'Come! Come! See the people from heaven!'"[19] Immediately after this he describes their boats—boats of a sort *he* had never seen.

According to Las Casas's précis, Columbus clearly defines this area in his *Journal* as the Earthly Paradise, in a passage Las Casas merely summarizes. Not that Columbus is slow or ignorant; rather he is a highly acute man who navigates that sea without end and gives account of everything marvelously. But he has never seen people naked before nor boats of that sort. *Both* sets of strangers identify each other as the natives of sacred territories, as figures from myths of origin enfleshed. (Years later, Montezuma will tell Cortés he believes the Spaniards have come from the land of the Aztec's ancestors and will hand over his crown, weeping.) But Columbus is as oblivious to this instructive irony as he is to the weight of consequence entailed in the plan he announces of enslaving his Edenic worshipers. He praises their virtue and generosity and innocence with the hand that writes romance, and with the

19. Columbus's equivalently persistent belief that he is worshiped everywhere he goes gets its pathetically funny comeuppance in an incident summarized by Las Casas from the *Journal*: "Returning to the place where they had left the boats, he sent some Christians to the place to which they had ascended, because it had seemed to him that he had seen a large apiary. Before those whom he had sent came back, many Indians gathered and came to the boats where the admiral had now collected all his men again. One of them went forward into the river near the stern of the boat and made a great oration, which the admiral did not understand, except that the other Indians from time to time raised their hands to heaven and shouted loudly: the admiral thought that they were reassuring him and that they were pleased with his coming, but he saw the Indian, whom he carried with him, change his expression and become as yellow as wax and tremble greatly, saying by signs that the admiral should leave the river because they wished to kill him." The admiral, however, will not flinch, and after approaching the enraged warriors with hawks' bells and brass rings, "pacifies" them, remarking in his journal that "they are people like the others whom I have found, . . . and they have the same belief and think that we have come from heaven" (Monday, Dec. 3).

other includes them in the *Letter*'s closing list of the islands' commodities, between aloe wood and rhubarb.

To complain of the inhumanity apparent in this contradiction would be a cheap shot—only the most remarkable men of Columbus's era were alive to the injustice of slavery, and Las Casas, West Indian slavery's most vocal opponent, was capable of proposing that the Spanish import Africans to the Indies to lighten the burden of the natives there. But the issue is pertinent to a discussion of the romance elements in the literature of discovery. Slavery and genocide were, at least to the West Indians, the central facts of the period. Despite the essential humanity (or practicality) of the Spanish kings, who objected vocally to both practices, they occurred almost everywhere in the Indies. The literature on which the administration of the area heavily depended, the long string of *cartas-relaciones* which started with the first letter of Columbus, must have been a contributing factor. And yet it was not all produced by cruel and savage men: Columbus, at any rate, was promoted as a candidate for canonization by a number of nineteenth-century French historians.[20]

Literature has a life of its own. The constraints of genre, convention, decorum can darken perception of historical actualities if they are too radically new, if they do not fit the categories of event and topic that old literary forms developed to encompass. In "Of Cannibals," Montaigne explains his dependence on the word of mouth of illiterate sailors for information about the New World: "For, subtile people may indeed marke more curiously, and observe things more exactly, but they amplify and glose them: and the better to perswade, and make their interpretations of more validitie, they cannot chuse but somewhat alter the storie" (*Essayes*, 1, 220). This judgment may underestimate the power of literary convention over literate men; whether Columbus deliberately "altered his story" is not clear. I suggest that the nature of his literary heritage altered his story, not only in the telling but in the event itelf.

The magnetic attraction of the mode of romance for traveler and travel writer both is easy to understand. The traveler's isolation in

20. According to Jane (*Select Documents*), these historians and biographers of Columbus included Count Roselly de Lorgues (*L'ambassadeur de dieu*, 1874), the Marquis de Belloy (*Christophe Colomb et la découverte du Nouveau Monde*, 1865), and Leon Bloy (*Le révélateur du globe*, 1884). See *Select Documents*, 1:xviii n.

a foreign culture and the relative freedom of movement inherent in his situation can easily reawaken the arrogant narcissism of the infant. Thus, perhaps, the tendency toward self-effacement in the early pilgrimage accounts, the attempt to replace the experience of the fleshly first-person with the ghostly traces of Christ and his antitypes. Romance is an unseemly mode for the pilgrim. But it is a dangerously appealing one for the colonizing explorer.

Unlike Dr. Chanca, Columbus was no blatant xenophobe. Unlike Sepúlveda, he did not argue that the Indians had no human souls. But on the testimony given by his *Letter* it would seem that he moved too easily between life and art, and his too lovely Indians are no more palpable, in the end, than the *twimenn* of *Wonders*. Thus they fit as naturally into his list of commodities as they do into the figure of the Golden Age. They are part of the stage set of his romance: consciousness and event belong to the admiral alone, and the *Letter* reaches its climax of intensity recounting that astonishing November stroll of his among the gossiping night-ingales. When pressed to render the islands appealing to another palate, he makes the same materials yield other flavors, and the "thousand kinds" of trees and flowers, the noble savages, the beautiful meadows and mineral sands become aloe, gum mastic, spices, slaves, and monetary metals.

The *Journal*

Unlike the *Letter*, the *Journal* of the first voyage is, naturally enough, a narrative, and being written as its experience unfolds. Although not by any means a private diary—it is addressed throughout to "your Highnesses"—it is unlikely that it was intended for publication in those paranoid days of commercial and colonial competition between Portugal and Castile: it is too full of usable information.[21] The literary and political contingen-

21. Neither Iberian government wanted to share the wealth, with anyone—a fact that has some bearing on the literary history of travel to the New World. R. A. Skelton quotes an Italian agent writing from Lisbon after Cabral's voyage: "it is impossible to get a chart of this voyage because the King has decreed the death penalty for anyone sending one abroad" (*Explorers' Maps*, 33). After the 1493 Barcelona edition of Columbus's *Letter* (reprinted once, in Valladolid in 1497), it was twenty-nine years before another eyewitness report from the New World was published in Spain. A copy of a letter of Manuel I to Cabral came out in Rome and

cies that guided its writing permitted a different sort of document from the *Epistola de insulis nuper inventis*, richer and more complex. Its format, as obvious a structure as it may seem to us in the latter days, exhibits a new approach to the task of recounting a journey. Although ships' captains had long kept logs and drawn peripluses, this journal, even in the abridged version that has come down to us, is far too elaborate to be called a log. I know of no full-fledged journal of travel published in Europe, or circulated in manuscript, before Columbus wrote his. (Although Felix Fabri had very recently organized his long tale of pilgrimage into books and chapters representing months and days, that account was composed after the fact.)

The *Journal* does share one important element with the *Letter*—the unabashed ego of the author as romance hero. The story of Columbus's great adventure begins, a little oddly, in the second person, grafting itself onto the story of Ferdinand and Isabella's recent conquest of Granada, but when it turns to the first person it proceeds immediately to ennoble its author for the part:

therefore, after having driven out all the Jews from your realms and lordships, in the same month of January, Your Highnesses commanded me that, with a sufficient fleet, I should go to the said parts of India and for this accorded to me great rewards and ennobled me so that from that time henceforward I might style myself "don" and be high admiral of the Ocean Sea and viceroy and perpetual governor of the islands and continent which I should discover and gain and which from now henceforward might be discovered and gained in the Ocean Sea, and that my eldest son should succeed to the same position, and so on from generation to generation. And I departed . . . .

This generic ego is somewhat obscured by the fact that long stretches of the *Journal* appear only as summarized, in the third person, by Las Casas, but shines even through summary at the moments of highest drama: when the admiral manages to draw into his own person the first sighting of land in the New World and draws the marked straws in three out of four pilgrimage lotteries held during the storms that almost prevented the return of the

---

Milan in 1505, but never in Portugal. Pizarro's *Letter* came out in Venice. Of twenty-five editions of Vespucci's *Letter* between 1503 and 1506, not one was published in Spain or Portugal.

expedition. It is also featured in his mounting antagonism to the forceful Capt. Alonzo Pinzón of the *Pinta*, who apparently entertained competing delusions of grandeur and who Columbus feared would try to beat him back to Castile with the news of the discovery. (Pinzón's is the only name mentioned with any frequency in the *Journal*, which lacks the opening catalog of names customary in chronicles. The New World, as it turned out, would never be big enough for all its heroes, who stole each other's glory and reconquered each other's conquests with a tragicomic repetitiveness.)

Las Casas quotes Columbus directly in one of the *Journal*'s most telling statements:

Sunday, Sept. 23rd . . . As the sea was calm and smooth, the people murmured, saying that, as there was no great sea, it would never blow so as to carry them back to Spain. But afterwards the sea, without wind, rose greatly, and this amazed them, for which reason the admiral here says: "So that high sea was very necessary for me, because such a thing had not been seen save in the time of the Jews, when [those] of Egypt came out against Moses who was leading them out of captivity."

This may seem reminiscent of Fulcher of Chartres's tendency to see in the gestes of the Crusaders fulfillments of biblical prophecies, but there is a twist: this event is not presented as a fulfillment of the divine intention (though later it will be), but as *analogous* to a scriptural case of divine intervention. Analogy equalizes its matters. Columbus here is not merely a chosen instrument of mysterious Providence, but an actor equal in stature to Moses. In the difference between his and Egeria's allusions to the Exodus may be registered one of those rifts in the flow of the *longue durée* to which Braudel instructs us to pay our closest attention. The time-honored relation of traveler to landscape is here entirely reversed: instead of the anonymous "I," invisibly following in the overwhelming footsteps of biblical or legendary heroes, we have a new Moses whose unarticulated desires control the landscape in his wake.

This remark of Columbus's is not an isolated instance of self-aggrandizement among his writings. In his letter to Juana de la Torre, written on the return leg of the third voyage, Columbus says: "Of the new heaven and of the new earth, which Our Lord made, as Saint John writes in the Apocalypse, after he had spoken of it by the mouth of Isaiah, He made me the messenger and He showed me where to go" (Jane, *Select Documents*, 2:48). In an account of a moment of danger and despair during his fourth voyage, he writes to the king and queen of hearing a voice in his sleep berating him for his lack of faith and saying:

What more did He for Moses or for His servant David? Since thou wast born, ever has He had thee in His most watchful care. When He saw thee of an age with which He was content, He caused thy name to sound marvellously in the land. The Indies, which are so rich a part of the world, He gave thee for thine own; thou hast divided them as it pleased thee, and He enabled thee to do this. Of the barriers of the Ocean sea, which were closed with such mighty chains, He gave thee the keys; and thou wast obeyed in many lands and among Christians thou hast gained an honourable fame. What did He more for the people of Israel when He brought them out of Egypt? Or for David whom from a shepherd He made to be king in Judaea? (Jane, *Select Documents*, 2:90–92)[22]

Who knows how much of this sort of thing Las Casas might have edited out of the first *Journal* itself; but even if the analogy between Columbus and Moses is the only instance that was ever

---

22. Around 1500–1501, while waiting in Granada for justice to be done in the matter of his arrest and imprisonment during the third voyage, Columbus drew up for the king and queen a "Book of Prophecies," a collection of every passage in the Bible, as well as in other ancient writings, that could have been construed as prophesying the discovery of America. Most of his explicit presentation of himself as a fulfiller of prophecies seems to date from this period. The reference in the letter from the fourth voyage to the chains of the ocean comes from the following lines of Seneca's *Medea:*

> venient annis saecula seris,
> quibus Oceanus vincula rerum
> laxet et ingens pateat tellus
> Tethysque novos detegat orbes
> nec sit terris ultima Thule.
> (ll.375–79)

("There will come an age in the far off years when Ocean shall unloose the bonds of things, when the whole broad earth shall be revealed, when Thethys shall disclose new worlds and Thule not be the limit of the lands"; Loeb Classical edition, 261.) Next to this passage in his copy of the *Tragedies*, Ferdinand Columbus wrote, "Haec profetia impleta est per patrem meum . . . almirantem anno 1492." See Morison, *Admiral of the Ocean Sea*, chap. 5. For a heavily researched analysis of Columbus's apocalyptic self-understanding, see Pauline Moffitt Watts, "Prophecy and Discovery: On the Spiritual Origins of Christopher Columbus's 'Enterprise of the Indies.'"

there, it is sufficient to give us a reading of the very profuse references and apostrophes to "Nuestro Señor" throughout. As Cecil Jane noted long ago, Columbus sees himself as a man with a Divine Mission, under the special protection of God. Additionally we can say that his God is very much a feudal Lord, bestowing gifts and titles to reward the service of his faithful vassal, and that his mission bore the savor of *aventur* despite his apparently eschatological understanding of it.

It would be easy enough to make a case for Columbus as megalomaniac, as indeed some have done, if we were not looking at his works in the context of their literary nature and lineage. This elevated notion of mission, besides being (as it turned out) not inappropriate to the historical importance of the discovery, is appropriate as well to the literary genres of chronicle and romance. What is not immediately apparent from the format of the *Journal*, looked at from an age of generically self-conscious journals and "travels," is that it belongs to those earlier genres, at least as a changeling child. Nor is this immediately apparent to us as readers of early travel accounts, for Columbus is new in making himself a romance hero: until Mandeville our "narratives" and descriptions have been nearly without protagonists, and even Mandeville is not a hero (a hero cannot hang up his boots "for gowtes Artetyke, that me destreyneth").

It is not a great surprise, however, to find these strains of romance in a travel account produced in the age of the *Morte D'Arthur*, *Amadís of Gaul*, the *True History of the Conquest of Florida*, and the *Luisiads*. Nor is it surprising to consider that a new flowering of heroic romance coincided with the "Age of Discovery" and the insurgence of humanism. But attention to such large coincidences is outside the proper scope of this analysis. The literary question is: Given a detailed travel account whose first-person author inhabits his book not as intercessor (like Egeria), nor as institutor of reality (like Marco Polo), but as hero, what changes can we detect in the character of the narrator's attention and in the objects of that attention?

The most notably unusual focus of attention in the *Journal* is on the natural beauty of the places visited. Although this topic has been essential to travel writing since the eighteenth century, it is not one we have encountered so far in this study. Egeria expressed awe at the sublimity of the scriptural landscape, but appeared to see the sublimity as a kind of topographical allegory referring to the sublimity of the God who had moved and spoken there. Her *descriptio*, and that of most other pilgrim writers after her, focused chiefly on sanctified buildings and religious monuments. Marco Polo, William of Rubruck and, to some extent, Mandeville enlarged the visual horizon, but with a practical eye toward the productivity or difficulty of the terrain through which they passed. Columbus records impressions of a purely aesthetic nature so often and with such emphasis that O'Gorman passes over Camoens to hand him the laureateship of the New World, and José Maria Gárate Córdoba begins his *La poesia del descubrimiento* with a treatment of "La poesia en prosa de Cristobal Cólon."

Both writers credit Columbus with a sensuous realism and a freedom from "artificial" Arcadian fictions which is, as I have shown, an inaccurate response to his ordering images. But they are responding to *something* fresh in the text of the *Journal*, and that may be that it allows room for such impressions at all. They are of no practical use to "your Highnesses," nor to science (e.g., from the entry for Oct. 21: "There are, moreover, trees of a thousand types, all with their various fruits and all scented, so that it is a wonder. I am the saddest man in the world because I do not recognize them, for I am very sure that all are of some value."). They are expressly denied the status of information, and although the summery beauty to which the impressions refer is later part of Columbus's evidence for having approached the Earthly Paradise, they appear in the *Journal* as spontaneous overflowings of emotion, as records of private pleasure, private *experience*.

The license that permits the interruption of private experience into geographical narrative comes from the conflation here of romance hero and travel writer. Columbus is not simply privileged by his travels to give an account of the parts in which he has journeyed: he is the onlie begetter and leader of the expedition, its First Cause. His relation to the event of the journey is felt and expressed as active, heroic, and crucial. It is difficult to separate observer from observed in the account of one who considers the observed territory "his." Columbus need feel no pressure to suppress the emotional reactions in which he and the islands are blended, because his presence as an experiencing character is necessary and central to romance.

The expostulations are quite consistent in their formulas, so it will do to quote from one, from the entry for October 21:

If the [other islands], which have been already seen, are very lovely and green and fertile, this is much more so, and has large and very green trees. There are here very extensive lagoons, and by them and around them are wonderful woods, and here and in the whole island all is green and the vegetation is as that of Andalusia in April. The singing of the little birds is such that it seems that a man could never wish to leave this place; the flocks of parrots darken the sun, and there are large and small birds of so many different kinds and so unlike ours, that it is a marvel.[23]

He goes on, as quoted above, to complain of his botanical ignorance: this complaint is another of his formulas. Sometimes there is the additional presence of nightingales or of mountains that appear to touch the sky; frequently there are pleas for belief, or the figures of "inexpressibility" and "outdoing" (e. g., "if the others . . . are very lovely . . . this is much more so").[24]

"Lovely," "green," "fertile," "extensive," "wonderful": not only is the account heavily adjectival, but the predicates are evidence of sensibility. They record not so much the external features of a topographical landscape as the internal features of a landscape-as-private-experience. Trees, flowers, lakes, and birds are not relayed as the objects of an ecosystem but as instances of pleasure. And over and over, what this all adds up to "es maravilla," is a marvel—

23. "Yo no les dejé tocar nada, salvo que me salí conestos capitanes y gente á ver la isla; que si las otras ya vistas son muy fermosas y verdes y fértiles, esta es mucho mas y de grandes arboledos y muy verdes. Aquí es unas grandes lagunas, y sobre ellas y á la rueda es el arboledo en maravilla, y aquí y en toda las isla son todos verdes y las yerbas como en el Abril en la Andalucía; y el cantar de los pajaritos que parece que el hombre nunca se querria partir de aquí, y las manadas de los papagayos que ascurecan el sol; y aves y pajaritos de tantas maneras y tan diversas de las nuestras que es maravilla" (Navarrete, *Colección de los viages y descubrimientos*, 1:35–36).

24. The inexpressibility topos sometimes leads the admiral beyond mere unaccommodated rhetoric (as when, on another voyage, he gets his men to sign a notarized oath attesting that Cuba is so large it cannot be an island): "Nov. 27th . . . He went on, telling the men whom he had in his company that, in order to give an account to the Sovereigns of the things which they had seen, a thousand tongues would not suffice for the telling nor his hand to write it, for it seemed to him that he was enchanted. He wished that many other persons, prudent and creditable, could see it, he says, being certain that they would not praise it less than he does."

a label that evaluates rather than describes its object, in terms of an alienated, admiring subjectivity.[25]

In fact what is happening here, quietly enough, is the transformation of place into event (in the psychological or neurological sense of the word). With a first-person narrator so abundantly entitled to presence in his narrative as is the hero-writer Columbus, the objects of his attention are quite naturally rendered as experiences rather than as existences independent of the writer. This difference from the annunciatory quality of Marco Polo's renderings can be seen in the difference between his and Columbus's syntactical habits. Marco prefers the minimalist copulative *to be* and the predicate nominative: "There is X." Columbus likes the predicate adjective: "X is beautiful, looks green, seems like Spain," and in fact he often tends away from the verb *to be*; his copulatives are not near-mathematical equal signs, but carry psychological content—"seems," "looks," "smells," "sounds."

This feature of the *Journal* exhibits, at the level of language, the principle that is manifest at the structural level in an almost unprecedented degree of narrativity. Although we have seen in the early pilgrimage accounts the incursion of experienced time into the originally static itinerary format (days replacing miles, past tense replacing, here and there, the habitual present), that time was ritual time, in which the pilgrim traveled *in illo tempore* on a kind of liturgical tape loop. But the *Journal* of Columbus has a plot—structured episodically, like the plots of romance, by *aventur*, but nevertheless imparting to the text those possibilities of change, suspense, growth, epiphany, *outcome* which differentiate the *Adventures of Robinson Crusoe* from the *Travels of Marco Polo*.

It could of course be argued that a journal could hardly help being narrative and episodic. Looking ahead ninety years to another *Journal*, Montaigne's account of his travels to the spas of

25. Here is a passage from a modern travel journal that shares the same subjective sense of landscape: "Small clouds are shining in the blue. We rise by gentle slopes to a panorama of dun rolling country, chequered with red and black plough, and sheltering grey, turreted villages in its folds; breaking against the far mountains into hills streaked with pink and lemon; bounded at last by range upon range of jagged lilac. The twin peaks above Tabriz go with us. So do a flight of yellow butterflies. Far below a horseman approaches. 'Peace to you.' 'Peace to you.' Clip, clop, clip, clop, clip, clop. . . . We are alone again" (Robert Byron, *Road to Oxiana*, 65).

Switzerland and Italy in search of relief for his ailing kidneys, one finds, however, a marked tendency in the direction of *descriptio*, as well as a degree of self-effacement surprising in the author of the *Essais*. But this is not a completely fair comparison. The nature of Montaigne's journey was so irreducibly private that it could hardly have served even him as a goad to narrativity (at one point he remarks ruefully, "It is a stupid habit to keep count of what you piss"; *Travel Journal*, 124). And the opportunities for pure description were profuse, as Montaigne was traveling in a terrain that offered, besides natural beauty, a host of historically and artistically significant sites and objects.

One could say then that it was the inherent eventfulness of Columbus's journey that provided the ground for the *Journal*'s narrativity, and that would be partially true. But surely Nearchus's naval exploration of the Indian and Persian coasts during Alexander's conquest—the first such within recorded memory in its time—would constitute an equivalently eventful material. The journal of Nearchus has reached us only through the epitomes and quotations of Arrian and Strabo; while we cannot assume anything of the rhetorical nature of the original first-person account, what is missing in Arrian's epitome is instructive. Although the account is more than a verbal chart, and recounts important battles, storms, and quarrels among the leaders of the expedition, it is almost entirely lacking in minor event, in the personal and social action that fills the space between the climactic moments of Columbus's adventure. Such personal or social events as are recorded in the *Indica* involve, significantly, Alexander himself (who is marching his troops overland in the same direction and occasionally encounters members of the fleet), and his emotions rather than those of Nearchus are reported. Alexander's power as a romance hero is so great that he appears to crowd all other consciousness out of accounts of his wars, even when, as in the *Indica*, he is not the main character. At the other end of the scale, the *Indica* lacks as well the linguistic presence of the journey's motive, as a measure against which events can be seen as parts of a progress, parts of a plot. The motive of exploration and discovery is explicitly referred to only during the report of a quarrel between Nearchus and his helmsman about whether to take a short cut at the mouth of the Persian Gulf (XXXII, 9–12).

Columbus, on the other hand, is continually reminding us of his purpose, although he is inconsistent in his phrasing of it, and continually involved in the briefer "events" of consciousness: decision, disappointment, alarm, ecstasy, resentment, deceit, manipulation, surprise, curiosity frustrated or satisfied, prayer, and, perhaps above all, naming. (Only one act of naming is recorded in all of the *Indica* [xxi, 10]; Columbus names everything in sight, even big rocks.) The space between well-defined episodes or incidents is filled with verbs of action. Even descriptive digressions are woven of miniature event:

Oct. 11th . . . They all go naked as their mothers bore them, and the women also, although I saw only one very young girl. And all those whom I did see were youths. . . . They do not bear arms or know them, for I showed to them swords and they took them by the blade and cut themselves through ignorance.

Oct. 16th . . . These people are like those of the said islands and have the same speech and manners, except that these here seem to me to be somewhat more domesticated and tractable, and more intelligent, because I see that they have brought here cotton to the ship and other trifles for which they know better how to bargain than the others did.

Oct. 19th . . . All the other things and lands of these islands are so lovely that I do not know where to go first, and my eyes never weary of looking at such lovely verdure so different from that of our own land. . . . When I arrived here at this cape, there came from the land the scent of flowers or trees, so delicious and sweet, that it was the most delightful thing in the world.

This miniaturized narrativity is a reflection of the grosser narrativity provided by the writer's strong sense of purpose. At moments of decision, it is the Mission that directs Columbus, and he refers to one or another of its avatars in recording almost all such moments, and at other kinds of cruxes as well. I quote here a number of his characterizations of the Mission, since a progression can be observed among them that deserves some comment. The Mission changes its nature over time. As a result, the stream of events recorded in the *Journal* appears more than merely episodic: it embodies a transformation:

Sept. 19th The admiral did not wish to be delayed by beating to windward in order to make sure whether there was land in that direction . . . because his wish was to press onward towards the Indies. And there is time enough, for, God willing, on the return voyage, all will be seen.

Oct. 3rd . . . the admiral believed they had left behind the islands which he had depicted on his chart. The admiral says here that it had not been his wish to keep beating about during the past week and on the days when he saw so many indications of land, although he had information of certain islands in that region, in order not to delay, since his aim was to pass to the Indies and, if he were to have delayed, he says that it would not have been good judgement.

Oct. 13th . . . here is also produced that gold which they wear hanging from the nose. But, in order not to lose time, I wish to go and see if I can make the island of Cipangu.

Oct. 15th . . . These islands are very green and fertile and the breezes are very soft, and it is possible that there are in them many things, of which I do not know, because I did not wish to delay in finding gold, by discovering and going about many islands. And since these men give these signs that they wear it on their arms and legs, and it is gold because I showed them some pieces of gold which I have, I cannot fail, with the aid of Our Lord, to find the place whence it comes.

Oct. 19th . . . I make no attempt to examine so much in detail . . . because I wish to see and discover as much as I can, in order to return to Your Highnesses in April, if it please Our Lord. It is true that, if I arrive anywhere where there is gold or spices in quantity, I shall wait until I have collected as much as I am able. Accordingly I do nothing but go forward in the hope of finding these.

Nov. 12th . . . So Your Highnesses should resolve to make them Christians, for I believe that, if you begin, in a little while you will achieve the conversion of a great number of peoples to our holy faith, with the acquisition of great lordships and riches and all their inhabitants for Spain. For without doubt there is a very great amount of gold in these lands. . . .

Nov. 27th . . . And I say that Your Highnesses must not allow any stranger, except Catholic Christians, to trade here or set foot here, for this was the alpha and omega of the enterprise, that it should be for the increase and glory of the Christian religion. . . .

Dec. 26th . . . And he says that he trusts in God that on his return, which he intended to make from Castile, he would find a barrel of gold, which those whom he had left there should have obtained by barter, and they would have found the gold mine and the spices, and in such quantity, that the Sovereigns, within three years, would undertake and prepare to go to the conquest of the Holy Places, "For so," he says, "I protested to Your Highnesses that all the gain of this my enterprise should be expended on the conquest of Jerusalem."

Of course, Columbus knew from the start that he went in search of the Indies, of gold, and of Christian converts, all at once. To the late medieval Christian each of these goals implied the others. And the order in which they succeed each other as focuses of attention is natural: the first step is physically to find the Indies, the next to find gold, and, when that material object begins to appear elusive, it is politic of him to concentrate on the spiritual profit Ferdinand and Isabella may reap from his expeditions.

This conceptual adaptivity, according to the geographer John L. Allen, is an essential quality in the successful explorer, whose quest begins in darkness:

At the outset of an exploratory venture, . . . field behavior and operations are based at least in part on the explorer's initial pattern of beliefs about the area. Routes are chosen, supplies are acquired, and other logistical decisions are made on the basis of preconceived notions about the nature and content of the lands to be investigated. As an expedition proceeds, the explorer may begin to recognize inadequacies and inaccuracies in his original images. He may modify his behavior accordingly, thus adding to the chance of his expedition's successful negotiation of unknown territory and to the fulfillment of its objectives; or he may realize that his objectives are ill-conceived or illusory. Conversely, an inability to realize the discrepancy between a pre-conceived image and an emerging reality may render an explorer unable to modify his behavior and may therefore cause his expedition to fail. ("Lands of Myth, Waters of Wonder," 46–47)

In short, at the center of exploration lies disillusionment—just as at the center of the Christian pilgrim's experience, Jerusalem, lies the frustration of achieving only the physical and not the celestial city. (In the next chapter we look at the ways in which such disillusionment could operate to restructure not only the exploratory venture itself, but the literary venture of the "exploration report.")

Allen does not touch on the process of reconceiving the objective in such a way as to avoid reconceiving its essential nature, which was the task of Columbus in his *Journal* (he dared not admit failure to his sponsors). But his remarks offer an insight into the narrative quality of Columbus's account, in its characterization of exploration as process rather than simply as a sequence of events. For process is to experience what "plot" is to "story" or chronicle. All we need for process to appear as plot in a record of events is a character in whose consciousness the process can be located. In the journal-romance of the Admiral of the Ocean Sea we have that character in full bloom.

In fact, we have seen a version of that character before: Friar William of Rubruck rendered his disappointing mission into the Mongol territory of central Asia with an equal attention to the minutiae of experience, and a marked imposition of plot on the series of events he recounts to his sovereign. Surely it was not through the decorum of romance that the friar sought license for his overwhelming presence in the letter to King Louis. His account is, if anything, an antiromance in its explicit disappointment, its emphasis on privation, humiliation, and failure. But I am not trying to claim that *only* the mode of romance could provide room for a central consciousness. All I am saying here is that *Columbus* is a romance figure, in a romance landscape, and that the *Journal*'s anomalous degrees of self-presentation and temporality can be best explained as resulting from the rhetorical exigencies of that literary mode.

Without question, a book-length study of the *Journal* as linguistic artifact is overdue—not because it is "great" or even "good" literature, but because it is literature at all. Poets may or may not be among the unacknowledged legislators of the world: travel writers quite definitely were, for a time. As long as the only available media for the transmission of crucial information were grafted onto artistic stock and shared in the generic restraints of the arts that supported them, the maps and narratives on which geographers and empire builders depended communicated more (and sometimes less) than information. Style, convention, rhetoric have a content of their own, and every genre has its implicit Weltanschauung. Where a literary text has become a cell in the body of history, historians must look beyond the notion of the more or less transparent "document" and investigate this cell with the techniques proper to its complex nature.

The history of colonialism is particularly open to linguistic study, as colonization is in part a linguistic act. At least it is by the linguistic domination of one culture over another that we have tended to define successful political aggression as conquest, colonization, or empire building: the Normans imposed their language on Britain and we say it was conquered. But after their invasion of Sicily they were linguistically absorbed, and Roger is not, as William was, "the Conqueror."[26] I could not begin to do justice to the scope and complexity of the linguistic aggressions reported in Columbus's *Journal*, and insofar as they are historical events, discussion of them would be out of place here. But insofar as they are plot events in a text I am treating as literature, they demand some mention. Together with the impressionism and consistent narrativity of this text, they constitute one of its most notable features.

Briefly, Columbus is obsessed with words, and in particular with names. The obsession with words as a general feature of the admiral's personality need not concern us: evidence that it was such a feature appears in Milani's study of the 121 words Columbus introduced—as Italianisms, Lusitanisms, and neologisms—into the Spanish language.[27] That he brought this obsession into his experiences in the New World and made it such a focus of his *Journal* is another matter. On landing, the admiral's first action was to call together the notary of the fleet and the captains of the two other ships "that they should bear witness and testimony how he, before them all, took possession of the island, as in fact he did, for the King and Queen, his Sovereigns, making the declarations which are required" (Oct. 11).[28] Natives then collected around the Span-

---

26. Summarizing the Spanish subjection of Venezuela, Las Casas says: "They haue slayne, and wholly disconfited great and diuers nations, so farre foorth as to abolishe the languages wonted to bee spoken, not leaving aliue that could skill of them" (I2r). See section 7, "Language," in Chiapelli, *First Images of America,* for articles on language changes (in both directions) during the contact period. In one of them, Stephen Greenblatt quotes the bishop of Avila from the ceremonial presentation of de Nebrija's *Gramatica de la lengua Castellana* to Queen Isabella: "Your majesty, language is the perfect instrument of empire" ("Learning to Curse," 562).

27. "It is to be hoped that the present work will show Columbus' rather considerable erudition; this aspect of the man has apparently remained hidden for five centuries. For example, he used terminology which was so new that it had not yet reached Spanish shores. This fact supports the general thesis in these pages that Columbus was one of those who transmitted the new learning of the Renaissance into Spain" (Milani, "Preface"). Many of Columbus's new terms are reported in etymological dictionaries as entering Spanish through the writings of Las Casas, although when transcribing Columbus's writings, Las Casas tended to edit out the new terms as foreign or incorrect.

28. Performance of this magical rite was codified into law in 1513 with the adoption of the *Requirimiento,* a speech to be read by explorers, to whatever Indians

iards, and conversations in sign language were held. Columbus's last comment in the entry for that day indicates that he began immediately to teach them Castilian: "They should be good servants and of quick intelligence, since I see that they very soon say all that is said to them, and I believe that they would easily be made Christians, for it appeared to me that they had no creed. Our Lord willing, at the time of my departure I will bring back six of them to Your Highnesses, that they may learn to talk. I saw no beast of any kind in this island, except parrots." (Columbus is likewise unusually attracted to parrots, and the Tainos soon learn to bring them to him as gifts.)

From this first landing until he leaves the Indies (on which day his final recorded action is to name the last piece of land he sees— "Cabo San Theramo"—before hitting the open seas), Columbus complains continually of the language gap, violates his own principles of conduct to capture Indians to whom he can teach Castilian, bemoans his ignorance of botanical nomenclature, and names everything in sight.

Very few of his names were to stick, and even he allows the native name (or what he believes to be the native name) for Cuba to reassert itself in the *Journal* over his own (Juanna). Certainly it was important to have at least tentative names for islands, capes, bays, and harbors if maps were to be made and return expeditions organized. The *Journal* records as well the naming of lakes, mountains, valleys, uninhabited plains, shoals, points, "seas," rivers, and streams. On more than one occasion Columbus seems to have been inspired to the act of naming by sheer beauty: "Cabo Hermosa," "Valle del Paraíso," "Monte de Plata." "Cabo del Buen Tiempo" records the good weather attending the outward progress of the fleet on January 11, "Cabo del Elefante" the shape Columbus

---

were within hearing distance, upon their "discovering" a new territory. Beginning with a history of the world up to the time of the first pope, it ends by requiring the Indians to acknowledge the overlordship of the king of Spain. Otherwise "we shall take you and your wives and your children, and shall make slaves of them, and as such shall sell and dispose of them . . . and we shall take away your goods, and shall do all the harm and damage that we can do, as to vassals that do not obey" (quoted in Lewis Hanke, *Aristotle and the American Indians*, 16). According to Hanke, the reading of the *Requirimiento* was the Spanish solution (for a while) to the problem of "how to make certain that conquests proceeded according to just and Christian principles" (15). Since it was never explained, often read without an interpreter, and sometimes whispered among the trees in the night while its audience was asleep, the Spanish solution was clearly not imagined as a discursive gesture. The response desired of the Indians was more liturgical than political.

saw in that headland.[29] And there are almost no native names in his nomenclature. (The *Letter* records his dispensing new names immediately after it announces the discovery and the taking of possession—noting in the case of "San Salvador" that "the Indians call it Guanahini.")

No other explorer of the New World gave so many names—or if he did, they do not make their way into the narratives of the expeditions. Vespucci's two "Letters" recounting his voyages of discovery mention only three place-names: two native and one mythical ("Antiglia," probably Haiti).[30] Even Cortés uses native names, "christening" only those towns he has established himself.

This explicit passion for naming and the recording of acts of naming might help to explain Columbus's formula of regret over his ignorance of plant names. Of course, he has good practical reason for this regret: he cannot report the discovery of spices if he cannot ascertain their presence. (Why *didn't* he bring a botanist?) But the formula quickly becomes redundant, and its frequency seems underdetermined—particularly as it tends to emphasize to his royal readers his failure to find spices.

Our hero considers himself to be exploring in or near the Earthly Paradise,[31] and in such a connection his preoccupation with naming takes on a special significance. If he can equate himself by analogy to Moses, why not to Adam? As "high admiral of the Ocean Sea and viceroy and perpetual governor of the islands and

29. According to Morison, "Haut Piton does suggest a huge elephant coming down to the Tortuga channel to drink, but Columbus had never seen an elephant. The association was probably a literary one" (*Admiral of the Ocean Sea,* 281–82). This was one of two topographical shapes Columbus records in his first journal; the other, a headland like a minaret (which Morison also recognized during his retracing of the First Voyage), he does not, for once, bother to name. As will be mentioned again later, the presence of elephants was necessary if these islands were to be truly "Indian." Naming might have been an activity useful for filling in the blanks, sketching into the record and somehow into the very being of the new lands features that ought to have been there but were not. In this light it would be interesting to consider the number of Spanish place-names Columbus left behind after his first voyage (Guadalquiver, Española, etc.), and the religious and animal names of the third (Bocas del Dragon, Boca de la Sierpe, for starters), and the largest single category of names: women's names. (Columbus named the Virgin Islands for the mythical and saintly travelers Saint Ursula and the 11,000 virgins, thus at one stroke introducing 11,001 women into the lonely seas of Paradise.)

30. See Amerigo Vespucci, *Navigationes,* in Martin Waldseemüller, *Cosmographiae Introductio . . . .*

31. February 21: "In conclusion, the admiral says that the sacred theologians and learned philosophers were right in saying that the earthly paradise is at the end of the east, because it is a very temperate place, so those lands which he had now discovered are, he says, 'the end of the east.'"

continent" which he is "discovering and gaining," he is in a sense
the legitimate and local successor to that first man to whom
Nuestro Señor gave "dominion over the fish of the sea, and over the
fowl of the air, and over every living thing that moveth upon the
earth" (Gen. 1:28).

After God put Adam into the Garden of Eden "to dress it and to
keep it," he brought the living things to him "to see what he would
call them" (Gen. 2:15, 19). But Columbus cannot name the beasts
and plants of a postlapsarian Eden: the intervention of historical
time disrupts the analogy between himself and our First Father. If
the freedom and plenty of Adam in Eden before the Fall make up
the archetype of the romance scenario, then even the high admiral
in his own New World cannot quite make the dream come true.
But he scurries to conceal this. He names profusely what he *can*
name, rejects or ignores many native names (even for non-European items such as tobacco), and persists in describing his Paradise
as not yet "dressed or kept" (e.g., Oct. 16: "on a single tree, there
are five or six different kinds [of leaves] all so diverse from each
other. They are not grafted, for it might be said that it is the result
of grafting; on the contrary, they are wild and these people do not
cultivate them.").[32]

In nothing does Columbus less resemble the Traveler than in the
extraordinary possessiveness displayed in his propensity for naming and his avoidance of native words. (Vespucci records four common nouns in an account about one-tenth the length of Co-

32. The issue of dressing and keeping a Paradise is actually somewhat complex,
and Columbus (as well as Las Casas) reflects the complexity in his contradictory
images of garden and wilderness. A garden is an image of nature cultivated and
formalized, but Eden is also an image of leisure. The original Garden of Eden
belonged to another order of reality, in which nature was less than man but somehow not in need of aggressive pruning or taming, not "wild." In that nature, the
beauty and harmony to which our gardens are nostalgic monuments was natural.
After the Fall, "we must *labor* to be beautiful." So Columbus is torn between seeing
a nature that needs him and one that does not—not a contradiction for Adam and
Eve, but a vital one for the Renaissance Genoan. He speaks of plains that could be
cultivated and crops that could be sown or gathered for increase and profit. He also
speaks of freakish botanical beauties that one might imagine only an expert gar-
dener could produce: "I observed upon a single tree blossoms, pods unripe, and
others burst open" (Nov. 4). Tasso and Spenser put such trees in their paradises,
where even the minor mortality of the seasons has no place. But those paradises are
equipped with their proper inhabitants, immortal gardeners never seen at work but
recapitulating that equally invisible and unimaginable horticulture of Adam and
Eve. The decorative Indians of the *Journal* cannot be allowed this role, and so the
admiral must spice his Paradise with aboriginally fallow land (called "fallen land"
on an early English map of Barbados).

lumbus's *Journal*, which by my count mentions only ten—three of them words for *gold*.) And yet the record shows that Columbus was not uninterested in the Taino's culture. Despite his oft-repeated insistence that the Indians have no "religion," he commissioned, during his second voyage, "one Friar Roman [Ramon] who knew their language to collect all their ceremonies and antiquities," which collection has come down to us through its incorporation into Ferdinand Columbus's *Historie*.[33] But native peoples possessed of a usable language and systematic culture are somehow too threateningly three-dimensional for the first *Journal*, and the Indians must remain ornamental; they must look and seem and appear but never be, and they must look/seem/appear as charming, gentle, graceful as the nightingales, as quick to learn Castilian as the parrots, as ripe for cultivation as the "Valle del Paraíso."

Coda: Las Casas

Columbus's epistles from the New World acted as a prism through which an old cosmography was refracted into the colors of romance. It was the first time this had happened in a European travel book, and it was not to be the last. Believers in a causal chain of literary influence might then see in Columbus the father of the modern traveler-hero, who becomes, in his book, a literary protagonist. I am not so sure. The writings of Columbus were quoted at length (and paraphrased, and plagiarized) in the important histories and cosmographies of his time, but nothing besides the *Letter* entered literary history whole. His works were not available as rhetorical models.

But his interpretation of the Caribbean and the network of images on which he relied to convey it left their mark, and the old worldview refracted through his romances died hard. Over a century later, Samuel Purchas would feel the need to devote a chapter of the book-length introduction to his *Pilgrimes* to contesting, with hilarious but earnest rationalism, the notion that "Ophir" was Española or Peru. He applied to that mythic identification an analysis guided by an interest in significant differences and local

33. For a complete translation of Friar Ramon's collection, see Edward Gaylord Bourne, "Columbus, Ramon Pane and the Beginnings of American Anthropology."

variation that is precisely lacking in the works of the admiral, to whom all "Indians" were the same and all the Indies one self-repeating Arcadian landscape.[34] Ophir, says Purchas, had supplied Solomon with ivory, and "an Elephant could not live in Peru, but by Miracle. For the Hilles are cold in extremetie, and the Valleyes, till the Incas made artificial Rivers were without Water, it never rayning there, whereas the Elephant delights in places very hote and very moist" (*Purchas His Pilgrimes*, 1:73–74). (This brief passage grants more independent selfhood to the elephants than Columbus's whole *Journal* does to the Tainos.)

Purchas's "Anagogicall" reading of the biblical excursion to Ophir, on the other hand, is eerily reminiscent of Columbus's "revised objective" as elaborated toward the end of the *Journal*. "Thus shall the Temple, and Church of God be edified, enriched, adorned, after we have arrived at Ophir, and have seen our owne weaknesse, and taken paines in myning Gods Treasures" (1:6). But Columbus did not "see his own weakness" in the Indies because he saw no Other in whom he could catch his reflection, as Mandeville so magnificently could at the end of *his* East.

Columbus of course did not create the allegorical and mythological response to the Indies. He simply ratified an understanding natural to the intellectuals of his day. And stay-at-home cosmographers and theologians seized on his implicit metaphors with more enthusiasm than did kings and soldiers. But we ought not underestimate the power of the "climate of opinion" at whose center he stood. Purchas was by no means the last to register some part of the view that would help inspire the settling of New England by "Pilgrims," or sputter its crowning degradation on the license plates of Saint Thomas, the "American Paradise."

Bartolomé de Las Casas is at least as important to the history of

---

34. Making his own first landfall the New World in the bay of Rio de Janeiro, Lévi-Strauss remembers Columbus's generalizing passage, in the *Letter*, about the beauty of the Caribbean islands and finds its suppression of differences emotionally true: "That's America: the continent makes itself felt at once. It is made up of all the presences which enliven, at the end of the day, the misted horizon of the bay; but to the newcomer these shapes, these movements, these patches of light do not stand for provinces, or towns, or hamlets; he will not say to himself 'There's a forest' (or a stretch of open country, or a valley, or a 'view'); nor will he see them in terms of the activity of individuals, each enclosed within his own family and his own occupation and knowing nothing of his neighbors. No: it all strikes him as an entity, unique and all-comprehending. What surrounded me on every side, what overwhelmed me, was not the inexhaustible diversity of people and things, but that one and single redoubtable entity: the New World" (*Tristes Tropiques*, 84).

New World description as Columbus (on whose writings his own often depended heavily). He was only in the loosest sense a travel writer; he had made the New World his home by the time he began to write his histories, and his books *were* histories. Like Herodotus (or John of Plano Carpini), he considered himself a kind of primary source, rather than the protagonist of an adventure. But a brief look at his *Brevisima relación de la destruycion de las Indias Occidentales* will make an appropriate coda to this chapter about the romance of the New World. There is no question of its influence on later writing and on opinion—the book is largely responsible for the "Black Legend" of the Spanish conquests (which has insidiously contributed to the widespread contempt for Latin America that shapes some of the political history of our own time). But oddly enough, considering its unrelieved grimness, almost despair, it feels closer in emotional color, conception, and rhetoric to the writings of Columbus than to any other document of New World experience.

Las Casas was responsible for the publication of much of Columbus's writing about the New World through his inclusion of it in his own *Historia de las Indias*. He spent a great deal of time editing, writing about, and thinking about Columbus. And he spent most of his adult life in the world Columbus had just discovered—in 1510 he became the first Christian priest to be ordained there. He admired the discoverer, but not uncritically, and has especially harsh words for Columbus's indication of the ease with which the "cowardly" Tainos of Española might be conquered:

Note here, that the natural, simple, and kind gentleness and humble condition of the Indians, and want of arms or protection, gave the Spaniards the insolence to hold them of little account, and to impose on them the harshest tasks that they could, and to become glutted with oppression and destruction. And sure it is that here the Admiral enlarged himself in speech more than he should, and that what he here conceived and set forth from his lips, was the beginning of the ill usage he afterwards inflicted upon them. (Quoted in Morison, *Admiral of the Ocean Sea*, 291)

What words had begun, Las Casas seems to have thought, words could end, and he set himself the literary task of undoing the harm Columbus had initiated when he "enlarged himself in speech." The *Brevisima relación* is in some ways just such a *descriptio* permeated with event as was the *Journal*. Its perception is as infernal as Columbus's was paradisal, but through the painfully detailed itemizations of slaughter and torture and rape emerges an oddly similar imaginative landscape: a luscious Eden peopled with "sweete lambes," "silly creatures," and "children." The intruding Spaniards are "Lions," "Tygres," "Divels," "everie one more cruell then other" (G3r), and he names none of the tyrants he accuses (even as Columbus avoids naming Spaniards in his *Journal*): "their memorie is now abolished from the face of the earth, as if they had never beene in this world"; I4r). Columbus's "thousands of kinds" of unnameable birds and trees are replaced with thousands, and sometimes "millions," of anonymous souls, "perished without faith and without Sacramentes." There are abundances here, as in any paradise, and as always they stagger the writer into the noisy silences of *occupatio*, "outdoing," "inexpressibility." But they are abundances of "villanies," vastnesses of "desolation," absolutes not of desire but of shame.

"I saw there so great cruelties, that never any man living eyther have or shall see the like" (B4v). Las Casas is fiercely brokenhearted, and his emotion overwhelms the explicit content of his book. It is full of what looks like information, but that information is so formulaic that it comes to seem merely the medium of his emotion: even the numbers quoted are more like the figures of rhetoric than of arithmetic. (Some slaughters or desolations are of "millions," some of "thousands"; in some places there are "hardly two hundreth," in others "no more than 2000" natives left—the numbers are an index of outrage, not of population densities.)

What has broken Las Casas's heart is the second Fall he witnessed in the Eden of Columbus:

The people of [Yucatan] were the most notable of all the Indies, as well in consideration of their policie and prudence, as for the uprightnes of their life, verily worthie the training to the knowledge of God, amongst whom there might have been builded great Cities, by the Spanishe, in which they might have lived as in an earthly Paradise, if so bee they had not made themselves unworthie, because of their exceeding couetessnesse, harde heartednes, and heynous offences. (F3v)

Thus, even the gold has been lost:

I say, that by the report of the Indians themselves, there is yet more golde hidden then is come to light, the whiche because of the uniustices and cruelties of the Spaniardes, they woulde not discover, neyther ever will discover, so long as they shall bee so euyll entreated. (L1r)

In Las Casas's understanding, the mining of the gold and its meaning (divided and then stitched together allegorically in Purchas's later "Anagogicall application of Solomon's Ophirian Navigation") are compacted utterly. This is for him not an *image* of Paradise despoiled and closing its gates again but the thing itself—as real to him as the same "paradise" was to him who, fifty years earlier, had at last been "given the keys."

This habit of literalism, in the writing of men whose places in history were secured at least in part by documents of interpretive description, was not without result in the world of events. As Las Casas himself says of Columbus, "what he here conceived and set forth from his lips, was the beginning of the ill usage he afterwards inflicted upon them." Las Casas, of course, intended nothing but good. But the objects of his intentions, those "sweete lambes" and "wild Christians," never existed outside of the collective romance to which he added his anomalously outraged pages.

Outrage did not lead Las Casas quite to despair: he gives warnings and advice to "your Majestie" (King Charles, by now), and both call on images familiar from Columbus—the Indies as a garden needing to be dressed and kept, and the Indies as a woman:

if his majestie doe not take some order therein in some time . . . they wil in a short time make an end of them in such sorte, that there will bee no more Indians to inhabite the lande, but that it will remaine a wildernesse without being manured. (M1r)

I say, sacred Majestie, that the way to redresse this countreye, is that his Majestie deliver her out of the power of Stepfathers, and give unto her an husbande whiche may increase her as is reason, and according as thee discerneth. (G3v)[35]

Las Casas had influence with the king, if not with his colonial administraters. He won important political concessions, and the lot of the Indians would have been even worse without the efforts in their behalf of the bishop of Chiapas. But his imagery had influence too, and what he had inherited from Columbus was passed on to all of Europe. That helpless daughter of bad stepfathers reappears in England, in Chapman's "De Guiana, carmen Epicum" (1596, a *propemptikon* to Lawrence Keymis's colonizing explora-

35. Las Casas is actually quoting here, from a letter sent to the king by "a Bysshoppe of this Province" (Saint Martha).

tion of Guyana), this time looking to Elizabeth for a mother, rather than to Charles or Phillip for a husband: "bowing her mightie breast, / And every signe of all submission making, / To be her sister, and the daughter both / Of our most sacred Maide" (in Keymis, *A Relation of the Second Voyage to Guiana*).

The English did not reject the Spanish romance, but they fed upon the image of the Fall in the *Brevisima relación*, which permitted them to see their role as typologically redemptive, and innocent. Chapman goes on to invoke a favoring wind that will set "their glad feet on smooth *Guianas* breast, [!] / Where (as if each man were an *Orpheus*) / A world of savadges fall tame before them, / Storing their theft-free treasuries with golde."[36]

The imagery of romance eventually permeated the corpus of New World description, from medical tract to exploration report to *historia*. De Bry's *Great Voyages* (1590–1634) opens with an engraving of Adam and Eve standing beneath the Tree of Knowledge, in that first Paradise to which all romance landscapes refer. The New World was clearly seen as a second chance, a clean slate. But the snake in the Tree is huge, and Adam looks (as well he might) aghast.

Columbus's application of the wide range of paradisal imagery to his discoveries is easy enough to point to, and its demonic usages in later European representations of the conquests of America, Africa, and the East are easy to condemn. This imagery performed a terrible task of self-deception for those who wielded it, authorizing and excusing (and, inadvertently, confessing) what can only be termed abominations. At the same time, the works of Columbus herald a literary development in the scope and focus of travel literature which, though essentially formal, is inextricably involved in the production and transmission of that imagery. When Columbus imposed on his "new heaven and new earth" the generic egotism and greed of romance, he also opened up the travel account to a subjectivity and narrativity new to the form and essential to its later masterpieces. The autobiographical and experiential bent and the ample sensibility of the modern genre bear the stain upon them of original sin: it was in the self-love of conquering heroes that the travel memoir was born.

36. Opheus had been alluded to before in a similar connection, by Robert Baker in his verse travel letter, "Voyage to Guinie." There the writer sees the West African coast as Hell, in which the European search for gold is likened to Orpheus's journey to the Underworld in search of Eurydice. (See chap. 6, n. 11, for a passage from this account.)

Cordiform world map. Venice, c. 1590. Courtesy of the John Carter Brown
Library at Brown University.

6

"Inward Feeling"

Ralegh and the Penetration
of the Interior

English travelers of the sixteenth century played a major
role in ushering in the long era of England's dominance
as a world power: it was they who found and took the first outposts
of that empire upon which, eventually, the sun stopped setting.
They were an articulate and voluble lot, as the sheer length of
Hakluyt's and Purchas's collections of voyage literature proves.
The written record of their achievement not only documents the
rise of English colonial and commercial power, but takes its place
in English literary history as well. As John Livingston Lowes, R. R.
Cawley, and, more recently, Percy G. Adams have shown, their
letters and books provided a rich vein of mostly vernacular prose
from which the poets, playwrights, and novelists of England's
emerging literary greatness would draw raw material, narrative
models, and inspiration itself.[1] One of the first major texts of the
English Renaissance was Thomas More's *Utopia* (1516), a high-
minded parody of such travel *descriptio* as Marco Polo's enamored
disquisition on the customs and government of Cathay.

More's *Utopia*, stimulated by Vespucci's four "Letters," "that
are now published" (and which may be forgeries), is also in a sense

---

1. John Livingston Lowes, *The Road to Xanadu: A Study in the Ways of the
Imagination* (1927); Robert R. Cawley, *Unpathed Waters: Studies in the Influence
of Voyagers on Elizabethan Literature* (1940); Percy G. Adams, *Travel Literature
and the Evolution of the Novel* (1983). None of these works, with the exception of
Adams's, has much to say about the literature of travel per se, and as Adams's chief
interest is in the eighteenth century, he tends to assume an unchanging and
undifferentiated nature in earlier travel literature. These books taken together,
however, make an impressive case for the importance of such literature to writers,
if not to critics.

the first piece of travel literature produced in England's Age of Discovery, though it was followed by a long pause in English exploratory activity. By the time the itch to discover returned, almost half a century later, *Utopia* appears to have worked some changes (not, of course, singlehandedly) in the rhetorical situation of the travel writer. In the discourse of travelers, entrepreneurs, and propagandists, the *fictionality* of Utopia (Noplace) had been established as an opposite pole to the geographical reality of the lands they hoped to discover and exploit (principally, North America, Guiana, and Cathay). The letter to his brother which opens Humphrey Gilbert's *Discourse of a Discoverie for a New Passage to Cataia* (1576) begins this way: "Sir, you might justly have charged mee with an unsettled head if I had at any time taken in hand, to discover Utopia, or any countrey fained by imagination: But *Cataia* is none such, it is a countrey, well knowen to be described and set forth by all moderne *Geographers*" (iiir). Twenty years later, in the preface to his account of the second expedition to Guiana, Lawrence Keymis rouses his readers to shame for their current timid inaction:

If we should suppose our selves now to live in the dayes of King *Henrie* the seventh of famous memorie, and the strange report of a West *Indies* or new world abounding with great treasure should entice us to beleeve it: per-haps it might be imputed for some blame to the gravitie of wise men, lightly to be carried with the perswasion and hope of a new found *Utopia*, by such a one as *Columbus* was, being an alien, and manie wayes subject to suspition. But since the penance of that incredulity lyeth even now heavie on our shoulders . . . let it bee farre from us to condemne ourselves in that, which so worthilie we reproove in our predecessors; and to let our idel knowledge content it selfe with naked contemplation, like a barren womb in a Monasterie. (*A Relation of the Second Voyage to Guiana*, unpaginated)

Utopia is now a term in the cosmographical imagination: a "Noplace" against which real places stand out (one hopes) in stark relief, and which draws into itself the projective desires that had led Marco Polo and Columbus to the brink of fiction in their accounts of other worlds. The popularity of More's fiction has provided the base for a whole new genre of harmless travel fiction, in which desire for a better (or different) world can be expressed and satisfied without corrupting the sources of practical geographical knowledge.[2]

Or so the theory might run—practice, as always, lags a bit behind it.

The search for the Northwest Passage for which Gilbert is propagandizing and that for El Dorado, which motivated the expeditions of Ralegh and Keymis to Guiana, were the most fantastical and quixotic of the English Age of Discovery. The Northwest Passage and El Dorado are today synecdoches for the Other World of optimistic fantasy. And Gascoigne's preface to Gilbert's book ends with a statement that would have made a nice epigraph for *Utopia* itself: "To conclude, whereas other *Cosmographical* workes doe but shew us things already knowen and treated of, this *Discoverie* doeth tend to a very profitable and commendable practise of a thing to bee discovered" (iiiir).

In 1585, Gabriel Chappuys brought out in Paris an encyclopedia divided into twenty-four sections devoted to distinct geographical areas, of which Utopia was one.[3] Ambivalence about the relation between Noplace and real places continued well into the seventeenth century. As More had tied Utopia to the New World by sending Hythloday to America with Vespucci, Cyrano de Bergerac's protagonist in *Les estats de la lune* (1657) ends up in Canada ("New France") on his first attempt to reach the moon. The division of travel literature into fictional and nonfictional kinds was complicated by the more gradual division of the geographical world picture into real and unreal places.[4] And this process was

2. Philip Gove's bibliographical study of eighteenth-century travel fiction, *The Imaginary Voyage in Prose Fiction*, establishes *Utopia*'s primacy as a model in the literary history of Christian Europe. In this connection Gove quotes E. A. Baker on the cyclical aspect of the relation between travel literature and prose fiction: "Fabulous voyages have always played a momentous part in the establishment of prose fiction as a new literary genre. They first appear as attested records of travel in the vast regions known to all mankind; and then merely as the picturesque framework for a Utopia, as in Plato's account of Atlantis in the *Timaeus*; for love adventures, as in *The Incredible Things beyond Thule*; or for satire, as in Lucian's *True History*. . . . The ancients likewise had their Mandevilles and their Defoes, as well as their Swifts and their earnest delineators of various kinds of Utopias" (*History of the English Novel*, 1:36, quoted in Gove, 17).

3. *L'estat, description et gouvernement des royaumes et républiques du monde, tant anciennes que modernes.*

4. Cawley (*Unpathed Waters*, 73) notes Ralegh's frustrated inquiries after an island that, it turned out, had been included on his map at the request of the

complicated, in turn, by the generic ambivalence of the inherited rhetoric of travel. Not only was the actuality of any given spot on the traditional map a problem to determine, but the language of geographical description was freighted with its own history of figurative and metaphysical usage. Some discussion of the state of the art as it stood by the mid-sixteenth century is necessary before we can look in any detail at an English travel account.

Little or no cosmography was available in England in the vernacular until the 1550s, when William Cunningham brought out *Cosmographical Glasse* (1559). The work is a dialogue in which a well-read but confused student of the subject finds inner peace through his master's ability to organize and categorize the information floating loose among the Latin and Greek classics. It offers extremely sketchy and outdated information on America—which in Cunningham's mind includes "Archay Chersonesus," a legendary name translating roughly into the Malaysia of real geography. The *descriptio* of this work includes, cautiously, the Plinian monsters, and the small *mappa mundi* among the illustrations bears not the slightest visible relation to the shape of the terrestrial world even as the rest of Europe knew it then.

Within the same decade, however, Richard Eden had translated and published the section on the New World from Sebastian Münster's *Cosmographiae* (calling it *A Treatyse of the Newe India*) and Peter Martyr's first three *Decades*, complete with exhortatory prefaces of his own.[5] Thus, England's reading public was introduced to the New World at several removes. Münster and Martyr were both *writers*: they composed their descriptions out of the written and oral accounts of travelers in a spirit close to the aesthetic of López de Gómara. The Spanish historian includes on the first page of his *Istoria de las Indias* a list of "Los istoriadores de Indias" and then says dismissively: "All the others being printed write their own, and they are brief. Therefore they are not entered in the number of

---

cartographer's wife, "that she, in imagination might have an island of her own" (quoted from Ralegh, *Works*, 4:684).

5. Sebastian Münster, *A Treatyse of the Newe India* (1553); Pietro Martire d'Anghiera, *The Decades of the Newe Worlde or West India* (1555). The originals of these translations, Münster's *Cosmographiae universalis* and Peter Martyr's *De rebus oceanis et orbo novo decades tres*, were published, respectively, in 1544 and 1533.

historians. If that were so, all the captains and pilots who gave account of their landings and navigations, which are many, one would call historians." This notion of the literatus's greater authority in the propagation of truth, by virtue of his *literary* skill, significantly inhibited the transformation of geographical understanding. In the English editions of Martyr and Münster, firsthand accounts have not only been worked up into literature, but then translated and finally enclosed in prefaces intended by Eden to soften the shock of the new: the first marginal note in his preface to *A Treatyse* is "Nothing new under the Sunne."

In this preface, Eden filters the New World through the familiar grids of legend and Scripture, as Columbus had. He says the matter of Münster's book

to some men might otherwyse seme in maner incredible, yf the lyke had not been sene in tyme paste, and approved by auctoritie of moste holy Scripture, which declaring the great wysdom, ryches, and noble viages of King Salomon, sayth that God gave him wisdom and understanding exceding muche, and a large heart, and that he prepared a navie of shippes, in the port of *Azion Gaber*, by the brinke of the redde sea, which sayled to Ophir, and brought from thence xxi score hundreth (whiche is xlii.M) weight of golde. (Unpaginated)

Münster himself is helpful in the same regard: he quotes Pliny and refers the reader to Marco Polo for a description of the Khan's magnificence (both men dead these two hundred and fifty years). He leads into Columbus from Marco, positioning America as an extension of the known East.

The slippery representation and ambivalent rhetoric of literary cosmography find their most sublime exemplar in Peter Martyr. As Columbus had in his *Journal*, Martyr confesses to an intoxicated imagination:

If I chance nowe and then in the discourse of this narration to repeate one thynge dyvers tymes or otherwise to make digression, I must desyre youre holynes [Pope Leo X] therwith not to bee offended. For whyle I see, heare, and wryte these thynges, mee seemeth that I am herewith so affected, that for verye joy I feele my mynde stirred as it were with the spirite of Apollo as were the Sibylles, whereby I am enforced to repeate the same ageyne. (132r)

His rhetorical sympathy with Columbus's voluptuous romance is manifested again in his synopsis of the discovery. The first event he recounts is that of the *Letter*'s climactic moment: "As they coasted along by the shore of certayne of these Ilandes, they harde nyghtengales synge in the thycke woodes in the month of November" (2r). Martyr sometimes surpasses Columbus in this tendency: "*Dryades*, or the natyve nymphes or fayres of the fountaynes" (23v) welcome the Spaniards when they land, and, although he does not believe that America actually contains the Earthly Paradise of Genesis, he uses the term constantly as an analogy.

The denial of radical otherness apparent in the familiar medieval, even Virgilian, imagery of writers like Münster and Martyr is nevertheless a step forward from the deeper denials of Stamler and Lilius, whose cosmographies, written earlier in the century, had elected not to describe the new lands at all, hinting that their status as fact was too dubious or at any rate too remote to matter. Since Stamler had actually met and spoken with Indians in Europe, this silence on his part would suggest a capacity for rejection of the new and alien which would be no simple matter to overcome. [6]

More's *Utopia*, contemporary with the works of Stamler and Lilius, is not only a satiric reflection of Europe's political and moral disgraces, it is also satiric and suspicious of the content of the new voyage literature. That his immediate response to the

---

6. "About the islands discovered I make no mention, but I am sending you the tracts about the newly discovered lands of Christopher Columbus, their discoverer, and Albericus Vespucci, . . . so that you may take a look at them. Notwithstanding I confess men of this sort and two young males to be among us, with whom as far as I was able I spoke, and looked at them very carefully" (Stamler, *Dyalogus . . . de diversaram Gencium sectis et mundi religionibus*, 1508 aiiiv). Zacharius Lilius, in *Contra antipodes* (1496), does not mention America; he simply proves that there is not and cannot be an "Antipodal region," nor people with spurs on their feet who walk "with feet opposite ours . . . which seems absurd and impossible" (fiiir). Joannis Cochleus in his edition of the *Cosmographiae Pomponii Melae* (1512), to which he appends a work of his own, is the most explicit and adamant of all about the "*novus mundus*": "Whether it be true or fabricated it contributes little or nothing to the knowledge of Cosmography and History. For both the people and the places in that land are obscure and nameless to us, nor are voyages made to that place without many perils. Consequently it is no concern of geography" (F1v). In his article "Not in Harrisse," E. P. Goldschmidt quotes from a 1498 commentary on Sacrobusto which acknowledges equatorial humans but describes them in language straight out of *Wonders of the East*: although they are kind and intelligent, they are "blue in color and with square heads; they appeared most strange to the Spaniards" (140).

reports of Columbus and Vespucci would be to delineate an even more impossibly innocent and abundant "Noplace" is not without suggestiveness in our context. The defensive claims of later English explorers that they are *not* writing *Utopias* indicate that the name came fairly quickly into the sardonic vocabulary of those who see fiction in anything strange or new. Almost a hundred years later, Keymis is still kicking against the traces of More's fictional appropriation of, and Martyr's Virgilian depiction of, the new lands: "In publishing this treatise, my labor principallie tendeth to this end: to remove all fig-leaves from our unbeliefe" (*Relation*, Preface). At the same time as providing a new and self-contained formal outlet for the imaginative impulses of potential Mandevilles, the *Utopia*, rhetorically indistinguishable from the description of an actual foreign nation, seems to have cast a shadow of doubt on those factual "relations" it parodied. Chappuys's careful abridgment allowed it to fit so naturally into his *L'estat, description et gouvernement des royaumes* that a careless reader might have remained unaware of its fictionality.[7]

In the context of a cosmographical rhetoric still heavily figural and allegorical, inclined to the accommodation of cultural fantasy, the rise (or rebirth) of the "imaginary voyage" was a development bound to initiate realignments in the travel writer's literary situation. But it was not the only development to stimulate new refinements of the genre. Münster's *Cosmographiae* touched off an explosion of geographical encyclopedism. Verbal and pictorial

---

7. Only a single introductory paragraph, and not one set off graphically in any way from More's text, marks the description of Utopia as fiction. Here is Chappuys's explanation for its presence in his collection, extracted from that paragraph: "Or avons nous bien voulu la mettre au rang de ces autres, pource qu'elle semble estre beaucoup plus resoluë et parfaicte, que celle de Platon, et à fin que de ceste lecture ainsi imaginée, le lecteur considerant les choses vrayes, qui sont continuës aux precedentes Républiques, puisse voir, que l'on peut tousiours, en la reformation ou constitution d'une nouvelle République, trouver quelque chose de nouveau qui soit bonne et profitable" (*L'estat*, xxiv). This sentiment reached its logical and poetically just conclusion in the New World, where, according to Todorov, "Vasco de Quiroga [who has been very impressed by *Utopia*] will organize two villages according to utopian prescriptions—one near Mexico City, the other in Michoacan, both called Santa Fe—which illustrate both his philanthropic spirit and the threatening principles of the utopian state." According to his description, these villages reproduced the details of More's book right down to the prohibition against dyed clothing: "we have here a fascinating play of mirrors, in which the misunderstandings of interpretation motivate the transformation of society" (Todorov, *Conquest of America*, 194–95).

atlases such as those of Waldseemüller and Ortelius, Chappuys and d'Avity, along with the great collections of *récits de voyage* by Ramusio, Hakluyt, Thevet, de Bry, and Purchas (of which Martyr's *Decades* was the important model), relieved the traveler-writer of several obligations. He need not be comprehensive beyond his own experience (as for instance Fulcher and Joinville had been about the more distant East). He need not organize his data according to conceptual categories. Others would do that for him. His most essential contribution had become the first-person narrative of experience, a work whose claim to the reader's attention had to do with the more properly literary features of story and personae. And the situation that made the encyclopedias and collections possible—the new accessibility of other worlds and the frequency of travel to them—also put a new pressure of veracity on the traveler. His reports could be, would be, verified or exposed. "The Relation of David Ingram," included in Hakluyt's first collection (*Divers Voyages*), had been discredited by the time of the expanded *Principall Navigations* and was deleted. Mandeville's *Travels* was included in both, but in Latin, one of the very few untranslated works in the collection (and available to Hakluyt in English).[8]

This suddenly expanded accessibility of geographical information provoked the need to maintain credibility, which had results of its own. Its intensity rendered the old rhetorical strategies inadequate. "No one would believe who has not seen," for instance, was a smug formula that operated in a world full of readers who *had* not seen and never would.[9] The reader recognized his own situation in the formula and felt his limited perspective directly

8. Richard Hakluyt, *Divers Voyages Touching the Discovery of America* (1582; rpt. 1964); idem, *The Principall Navigations, Voiages and Discoveries of the English Nation . . .* (1589). The latter, revised and enlarged, was published again in three volumes between 1598 and 1600, and a modern reprint is available (1903–5). My references in this chapter are to *Divers Voyages*, but all the texts I mention, other than Ingram's, are included in all the above-mentioned editions of the work.

9. More plays an early version of the novelist's line "It was like something right out of a novel" when he uses this formula in *Utopia*: "They do not keep it [gold] as a treasure, but in such a manner as I am almost afraid to tell, lest you think it so extravagant, as to be hardly credible. This I have the more reason to apprehend, because if I had not seen it myself, I could not have been easily persuaded to have believed it upon any man's report" (61). The incredible manner in which the Utopians keep their gold is as "chamber-pots and close-stools." What makes this a particularly vertiginous moment of "truth" is that More is here echoing the claim of actual travelers to the New World, who inevitably lyricize over the indigenous peoples' careless contempt for gold and their apparently moneyless cultures.

addressed, his inclination to disbelief thereby subverted. But the sixteenth-century reader was a potential traveler himself, or knew people who had traveled, or at any rate could easily flip to another description by another traveler in the same book. Disbelief, as Keymis notes almost wrathfully in his preface, was rampant.[10] But the Indies, East and West, *were* marvelous—not in the old, objectively understood sense of the word, but subjectively, relative to the familiar operations of European nature and culture. In an article analyzing the rhetoric of what he refers to as the "exploration report," Hans Galinsky pinpoints the issue: "Here one becomes aware of a basic problem of early overseas literature, which now faces the exploration reporter, a problem not initiated by the New World though intensified by it: how does one convey that subjectively true sense of the marvelous and at the same time keep the reporter's cardinal goal of conveying objective truth?" (Exploring the 'Exploration Report,'" 7). He touches on a couple of rhetorical solutions: comparison of new phenomena with both legendary and homey things at once, and the masking of the marvelous in quantitative expression (he quotes Hariot's claim that "foure and twentie houres labour" will provide a corn harvest sufficient for a year). What he does not touch on is the ultimate inadequacy of such solutions and the concomitant shift of interest in the form from depiction of abstract or uninhabited fact to the relation of the narratable facts of experience.

The antinarrative urge toward encyclopedism, which Ronald Swigger calls "a total order of words . . . in which human beings tell themselves what they know and understand about the universe"

---

10. Percy Adams quotes a number of complaints over this situation: "[William] Biddulph [in *The Travels of Certaine Englishmen into Africa, Asia, . . . Jerusalem* (1609)], unhappy with readers who 'will hardly believe anything but that which they themselves have seen' and who smugly dismiss anything strange with 'Travellers may lie by authority,' concludes bitterly, 'but they are liers themselves which say so.' William Wood, in New England twice in the first half of the seventeenth century, was quite upset by the common opinion concerning travelers. 'I would,' he said at the start of his New England's Prospect (1634), 'be loath to broach any thing which may puzzle thy belief, and so justly draw upon myself that unjust aspersion commonly laid on travellers, of whom many say, They may lie by authority, because none can control them.' And then he explodes, 'There is many a tub-brained cynic . . . , who because anything stranger than ordinary is too large for the strait hoops of his apprehension, he peremptorily concludes that it is a lie,' and so Wood rejects 'this sort of thick-witted readers'" (*Travel Literature and the Evolution of the Novel*, 95–96).

("Fictional Encyclopedism," 355), is easily discerned in most later medieval travel relations. It accounts for their characteristic inclusion of unattributed hearsay data and their reliance on Pliny, Solinus, and the Alexander romances for descriptions of phenomena they did not see but had to mention in order to be thorough. This imperative of comprehensiveness weakened for the European travel writer during the sixteenth century. An unwieldy increase of knowledge and event was matched by a proliferation of subgenres in the once (awkwardly) unitary sphere of travel literature. The traveler who wrote no longer produced a work informed by the multiple generic pressures of the *historia, cosmographia, itinerarium,* memoir, "imaginary voyage," and *carmen Epicum* (as Chapman labels his gilded proem to Keymis's *Relation*). He no longer had to produce The Book, only his own book.

Only in hindsight, of course, can we characterize the medieval travel book this way: before the literary division of labor took place, a writer did not really see himself as, was not, generically polyphonous. The travel relation of the relatively untraveled Middle Ages was a member of a class unified by subject matter. (To that extent it cannot perhaps be referred to as a "genre" in the modern sense.) The subject matter was the world outside of Home, and comprehensiveness was naturally a virtue in this undertaking. Ignorance was deep and universal, and the urge to tell oneself and others *everything* under those circumstances seems psychologically comprehensible even across the great gap in history between Marco Polo and ourselves.

The subgenres of the Renaissance, on the other hand, are unified within themselves more by the writer's postulated *relation* to the material, and the various relations demand distinct voices and strategies, and circumscribe the spaciousness of medieval coverage. The traveler wrote up his experience. The *istoriador* read them all and produced a comprehensive *Historia general de las Indias* in his study. The cosmographer read them all and produced *A Brief Description of the Whole Worlde* in his study. The cartographer gathered charts and sketches from pilots and gentlemen-sailors and produced the *Orbis theatrum.* The humanist statesman and the excited poet produced the *Utopia* and "De Guiana, carmen epicum," the *New Atlantis,* and *De navigatione.*[11] The great col-

---

11. Obviously, some category crossing took place: the most hilarious, that of travelers and navigators into the territory of the poet. Robert Baker rendered

lector gathered most of this into huge volumes, limiting his efforts to editing and translation and resisting the urge, as Pliny, Roger Bacon, and Mandeville had not, to transpose all this into his own single tone. What he left out of the collection brings us back to the most important split in the handling of the old *materia*: to the extent of the editor's ability to distinguish (an admittedly problematic limit), there is no imaginative or marvelous literature in Hakluyt, de Bry, or Purchas. The concatenation of Cotton Tiberius Bv, with its *Wonders of the East*, its scientific Greek geography, its prayer to the Trinity, and its genealogical tables between one set of covers, is no longer a serious possibility.[12]

This emerging scrupulosity of separation between accounts of such places as Utopia and Guiana, between the vastly metaphorical and the responsibly documentary, is certainly not a case of the clean break. Sir Walter Ralegh's *Discoverie of the Large, Rich, and Bewtiful Empire of Guiana* will provide us with a test case through which to investigate the difficulties of a literary transition taking place in a vacuum of language, and a chaos of symbols dislodged

---

accounts of his two voyages to "Guinie" in 1562 and 1563 in verse, fancying himself a second and more put-upon Orpheus combing hell, not for a woman, but for gold (the two were commonly confused):

> And Orpheus past I wot
>   the passage quietly
> Among the soules in Charon's boat
>   and yet to say truly
> I never read that he
>   paid for his passage there
> Who past and repast for to see
>   if that his wife there were.
> Nor yet that he paid ought
>   or any bribe there gave
> To any office, while he sought
>   his wife againe to have.
> Whereby I surely gesse
>   these men with whom that we
> Have had to do, are fiends more fierce
>   than those in hell that be.
>   ("Voyage to Guinie," 130–42)

12. Such a thing is not yet an impossibility, though. An early sixteenth-century Venetian codex called *Viaggiatori antichi* and described by Yule as containing a badly distorted text of Marco Polo includes, along with accounts of the journeys of Odoric, Ca'da Mosto, Cienza, da Gama, and Columbus, a life of Alexander the Great and a tract on the poverty of Jesus; "il codice termina con cose apocrife." However, the fact that the collection is a manuscript and not a printed book suggests a relatively unpretentious provenance.

from their *schema*. How is Ralegh to document another world, without any tradition behind him of simply denotative discourse? How is he to accommodate the attested and expected presences of the Other World, so precious to the European imagination, when the New World can no longer be situated on the old allegorical map on which they are at home? We have seen the effect of Columbus's reliance on the inherited languages of pastoral and heroic romance and anagogical geography in the description of the Caribbean islands. We have now to look at a text that aims to tell *"nothing but* the truth"—a thinner, more limited, more dependable and useful truth—about the mythical land of El Dorado.

The Problem of Words

The New World necessitated a new rhetoric for reasons having as much to do with perception and inadequate vocabulary as with politics and economics. Before he left, the Hungarian poet Stephen Parmenius, who was drowned on an expedition to New-foundland, had plenty to say in *De navigatione*, his *propemptikon* to Humphrey Gilbert. But in his brief letter, written on shipboard from Newfoundland to Richard Hakluyt, he is at more of a loss: "The manner of this Countrey, and people remayne nowe to bee spoken of. But what shall I say, my good Hakluyt, when I see nothing but a very wildernesse?" (*New Found Land of Stephen Parmenius*, 175).

That "nothing" may be the first perceptible fact of an entirely alien surround, for the discrete features of which one has no nouns. A newborn infant's almost unimaginably full visual field is undifferentiated and therefore indescribable. Even depth perception is an accomplishment of maturity. The shock of the terrain that has no known history, no cultivation, no apparent connection with the categories under which human—that is, European—life is apprehended, is analogous to the mysterious intellectual trauma of the infant. Perhaps one can read an adult's reaction to such a mass of unaccountable phenomena in the poignant appearance of "nothing" in the brief (fourteen words) glossary of "Indian" nouns provided by Peter Martyr in his *Decades*, or the last entry in the glossary to Robert Dudley's "relation": "*Non quo*, or *Non Quapa*, I know not, or I cannot tell."[13] And perhaps these are only the felicities of hindsight. But certainly Parmenius would not have found himself at such a loss confronted with Italy.

The New World was indeed full of things, but the articulation of them was an awesome linguistic and rhetorical challenge, sometimes openly shirked and sometimes eluded by rhetorical sleights of hand. The Nothingness of the written New World began as the refusal of writers like Stamler and Lilius to admit its existence, and was aided and abetted by the tendency of Columbus (among others) to describe it in paradisal negatives inherited from the rhetorics of pastoral and dream vision.[14] Parmenius's own *De navigatione* is full of this, describing America as "A world which has not felt the weight / Of Babylon, the Persian's might, nor known / Victorious Macedon," and where "No cares will then oppress the youth with age, / And labouring will not deprive a man / Of time to make a living through his own / Abilities" (lines 46–48, 153–56). Such negatives are eventually found crowded to the borders of texts, in prefatory poems and marginalia: there is a radical difference in style between Keymis's *Relation of the Second Expedition*

---

13. Quoted from Dudley's own brief account, included in *The Voyage of Robert Dudley . . . , Narrated by Capt. Wyatt, by Himself, and by Abram Kendall, Master*, 79. Despite their frequently glib equations (and their telling brevity), the appearance of glossaries in travel books and "histories" of the New World in the sixteenth century is a suggestive fact. They are a new feature of geographical literature (although Mandeville, not surprisingly, had included foreign alphabets). Peter Fleming, in *Brazilian Adventure* (1933), tells us that he included one in his book because, despite his best intentions, he found that he had used "foreign words" in the text. His explanation of why he uses "foreign words" points to underlying concerns that were *not* the concerns of medieval travel writers, but were beginning to surface in the Renaissance: "First of all, there are words like *batalõa* and *rapadura* and *mutum*, which denote things unknown outside Brazil, and which it is therefore impossible to translate. . . . Secondly, there are words of which a literal translation is for one reason or another inadequate. The word sandbank, for instance, gives you a very niggardly idea of what a *praia* is, and the word *plage*, which conveys an image nearer the truth, has unsuitable associations. Similarly, an *urubú* is a far more scurvy and less spectacular creature than the popular conception of a vulture. Thirdly, there are a few words which can be translated perfectly well, but which we, in conversation, never did translate: words like *jacaré* and *arara*. We never said 'There's an alligator', or 'There's a macaw', but—I suppose because of the presence of our men—always used the native words. So it is easier and more natural, when writing of these things, to give them the names under which they live in my memory" (133).

14. For the last word on these negatives and the origins of American literature, see Terence Martin, "The Negative Structures of American Literature."

to Guiana and Chapman's "Carmen epicum," which precedes the preface ("There *Learning* eates no more his thriftlesse bookes, / Nor *Valure* Estridge-like his yron armes. / There *Beautie* is no strumpet for her wants, / Nor *Gallique* humours putrefie her blood."). But how to fill the *Relation* if not with negatives like these, or with the positive images of Virgil and Ovid in the *locus amoenus*, or with the splendid grotesqueries of Herodotus, Pliny, Isidore, Marco Polo, Mandeville?

After the initial periods of rejection and indifference, America gradually became *the* place to talk about if one were talking about places (Hythloday sails with Vespucci, not with da Gama). But America was also the place that could not be talked about in the old ways. Despite its ineluctable imaginative suggestiveness, it was becoming the locus par excellence of commercial activity, political expansionism, new scientific knowledge. It was a bunch of real, palpable atoms, in furious spin. It could not be Paradise (does one *mine* Paradise or organize commerce with the *locus amoenus?*), and it had to be something.[15] Writers had to convey this Something without the help of classical authority or popular legend; even the dependable hoard of nouns with which travelers had so long managed their laconic, implicitly domesticating descriptions would no longer suffice. No honest eyewitness could get away for long with saying, "The king's castle was magnificent. The peasants' tribute was in the form of barley and swine." No king, no castle, no peasant, no barley, no swine. Cathay was homey and familiar compared with a place like Cuba. *Cacique, manioc, zemi* are *not* simple equivalents of king, barley, Jesus. Peter Martyr's glossary is a lie, "the thing which is not," as the Houyhnhnms would say.

Neither could the Matter of America be fully conveyed in sim-

15. To what extent the kind of attention American explorers had to pay was a brand new exercise of intellect can be seen by comparing the needs their knowledge had to serve with that served by the gleanings of medieval travelers. Even Roger Bacon's passionate plea, in his *Opus majus*, for knowledge based on experience and natural reason had put itself in the service, at least in the realm of geography, of scriptural exegesis. If we knew the exact topography of the Holy Land we could glean more from the Bible: "In this middle division [Egypt] is the city of Syene, of which Ezekiel speaks expressly in chapters xxix and xxx, saying 'From the land of Syene up to the ends of Aethiopia shall the foot of man not pass.' Syene is the lower limit of Aethiopia and the remotest part of Egypt, as Jerome states on Ezechiel" (1:332). He gives in this section a lengthy allegorized description of the River Jordan, as an example of the usefulness of geographical information.

iles, metaphors, and analogies: now that the New and Old Worlds were known to be actually and practically discrete, their difference had to be accounted for. Beyond their overt explanatory functions, such figures bespeak a sense of seamlessness between the new and the old that was not yet imaginatively earned. Difference must be acknowledged before the accommodating ritual of analogy even makes sense. But how to *express* difference in a genre whose rhetorical mainstay was the analogy and whose Matter had always been the Scripted, the legendary, the elaborately preconceived? If this is not Cathay, not Ophir, not the Earthly Paradise, can it be anything at all in a literary *schema* that has always existed to mediate between legend and the actual, faith and *connaissance*?

We cannot recognize the America of de Soto, Cabeza de Vaca, Darwin—even of Elizabeth Bishop—in Martyr's nymph-bedecked and Hyperborean Ophir, although he is quite certain that this continent is not the East of Marco Polo and Mandeville, is indeed the West, and somehow new. His West is not so new at all, at least as a matter embodied in the inherited style of its transmission. His underlying attitude is "we knew it all along" ("Nothing newe under the Sunne"). For Peter Martyr, and for Columbus, Fracastoro, Münster, Parmenius (until he gets there), there is already a style of thought and expression within which what O'Gorman calls the "being of America" could be recorded. And this amounts to yet another— subliminal—rejection of the New World. For America, to European history, was above all a challenge, a disruption, a catalyst of discontinuities.

The paradisal absences of winter, weaponry, and private property do not constitute an emptiness that might leave a writer speechless. On the contrary, those blanks, by virtue of their long literary history, invoke a picture of the very fullness of delight. The more mundane absences of monasteries, caravels, Jews, bishops, books, razors, hawks' bells, pigs, and peas are somewhat more baffling. "But what shall I say, my good Hakluyt, when I see nothing but a very wildernesse?" Parmenius is talking (or rather, not talking) about Newfoundland, a somewhat more homogeneous and uninhabited landscape than those of the West Indies, but the problem is generic all over the Americas. The man who wanted to describe the New World and its phenomena had no "terms," as Michel Butor puts it when he speaks of the syntax of the opposed experience of pilgrimage or the Grand Tour (journeys "to those places which speak, which tell us of our history and ourselves"; "Travel and Writing," 9). The Renaissance explorer had only the elemental words of sense experience. Even some phenomena we now consider "elemental" had to find new names. American nature was mountainous, riverine, tempestuous. *Waterfall, cataract, lagoon, whirlpool, swamp, keys, hurricane, tornado, thunderstorm*: as vernacular English words, all joined the language during the first century of the period of English exploration.

The *Oxford English Dictionary* gives first citations for both *waterfall* and *cataract* that are almost exactly contemporaneous with Ralegh's *Discoverie* and not likely to have been in general circulation yet. Thus Ralegh narrates, rather than simply declares, the existence of the one he sees near the confluence of the Orinoco and the Caño José:

We saw [the mountaine of Christall] a farre off and it appeared like a white Churche towre of an exceeding height: There falleth over it a mightie river which toucheth no parte of the side of the mountaine, but rusheth over the toppe of it, and falleth to the grounde with a terrible noise and clamor, as if 1000 great belles were knockt one against another. I thinke there is not in the worlde so straunge an overfall, nor so wonderfull to beholde: *Berreo* tolde mee that it hath Diamondes and other precious stones on it, and that they shined very farre off: but what it hath I know not. (101–2).[16]

Although one might take this "mountaine of Christall" as a member of the set whose instances run from folktale and medieval romance through the Big Rock Candy Mountain of the American hoboes, it is present in the *Discoverie* as a topographical encounter rather than merely as a sign of Paradise. A new noun, a new thing in the world, is necessarily *encountered*, has its conceptual birth in the circumstances that introduced it to the writer. That the paragraph constructs a comparison is less fundamental, and certainly less new, than that it constructs out of an object an event, depicts a process, descends to the morphological level of description in its attempt to convey a cataract without "cataract." (Ralegh's word "overfall" is the first usage with this meaning cited in the *Oxford English Dictionary*: he diverted it from its current reference—to

16. I cite by page number from the Hakluyt Society's diplomatic edition of the *Discoverie*, ed. ("with copious explanatory notes and a biographical memoir") Robert H. Schomburg (1848).

the turbulent meeting of contrary currents—and his usage quickly became obsolete. Its last listing is dated 1613, from Harcourt's *Voyage to Guiana*, and is probably an echo from his own book.)

Galinsky's example of the use of comparison to convey the marvelous, alien, and new without departing from the truth is culled from Piedro de Castañeda's *Relación de la jornada de Cíbola* (which first saw print in an American bilingual edition in 1904):

After going about 150 leagues, they came to a province of exceedingly tall and strong men—like giants. They are naked and live in large straw cabins built underground.
... When they carry anything, they can take a load of more than three or four hundredweight on their heads. Once when our men wished to fetch a log for the fire, and six men were unable to carry it, one of these Indians is reported to have come and raised it in his arms, put it on his head alone, and carried it very easily. They eat bread cooked in the ashes, as big as the large two-pound loaves of Castile. (Galinsky, "Exploring the 'Exploration Report,'" 6–7)

"Extremes touch," says Galinsky: "a familiar European myth, that of the giants, and familiar daily reality, the large two-pound loaves of Castile, are equally enlisted to guarantee the truth of a report on the 'real' giants of the new world." Galinsky is not interested in the literary prehistory of the "type" he is trying to establish: if he were he would know that this habit is not a defining characteristic of New World reportage. And he would note that the old similitude, in Castañeda as in Ralegh, serves a different function now. Castañeda's paragraph develops a single impression through a number of devices: comparison, anecdote, itemization of traits. These men are *big*, and he presents us with an entertaining variety of routes to this knowledge. He offers a form of verbal pleasure in the relative wealth of his detail and the rhetorical variety of its presentation. As a result we are left with knowledge about our narrator as well as about his "Indians": about the intensity of his impression, the affections of his imagination, the range of his associations, the nature of his curiosity. Ralegh gives us even more to chew on. His image of the Church and its clashing bells is odder than Castañeda's giants. How is a waterfall like a church? Why does he insert such a thing in this "very wildernesse?" (The link between church and waterfall appears elsewhere in the text as well: "There appeared some ten or twelve overfals in sight, every one as high over the other as a Church tower"; *Discoverie of Guiana*, 81.) The comparisons help us visualize the unfamiliar, but surely the connotations of spire and bells, or even the loaves of Castile, are atmospherically inappropriate?

So are the regal pavilions of the Seven Cities of Cíbola that cover the southwestern part of North America on Juan Martinés's map of 1578. So are the spires and towers huddled among the hills of the Caribbean islands in the woodcut accompanying the Basel edition of Columbus's *Letter* (see fig. 8).[17] The widespread imposition of Old World architectural forms on visual representations of the New World was a curious fact of contemporary iconography, and perhaps it influenced Ralegh. At any rate, his insertion of precipitous white church towers into our visual image of inland Guiana is not particularly *useful*, and it does not make his waterfall much less suspiciously marvelous. It is consoling to him and entertaining to his reader in its very incongruity. It is a sign, perhaps, of an underlying longing for home, and his particular perception is an ingredient in the encounter he is narrating. The spire and the clashing bells are, in short, expressive.

This wasteland, empty of churches and full of things for which there are no words, and to which neither Marco Polo nor Virgil nor the Bible can prepare the way, is Ralegh's Matter. The paradox of the superabundant wasteland, confronted by an inadequate vocabulary, gives rise at last to the art of close description and establishes narrative as the necessary structure of the travel "relation." The narrator's *experience* is the only object of which his knowledge can be comprehensive and to which his language can be equal. It is with this experience that he fills the wilderness and his relation.

Narrativity

The Discoverie of the Large, Rich and Bewtiful Empire of Guiana, with a Relation of the Great and Golden City of Manoa

17. For illustrations of these and countless other iconographic struggles with the New World, see R. A. Skelton, David B. Quinn, and W. P. Cumming, *The Discovery of North America*.

Fig. 8. Castles and churches in the Carribbean. From one of the first editions of Columbus's *Letter*. Basel, 1493. Courtesy of the John Carter Brown Library at Brown University.

*(which the Spaniards call El Dorado), etc. Performed in the yeare
1595. by Sir W. Ralegh, Knight . . . :* even the title is implicitly
narrative, and the author is presented as its protagonist in the
ambiguous "performed." The book is also a work of propaganda. It
ends with a long, summarizing panegyric to the enormous and
easily defensible wealth of the "Empire," and Ralegh's concluding
sentence suggests that he considers the work a preface to the as-
yet-unacted history of the territory: "To speak more at this time, I
feare would be but troublesome: I trust in God, this being true, will
suffice, and that he which is king of al kings, and Lorde of Lords,
will put it into her hart which is Lady of Ladies to possesse it, if
not, I wil judge those men worthy to be kings therof, that by her
grace and leave will undertake it of themselves" (120).

The element of propaganda in the account should not be forgotten, and it is characteristic of the "relations" of the first period of
British empire building: America did not reveal its commercial
potential quickly, and colonizers seeking colonists and investors
could not afford to be absolutely scrupulous in their interpretations of the new lands. The ease, then, with which such relations
slip into the mythic pattern of the heroic quest identified by
Galinsky and Adams is not purely a concomitant of the experience
of exploratory travel, but conditioned by the political necessity of
impressing one's sponsors, past and future.[18]

On the other hand, one must also impress them with credibility,
and Ralegh's loud protests against "malicious slander," in his
"Epistle Dedicatory" and the preface "To the Reader," indicate his
anxiety to be believable and believed. Already a published writer,
and known as a poet, he even uses that old chestnut, the *excusatio
propter infirmitatem* (Curtius's "modesty topos"): "I do humblie
pray that your honors wil excuse such errors, as without the
defence of art, overrun in every part, the following discourse, in
which I have neither studied phrase, forme, nor fashion" (x). This,
from the writer and courtier whom all will see reflected in Shakespeare's echoing phrase "the glass of fashion, and the mould of
form"! As we have seen, the topos has a special importance in
travel literature as a device for deflecting the suspicion that verbal

---

18. On the heroic quest, see Galinsky, "Exploring the 'Exploration Report,'" 19;
and Adams, *Travel Literature*, chap. 5, "Structure: The Hero and His Journey."

art distorts "the truth" and similitudes (on which the travel writer must depend) veil it. Its chances of being effective, however, in the hands of so elegant and exuberant a writer as Ralegh are nil. But he has better and more artful tricks up his pearl-encrusted sleeve.

His first sentence (embodying what was already a formula of the English genre) establishes the intensely and minutely narrative format. Without any preliminary situating of the voyage's events in a larger political-historical context, such as opens the *Journal* of Columbus, he plunges directly into the water:

On Thursday the 6 of Februarie in the yeare 1595, we departed *England*, and the sunday following had sight of the North cape of *Spayne*, the winde for the most part continuing prosperous; wee passed in sight of the *Burlings* and the rocke, and so onwardes for the *Canaries*, and fell with *Fuerte ventura* the 17 of the same moneth, where wee spent two or three daies, and relieved our companies with some fresh meate. (1)

The dates, numbers, and place names are profuse (if incomplete), familiar, and relatively mundane. We are not forced instantly to position ourselves in the New World, but continue on past "the *Gran Canaria* and so to *Tenerife*," losing "a small Gallego on the coast of *Spayne*, which came with us from *Plymmouth*." Narrativity is the point and exposition secondary. Only by the way do we learn the approximate size of the original fleet, the names of other captains, the preliminary point of destination.

The narrativity is complex, and will remain so. Events are displaced from the story's natural order (for effect, not, as with the medievals, because "I forgot to tell you before"), compressed into dependent clauses explaining other events, elaborated at a variety of lengths, motivated and rationalized, employed as frameworks for description, explicitly elided as "impertinent to my purpose"— and even constructed interpretively out of the absence of events: "we abode there 4 or 5 daies, and in all that time we came not to the speach of anie Indian or Spaniard: on the coast we saw a fire, as we sailed from the point *Carao* towards *Curiapan*, but for feare of the Spaniards, none durst come to speake with us" (2).

Ralegh does not shift gears upon arrival, as Columbus had in his *Letter*, from narrative to interpretive description. In fact he refers explicitly to a "description" and a chart that it is "my purpose . . . to send to your lordship [Charles Howard] in a few daies" (see fig. 9

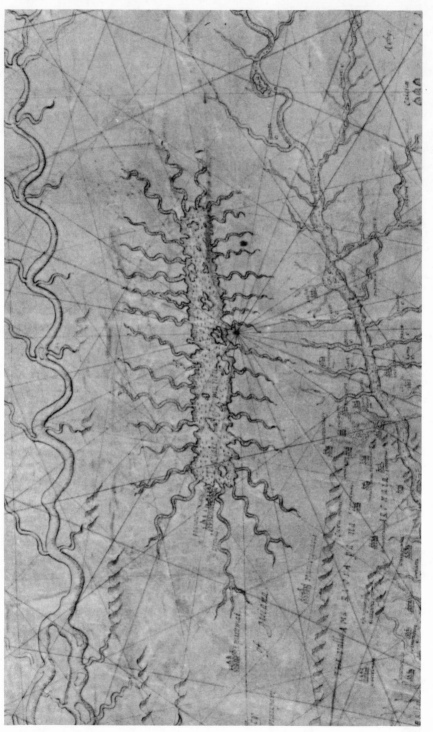

Fig. 9. El Dorado on a map attributed to Walter Ralegh, c. 1595. By permission of the British Library.

for a map attributed to Ralegh), and he relies on them (mentioning them at several points) to permit him a more pure narrativity in the *Discoverie* than might otherwise have seemed decorous. It is more than ordinarily important to him to build an air of solid circumstantiality about this relation: he has been accused of lying "hidden in Cornwall" throughout the expedition and wants to make it clear that "the rest were much mistaken, who would have perswaded, that I was too easful and sensuall to undertake a jorney of so great travel" ("Epistle Dedicatory," iv-v).

The strategic reliance on narrativity is a rhetorical enabling force as well. It allows him to convey the feel of an alien land, the character of alien people, even the taste of alien liquors. Sailing down a river, feasting with the native inhabitants on shore: the close narration of such activities makes scenery and culture far more accessible than do the static *descriptio* of the cosmographer or the lyrical transformations of Columbus's earlier accounts. Ralegh's verisimilitude refers to inner experiences, but those experiences are of phenomena and people outside himself, and thus their written reality is coextensive with his. His experience is made up of the features of the Other. The narration of Columbus is occluded by a dense veil of preconceptions: he has a word for everything, and an imaginary map to whose features everything he finds can be made to correspond. He has not found an empty wilderness but a Paradise familiar from every branch and level of his literary heritage. Thus, although he too describes experience and embeds his objects in encounter and event, the encounters are false "recognitions" and the objects are transformed reductively into literary clichés. The resulting picture is a dream, claustrophobically structured by the dreamer's private desires and fears.

But to be fair, Ralegh is not seeking to prove his own self-generated (and controversial) postulates in this adventure. El Dorado is not "his own invention," and for that reason he is not tempted to perceive Guiana as an extension of himself. In fact, he constructs his heroism with an approach almost exactly opposite to that of Columbus. He pictures himself as taking the torch from the last in a long line of illustrious—and Spanish—heroes who had made the quest their own. He does not initiate the mythic adventure (of which "many yeares since, I had knowledge by relation"), but before the true European history of Guiana can begin, he will conclude it.

Before leaving Trinidad "towards our proposed discovery," Ralegh took and burned its new capital, San José, and captured the governor, Antonio de Berreo (who had the year before ambushed an advance scouting party sent to the area by Ralegh under Captain Whiddon). Berreo had himself been trying to find El Dorado, having inherited the mission from his father-in-law, "taking his oth and honor to follow the enterprise to the last of his substance and life who since he hath sworne to me hath spent 300000 ducats in the same, and yet never could enter so far into the land as my selfe with that poore troupe or rather a handfull of men" (25).

Having taken Berreo aboard his ship and "used him according to his estate and worth in all things I could," Ralegh pumped him about Guiana. But he does not here, as often, simply report the conversation. Instead he goes back and then forward in time to outline briefly the origin, goal, and outcome of his whole project, proves out of the histories of Cieza de León and López de Gómara "how this Empire of *Guiana* is become so populous, and adorned with so manie great Cities, Townes, Temples, and threasures" (11), and proceeds to narrate the disastrous history of the Spanish quest whose last hero he has "displanted"—as he puts it, "the ends and tragedies of Oreliano, Ordace, Osua, Martynes, and Agiri" (23), as well as those of Ortalde de Saragosa, Pedro de Silvia, Pedro Hernández de Serpa, Hernán Pérez de Quesada, and finally Berreo himself.

The history ends as if it had been the indirect discourse of Berreo, and we are back on the ship in the captain's cabin: "After I had thus learned of his proceedings past and purposed: I told him that I had resolved to see *Guiana*, and that it was the end of my journey, and the cause of my coming to *Trinidado*. . . . Berreo was stricken into a great melancholie and sadnes, and used all the arguments he could to disswade me" (41–42). The "displanted" Spaniard delivers himself of the dire and detailed warning customary at the start of such a quest, and Ralegh comments: "Many and most of these I found to be true, but yet I [resolved] to make trial of all whatsoever hapned" (42).

The literary artifice of this long section is somewhat intricate for the genre (such as it is) in which it appears. The delayed exposition of events that precede a narrative's opening is familiar to the audiences of epic and novel (and of course romance finds a use for it, as a way of providing supernatural objects and mysterious events with genealogies). Such withholding of information is always part of a design on the reader: it obeys a manipulative impulse more familiar to us from literary narrative (and propaganda) than from the pragmatic storytelling of scientists, foreign correspondents, and "witnesses." We could have used this brief history of the quest before now: a thoroughly pragmatic writer might have begun with it. What, then, has Ralegh's artificial structure yielded him in the way of profits?

Ralegh needs both to control the reader's suspicions and enthusiasms, and to justify his unusual degree of storytelling. He wants from his readers more than mere approval, and he needs more than credibility to get it: he needs affection and vicarious involvement, and at the same time admiration. He must be not only hero, as Columbus was, but mere protagonist as well. (To adapt Bakhtin's distinction between epic and novel, the epic hero "stands on an utterly different and inaccessible time-and-value plane" from the reader; the novelistic protagonist is one of us, and the events of his story are "based on personal experience and thought." *Dialogic Imagination*, 122–123.) We must feel with Ralegh, be moved to want what he wants by seeing as he sees. His original cast of readers was a challenging mix: sponsors, potential but still-unwon comrades, the temperamental queen, the court in which his reputation was under siege. We have seen medieval writers play for credibility and Columbus play for power, but Ralegh here is playing for love—the special literary love in which a reader "identifies" with a fictional protagonist, the conditional love a reader awards to an author in whose work he has been brought to pleasure.

Why our pleasure in a narrative is increased in proportion to the rearrangement of its underlying story is a question best debated by narrative theorists; *that* it is increased appears to be a fact. Our specific pleasure in this text is consequent upon its ordering of the types of our involvement, and their total range. What we experience from the convolutions of Ralegh's opening movement is, first, the immediacy of pure action, in the imaginatively accessible waters of the *oikumene*; second, involvement in his emotional motivations, at once daring and "honorable"; third, a knowledge of total scheme and outcome, presented only when we have been softened by our vicarious share in the experience of the writer; fourth, the awe and admiration for Ralegh's heroism brought on by "the ends and tragedies" of his illustrious forebears in the adven-

ture; fifth, another vicarious involvement with his emotions when
the scene of Berreo's "melancholie" warning and Ralegh's gallant
dismissal of it is dramatized. Along the way we have been presented more or less painlessly with an outline of the area's complicated geography and politics, so that we are now oriented in the
New World by the same means as Ralegh had been to that point:
"for that by discourse with the Spaniards [in Trinidad] I daily
learned more and more of *Guiana*, of the rivers and passages, and of
the enterprise of *Berreo*, by what meanes or fault he failed, and
how he meant to prosecute the same" (6). Our pause, occasioned by
the narrative digressions from chronology, is parallel to Ralegh's
pause in Port of Spain to gather information. His pause is not
narrated but in fact *duplicated* for us: he is well aware of the
dangers of pure mimesis, commenting along the way that he will
"forbeare to name [all the tributaries of the Orinoco Berreo saw] for
tediousness, and because they are more pleasing in describing than
reading" (33).

He echoes Marco Polo's figure (or Rusticello's) in which reading
and writing are spoken of as forms of travel, and reader and writer
as traveling together, when he concludes the narrative portion of
the book: "Now that it hath pleased God to send us safe to our
ships, it is time to leave *Guiana* to the Sunne, whom they worship,
and steare away towardes the north: I will therefore in a fewe
wordes finish the discovery therof" (107). The figure has a greater
significance in this book, though, than in the more discursive and
less inhabited *Il milione*. If Ralegh has played his cards right—and
he has—we *have* been journeying with him, watching the days and
the river slide by from behind his eyes, changing as we travel out of
ignorance into sensible knowledge, out of suspicion into belief.
The book ends by requesting action on the part of its changed
readers: "[that] her majesty will give order for the rest, and eyther
defend it, and hold it as tributary, or conquere and keepe it as
Empresse of the same . . . if not, I wil judge those men worthy to be
kings therof, that by her grace and leave will undertake it of themselves" (120).

Roland Barthes might have called the *Discoverie* a "writerly"
text: "Why is the writerly our value? Because the goal of literary
work (of literature as work) is to make the reader no longer a
consumer, but a producer of the text" (*S/Z*, 4). And elsewhere,

"The text you write must prove to me *that it desires me*" (*Pleasure of the Text*, 6). At a starkly literal level (Keymis and Harcourt, who adore him, follow in Ralegh's footsteps with their own expeditions to Guiana and continue the production of his text with their own *Relations*), Ralegh's text answers both these requirements, as no other discussed in this study does except, to some extent, Egeria's. The juxtaposition of their works is not irrelevant: Ralegh refers to his journey as a "painful pilgrimage" ("Epistle Dedicatory," v), and "the Great and Golden Citie, which the Spaniards call El Dorado" fills a place in it analogous not to Egeria's Jerusalem, but to the celestial Jerusalem of which she no more than Ralegh achieves the sight. But most importantly, both writers work to effect some form of *active* participation on their reader's part—Egeria constructing a verbal rosary for her Venerable Sisters to use as a devotional tool, Ralegh a Siren's song that will lure the reader with him beyond the borders of the text and into the next expedition to Guiana.

Of course, the works are far more different than similar. With inadvertent allegory, one of Columbus's Indians is reported as telling his king "how the Christians came from the heavens and that they were seeking gold" (*Journal*, Dec. 14). It is a long way down from the celestial city to the gold mines of El Dorado, and the desires of Egeria's and Ralegh's texts are alike only insofar as they are desires. The habit of elaborating travel from desire has been consistent, as has, apparently, the habit of substituting a text for the elusive object of desire. But the nature of the object has changed utterly, and with it the ways of representing it, of alluring the reader to it. Egeria's "narrative" transcribes ritual motion, in which every movement is equally important and necessary: there are no anachronies, no ellipses, and no personalities.[19] Ralegh's

---

19. "Anachronies" is Gérard Genette's term (introduced in *Narrative Discourse*) for instances of "discordance between the two orderings of story and narrative"—a term that "implicitly assumes the existence of a kind of zero degree that would be a condition of perfect temporal correspondence between narrative and story." He points out that folklore narrative approaches this zero degree, but that epic and novel share the formal topos of a "beginning *in medias res*, followed by an expository return to an earlier period of time" (36). "Ellipsis," one of his "four basic forms of narrative movement," is the "leap forward without any return" (43). A fuller discussion of Egeria in light of Genette's terminology would be worth pursuing, as her "zero degree" is interestingly complicated by the ghostly presence of so many stories not her own.

narrative mimics the private and spontaneous experience of adventure, grounded in personality; it is organized by the rhetorical and aesthetic criteria proper to persuasion and pleasure.

Therefore, to quote Barthes for the last time, there are places "where the garment gapes," or in Valéry's more ethereal vocabulary, "there are *lacunae*; there is a God." Experience in the memory is neither continuous nor strictly chronological; it is warped out of the straight line by the varying heat of emotion. Columbus wrote something every day in his journal, even if "nothing" happened. Ralegh is more true to life: he elides, for instance, his whole return trip down the Orinoco, except for its entrance into the sea. He announces the absences of many geographical descriptions that are "more pleasing in describing than reading" or "were tedious, eyther to describe or name." He avoids a trip to the "mountaine of Christall" to see "what it hath," and above all and most artfully, avoids the relation of "the Great and Golden Citie of . . . El Dorado," promised by his title, by stopping "fower daies journey" short of the empire of Guiana itself. He will come back next year, with some of his readers, or so he hopes—and so we must hope.

In place of the climactic description we had expected, of the mysterious interior city paved with gold, we are given a brief political analysis of the Guianian situation from the lips of a knowledgeable and friendly border chief. This is an absolutely central absence—necessitated of course by the fact that there is no El Dorado—but most flirtatiously paraded "a farre off," suggested and erased, circumambulated by its geographical and political and historical positionings. We are rarely allowed to forget it for long and never allowed to see it. The experience that has filled the relation is in a sense negative, a frustration, a journey to nowhere: the actual "end of my journey" is the port of Morequito, an uninhabited landing near the border chief's village. But a frustrated desire is still an event, and so we have a narrative.

Description

Although this narrative is the crucial feature of the *Discoverie*, which obscures the failure of its object in a bustle of heroic activity, we are offered along the way a landscape of the country through which the story leaps and pirouettes. This is the one dependable clause in the travel writer's contract with the reader: objects will be provided for our view. As we have seen, objects were for a thousand years the main business of the travel account. From Egeria through Mandeville the text is a minimally narrative setting for the description of churches, tombs, volcanoes, rivers, strange plants and animals, jewels, monsters, and peoples presented as static figures in unusual costumes. This orientation toward things infected human beings with a thing-ness of their own: they have traits but no histories, characters but no apparent interaction with the traveler, titles but no names. (Outside of the Crusade chronicles, the one great non-European *person* presented to us in travel literature is Kublai Khan, metonymic for the splendid East even in Marco Polo's book and quickly becoming a faceless immortal like Prester John—succeeding accounts refer to him only as "the Khan.")

Ralegh does notice "things" in the old way, and even such *occupatios* as the following, with its copious list of things he will *not* name or describe, crowd out the sense of blank vacancy invoked by some New World reportage: "To make mention of the several beasts, birds, fishes, fruites, flowers, gummes, sweete woodes, and of their severall religions and customes, would for the first require as many volumes as those of *Gesnerus*, and for the rest another bundle of *Decades*" (109). But he declines the tasks of naming and itemizing, deferring to the new specialists, who are experts at extrapolation, classification, and exposition. He is telling a story: his book is not a *Description* but a *Discoverie*, and inert objects have no place in it. Reversing the emphasis of the medieval travel account, he tends to give us characters instead of objects, individual persons instead of monstrous races.

He aims to fill his wilderness, and he fares well in the task. He is obligated, in part, by his inability to give us the "Description of the Great and Golden Citie" itself, but his scope and opportunity are widened by the unusual amount of contact he pursues with the inhabitants. He is astonishingly diplomatic and unfailingly gregarious. Even Spaniards will talk to him, and his deadly rival Berreo tells him everything he needs to know before he sets off up the Orinoco. The speechless, undifferentiated, mythically innocent Indians of Columbus and Las Casas are nowhere to be found: the *Discoverie* leaves the head spinning with the various unpronounceable names of tribes, along with the natures of their languages, their varieties of sophistication, their histories and medical lore, their political relations with each other. And two of the longest passages in the work record private conversations with the border chief, Topiawari.

Ralegh's intentions are no better than those of Cortés, whom he emulates, and whose successful conquest of Mexico Todorov puts down to his communication skills: his ability to manipulate languages (verbal and otherwise), his curiosity, his resulting "perfected system of information." Todorov emphasizes Cortés's remarkable awareness of the need for reconnaissance, and his desire for the more complete dominance that comes with knowledge: "What Cortes wants from the first is not to capture but to comprehend; it is signs which chiefly interest him, not their referents" (99). Also like Cortés, Ralegh pays close attention to "internal" dissensions among the indigenous people, aware that he cannot conquer without native allies. But he is on a scouting mission this time, floating through alien territory on two or three barges and wherries with a hundred men, and cannot risk armed conflict. He must be scrupulous wherever he goes:

Nothing got us more love among them than this usage, for I suffered not anie man to take from anie of the nations so much as a *Pina*, or a *Potato* roote, without giving them contentment, nor any man so much as to offer to touch any of their wives or daughters: which course, so contrarie to the Spaniards (who tyrranize over them in all things) drew them to admire hir Majestie, whose commandement I told them it was, and also woonderfully to honour our nation. (61)

That this behavior was mostly cynical is manifested in his closing summation of "the easines of the conquest of *Guiana*":

To conclude, *Guiana* is a Countrey that hath yet her Maydenhead, never sackt, turned, nor wrought, the face of the earth hath not been torne, nor the vertue and salt of the soyle spent by manurance, the graves have not beene opened for gold, the mines not broken with sledges, nor their Images puld down out of their temples. It hath never been entred by any armie of strength, and never conquered or possessed by any Christian Prince. (115)

Ralegh's later prospectus for the said conquest ("Of the Voyage for Guiana") indicates that he fully intended these remarks as an incitement.

My point is that Ralegh's political ethics were about as low as those of any other Renaissance man of action: the startling three-dimensionality of his Indians is not a function of an unusual moral refinement. His thoroughgoing absence of xenophobia is such a relief that one is at first tempted to put it down to sentimental "humanity": the paragraph quoted above is a quick cure. War is the final topic and the next step for him as for William of Rubruck, Marco Polo, Columbus—generalization about the Matter of the Other in premodern European travel accounts seems generically embodied by the topic of invasion.[20]

It might be a less merely tidy suggestion than it sounds to put the fullness of Ralegh's Indians down to the cultural and historical vacancy (for him) of their territory. For the explorer and the writer both, people can fill the gap left by the apparent absence of things. If pilgrimage and the Grand Tour—travel to lands inscribed in and with our own history or lore—are "travel to places that speak," successful exploration may be "travel to people that speak." Where? is the explorer's great question: his Indian interpreters and pilots and political allies tell Ralegh where the navigable rivers are, where the food is, where the gold is, where his enemies are. Because he is narrating, this information is transmitted to us through the relation of conversations, events in which the Indians are necessarily characters, crucial characters.

Once the practice of narration is under way, the flesh of "gratuitous detail" forms almost spontaneously on the bones of information. Here is a passage from the description of Guiana itself (which Ralegh never quite reached), conveyed in the form of a conversation with Topiawari:

I asked what nations those were which inhabited on the further side of those mountains, beyond the valley of *Amariocapana*, he [Topiawari] answered with a great sigh (as a man which had inward feeling of the losse of his countrey and liberty, especially for that his eldest sonne was slain in a battel on that side of the mountaines, whom he most entirely loved,) that he remembered in his fathers life time when he was very old, and himself a yoong man that there came down into that large valley of *Guiana*, a nation from so farre off as the *Sun* slept, (for such were his own

20. See also the works of Piero Tafur and Bertrandon de Brocquière, two unusually gregarious fifteenth-century travelers to Asia Minor. And note that even Mandeville opens his book with a call for Holy War—although he quickly subverts it.

words,) with so great a multitude as they could not be numbred nor resisted, and that they wore large coats, and hats of a crimson colour, which colour he expressed, by shewing a peece of red wood, wherewith my tent was supported, and that they were called *Oreiones*, and *Epuremei*, those that had slaine and rooted out so many of the ancient people as there were leaves in the wood upon all the trees, and had now made themselves Lords of all. (76–77)

The encounter is narrated to its end:

After he had answered thus far, he desired leave to depart, saying that he had far to go, that he was old, and weake, and was every day called for by death, which was also his owne phrase: I desired him to rest with us that night, but I could not intreat him. (77)

Ralegh's evident and sympathetic interest in the language, behavior, and "inward feeling" of Topiawari is a far cry from that of the plunderer or the anthropologist. This "Indian" is revealed not as an object but as a subject, whose words and actions take over the text for many pages at a time and whose effect on English readers may have been quietly revolutionary. Topiawari is not only eloquent, knowledgeable, and susceptible to parental and patriotic love: he is real. That Ralegh manages to make him seem real and exotic at once, both alien and human, seems to me a sign of an accomplished widening of consciousness. He has no inclinations toward "soft primitivism"—none of the already clichéd virtues of the Noble Savage is featured in the *Discoverie* (except for the physical beauty of certain of the Indian nations; in at least one case, that seems to be the result of a specific sexual attraction[21]). His respect is understated or implied: where Columbus took six Tainos back to Spain "to learn to speak," Ralegh leaves two Englishmen with Topiawari "to learne the language" (96). He does

21. "That *Cassique* that was a stranger had his wife staying at the port where we ankored, and in all my life I haue seldome seene a better fauored woman: She was of good stature, with blacke eies, fat of body, of an excellent countenance, hir haire almost as long as hir selfe, tied vp againe in pretie knots, and it seemed she stood not in that aw of hir husband, as the rest, for she spake and discourst, and dranke among the gentlemen and captaines, and was very pleasant, knowing hir owne comelines, and taking great pride therein. I haue seene a Lady in England so like hir, as but for the difference of colour I would haue sworne might haue beene the same" (66).

not mention the propagation of the One True Faith (though he will harp on it like any other, later, in his outline of the means of conquest, prepared for the government).[22] He is almost never judgmental, and when he is, only with respect to specific people. He is a narrator—of a radically social experience.

This is not to say that Ralegh neglects the nonhuman landscape. On the contrary, he falls in love with it. The love may be annexed to his desire for El Dorado; the river is the way in—the only way, according to Ralegh—to the Bewtiful Empire of Guiana. But since he is in love, he does not usually deal with this landscape as though he were providing information. (That task, after all, belongs to the "description" and the chart.) It is the mise-en-scène of his story, and it is also the only set of clues available to the maddeningly hidden wealth of his unreachable destination. Thus, as narrative has stood in for achievement, and people for objects, the way there must stand in for the destination; again, this translation is an important task. The way there is all he knows, all he can offer his potentially active audience with any certainty, but it must not seem to overwhelm the importance or the reality of the unseen, unproven Citie. He is cruder in his closing summary than in his narrative: "Where there is store of gold, it is in effect nedeles to remember other commodities for trade: but it hath towards the south part of the river [i.e., toward the border of Guiana], great quantities of Brasill woode, and of divers berries, that die a most perfect crimson and Carnation" (113).

The descriptions of landscape or environment are of two kinds, both expressive in their function: one pictures extremity and the other a complicated beauty. Extremity consists of weather, heat, navigational difficulties, bewilderment. This picture operates to make heroes of "that poore troupe or rather a handfull of men" who survived to a man the "perils . . . diseases . . . ill savours . . . the care and labour of such an enterprize" ("To the Reader," xiii). If

---

22. The document attributed to Ralegh, "Of the Voyage for Guiana" (the English apparently use "voyage" where the Spanish say "pacification"), in which he outlines the reasons that country can and should be conquered, and "the meanes to subdue it," is included in the appendix to Warner's edition. It echoes almost all the most ethnocentric and jingoistic justifications of the Spanish actions in the West Indies and suggests the degree to which, in the *Discoverie* at least, rhetorical form can be responsible for vision and content. It is discursive rather than narrative, and it is as cynical and disregarding of the "Indians'" freedoms as anything of Cortés's or de Soto's.

circumstantial narrative has made Ralegh's presence in Guiana credible, then these harsh descriptions make of his desire to return a proof of the existence of gold:

But it shall bee founde a weake pollicie in mee, eyther to betray my selfe, or my Countrey with imaginations, neyther am I so farre in love with that lodging, watching, care, perill, diseases, ill savours, bad fare, and many other mischiefes that accompany these voyages, as to woo my selfe againe into any of them, were I not assured that the sunne covereth not so much riches in any part of the earth. (83)

His first description of landscape is of the complicated delta of the Orinoco (formed by seventeen large branches and a great many smaller ones, ninety miles wide and thirty-six miles deep). It is a characteristically active and temporalized description, framed by the situation of the pilot's ignorance:

and if God had not sent us another helpe, we might have wandered a whole yeere in that laborinth of rivers, ere we had found any way, either out or in, especiallie after we were past the ebbing and flowing, which was in fower daies: for I know all the earth doth not yeeld the like confluence of streames and branches, the one crossing the other so many times, and all so faire and large, and so like one to another, as no man can tell which to take: and if we went by the Sun or compasse hoping thereby to go directly one way or other, yet that waie we were also carried in a circle amongst multitudes of Ilands, and every Iland so bordered with high trees, as no man could see any further than the bredth of the river, or length of the breach: But this it chanced. . . . (46)

and then comes another narrative episode. Two, in fact, and inserted here and there in phrases and dependent clauses are more descriptive clues: "the people on the banks shadowed under the thicke wood gazed on with a doubtfull conceit" (47). "Those people which dwell in these broken Ilands and drowned lands are generally called Tivitivas" (48). (Note that the *subject* in both sentences is "people.")

Later, on a trip for food down a tributary, they almost "gave up the ghost" before finding a village:

it was as darke as pitch, and the river began so to narrow it selfe, and the trees to hang over from side to side, as we were driven with arming

swordes to cut a passage thorow those branches that covered the water. . . .
We began to doubt, suspecting treason in the Pilot more and more: but the
poore olde Indian ever assured us that it was but a little farther, and but
this one turning, and that turning, and at last about one a clocke after
midnight we saw a light, and rowing towards it, we heard the dogs of the
village. When wee landed we found few people. (56)

And so, consequently, little in the way of narrative, and the village
is not described. The river was the scene of fear, heroism, treach-
ery, and so we are given to see it, dark, overgrown, uninhabited.

But the next day, fed and rested and loaded with food for the
others (waiting at anchor back in the main river), Ralegh's mood
has changed, and he sees the country in a different light:

On both sides of this river, we passed the most beautifull countrie that
ever mine eies beheld: and whereas all that we had seen before was nothing but woods, prickles, bushes, and thornes, heere we beheld plaines of
twenty miles in length, the grasse short and greene, and in divers parts
groves of trees by themselves, as if they had been by all the art and labour
in the world so made of a purpose: and stil as we rowed, the Deere came
downe feeding by the waters side, as if they had beene used to a keepers
call. (57)

This is Ralegh's beauty, and it is one of the strangest aspects of
his book. All the beauty of the river country is English beauty, and
the more so the closer he gets to Guiana itself. At the limit of his
journey he encounters the valley of Ameriocapana, "whose plaines
stretch themselves some 60 miles in length, east and west, as fayre
ground, and as bewtifull fieldes, as any man hath ever seene, with
divers copses scattered here and there by the rivers side, and all as
full of deare, as any forest or parke in England, and in every lake
and river the like abundance of fish and fowle, of which *Irrapar-
ragota* is Lord" (98). In Dorothy's immortal words, there's no place
like home. But certainly Ralegh's Noplace is much more like
Home than Thomas More's: deer parks along the river, waterfalls
like churches, spume that "we tooke . . . at the first for a smoke
that had risen over some great towne" (81), the *cacique*'s wife of
whom "I have seene a Ladye in England so like her, as but for the
difference of colour I would have sworne might have beene the
same" (66).

Although it is in his perception of beauty that Ralegh seems most closely to approach the literary trompe l'oeil of Columbus and Martyr, their habit of imposing the Golden Age and the *locus amoenus* over the otherness and difference of the West Indies, the differences are notable. If Ralegh's language expresses an imposition of desire over fact, for one thing, the desire is different: it is for home, and in its present tense. Henri Baudet, in his essay on the role of the Earthly Paradise in European thought about and contact with non-European worlds, has this to say about the earliest stirrings of the Age of Discovery: "[Because the Nile was said to have its source in Ethiopia,] the renewed interest in Ethiopia now created the possibility of locating the geographical whereabouts of Paradise. . . . The image thus became a geographical reality. It was removed from a distant past to a distant present. . . . The distance became a matter of geography" (15). If this is so, and it certainly seems sensible from what we have seen so far, then Ralegh's attitude displays yet another transformation of the locale of the Great Good Place. Paradise is now the image of home as it appears from across the Threshold of the Known.[23] Ralegh's presentation of the homely version of Paradise is particularly poignant because he was so close to the last postulated location of the geographically reachable Eden: it was the enormous force of the Orinoco's disemboguement into the Gulf of Paria that stimulated Columbus to his the-

---

23. Ralegh is not alone in his injection of nostalgic *amor patriae* into the beauty of the New World. Bartholomew Gosnold's Virginia is "replenished with faire fields, and in them fragrant Flowers, also Medowes, and hedged in with stately Groves, being furnished also with pleasant Brookes, and beautified with two maine Rivers that (as wee judge) may haply become good Harbours" (Purchas, *Purchas His Pilgrimes*, 18: 309). John Brereton and his comrades "stood awhile like men ravished at the beautie and delicacy of this sweet soyle: for besides divers clear Lakes of fresh water (whereof wee saw no end) Medowes very large, and full of greene grasse; even the most wooddy places . . . doe growe so distinct and apart, one free from another, upon green grassie ground, somewhat higher than the Plaines, as if Nature would shew her selfe above her power, artificiall" (Purchas, 18:315). After a long paean to a Virginian river, James Rosier compares it to (among others) both Ralegh's Orinoco and the Thames: he stops short at the Thames ("I will not preferre it before our River of Thames, because it is Natale solum, England's richest treasure"), but goes on to say that *if it were in England*, "I would boldly affirme it to be the most rich, beautiful, large, and secure harboring River that the world affordeth" (Purchas, 18:351). Of course this feature of the voyage reports (an expansion of Columbus's formula "like Andalusia in April") also serves the practical function of eliding difference in a bid to elide the fear of potential colonists—that abiding fear of difference that in fact sent many early colonists home on the next ship.

ory of the pear-shaped earth down whose nipple of Paradise the Orinoco ran into the sea.

The Matter of the paradisal goal is perfectly evident in the *Discoverie*. El Dorado is a literalization of the celestial Jerusalem, which was also paved with gold and walled with precious stones; Ralegh calls his journey to it a "painful pilgrimage"; he begins it in a "laborinth"; he sees it as the ultimate possession of the quasi-divine "Lady of Ladies" (Spenser's Gloriana, after all), with whose portrait he incites the Indians to idolatry.[24] He goes through hell and high water to reach it, and sees signs of it, as Columbus had, everywhere.

These signs form another aspect of Ralegh's descriptive presentation of the country. Although he rarely devotes a whole passage merely to describing a sign of precious minerals—notice of one always leads him more or less immediately into a discursive digression—the account is scattered with them throughout, like the earth itself, where "every stone that we stooped to pick up promised eyther golde or silver by his complexion" (82). The banks of the Orinoco are "for the most part of a blew metelline colour, like unto the best steele ore, which I assuredly take it to be: of the same blew stone are also divers great mountaines, which border this river in many places" (69). In a basket abandoned by an escaping Spaniard he finds "quick silver, saltpeter, and divers things for the triall of mettals, and also the dust of such ore as he had refined, but in those *Canoas* which escaped there was a good quantity of ore and gold"—or so he assumes (59). "Wee returning the same daie to the rivers side, sawe by the way many rockes, like unto Golde oare, and on the left hand, a rounde mountaine which consisted of minerall stone" (100). "In *Guiana* itself I never saw *Marcasite*, but all the rocks, mountaines, all stones in the plaines, in woodes, and by the rivers sides are in effect thorow shining, and appeare marveylous rich, which being tried to be no *Marcasite*, are the trew signes of rich mineralles" ("To the Reader," xi). Then there is the "mountaine of Christall" Ralegh forbears to visit, and

24. "I showed them her majesties picture which they so admired and honored, as it had beene easie to have brought them idolatrous thereof. The like and a more large discourse I made to the rest of the nations both in my passing to *Guiana* and to those of the borders, so that in that part of the world her majesty is very famous and admirable, whom they now call *Ezrabeta Cassipuna Aquerewana*, which is as much as *Elizabeth*, the great princesse or greatest commaunder" (9).

the Orenoqueponis' promise, upon being shown sapphires, to bring him "to a mountaine, that had of them verye large pieces growing Diamond wise" (83).

But most of the mineral presence reaches us thirdhand, via the accounts of Indians, of "historians," of Berreo, of the "letter written into *Spaine* which was intercepted, which master *Robert Dudley* told me he had seen" (21). Dudley's account of the letter "confirms" the first "firsthand" appearance of gold in the *Discoverie*, an appearance astonishing in what it signifies to Ralegh and about Ralegh. It is not in fact an authentic firsthand encounter, but sneaked in under cover of a discussion of the Indians' drinking celebrations "which I have seen":

All those that pledge [the Emperor] are first stripped naked, and their bodies annoynted al over with a kinde of white Balsamum . . . of which there is great plenty and yet very deare amongst them, and it is of all others the most pretious, whereof we have had good experience: when they are annointed all over, certain servants of the Emperor having prepared gold made into fine powder blow it thorow hollow canes upon their naked bodies, untill they be al shining from the foote to the head, and in this sort they sit drinking by twenties and hundreds and continue in drunkennes sometimes six or seven daies together. (20–21).

This is one of the most staggering images of abundance, excess, and conspicuous consumption ever distilled by a Western traveler, and certainly worthy to set in the heart and on the high place of this journey through Noplace. But perhaps most significantly it is an image compounded both of gold and of people: for *El Dorado* really means "the Golden *Man*," and this legend of the Emperor's festive annointment is the source of the name. How deeply satisfying this image is to Ralegh is registered in the fact that this is the only place in his book where he does not carefully distinguish between second- and firsthand knowledge (faith and *connaissance*): in fact he seems to be purposely blurring the boundary.

This passage inserts another new element into the old images of desire through which the early writers understood the new lands: the central figure is human, the destination then imaginable as an encounter; the climax will be social. Columbus's ruling image is introverted. The human absence he perceives in his Paradise, which is merely *decorated* with Indians, allows him the interior pleasures of sensation and singularity. In Ralegh's earthly heaven, the "shining" ones "sit drinking by twenties and hundreds and continue in drunkennes sometimes six or seven daies together," and he practices his social skills all down the river: "we that were weary, and hotte with marching, were glad of the plenty, though a small quantitie satisfied us, their drinke beeing very strong and heady" (103).

The Similitude

We have already seen that Ralegh's text differs from those of his predecessors in its ample provision of detail and in the particular figuration of its hidden desires. Narrativity has been adduced as both cause and result of these differences. The man who seeks human contact must narrate his account of it; narrativity stimulates the literary production of detail. Being a sequential structure dependent on "cause and effect," narration must include the causal ingredients of character and mise-en-scène. Other people enter the picture, as agents, and scenery stirs and reflects the desires and fears of the narrator. But Ralegh's break with the past is not purely a matter of his narrativity. The similitude, crucial trope of travel literature and its epistemological weak spot, achieves a new function in the text of the *Discoverie*.

This study has had occasion before to touch on the fraught critical history of the similitude: its responsibility under the form of metaphor for creating the grotesque organic life reported and believed to flourish beyond the *oikumene*, and its converse function of denial in equating the things of Elsewhere with the things of Home. The concern medieval commentators express about the deceitfulness of "images" was not unwarranted. The literalism we have seen in the production and transmission (and, by implication, the reception) of the travel writer's similitudes materially inhibited both sympathy for other human cultures and the increase of knowledge about them. The marvelous is marginal, biologically and culturally, although it may be used as a figure for central and interior desire. The marvelous is also, in part, a rhetorical phenomenon. A brief enough description, especially when communicated as a distortion of the familiar rather than as something *essentially* different, produces a marvel. Any description isolating its object

from the temporal and environmental matrix in which it is natural
produces an icon; if the image's lack of dimensionality is received
as characteristic of the object described, rather than of the description itself, we are automatically possessed of a thing less real, less
explicable, than the things-in-context that make up Home.

Mandeville's more extended *descriptio* offered an initial solution to this rhetorical problem. But a large part of the problem lies
in the distance—or rather, lack of it—between tenor and vehicle.
Todorov offers a graphic example of this collapse of metaphor in
speaking of what he perceives as the difference between Aztec and
Spanish understanding of the symbolic. He describes and then
comments on an Aztec ritual in which celebrants don the flayed
skins of sacrificed victims, believing themselves to be participants
of the dead "gods" whose skins they wear:

Here the object of the representation remains present, in appearance at
least (the skins); what symbolizes is not really separated from what it
symbolizes. We have the impression that a figurative expression has been
taken literally . . . ; curiously, we ourselves have the expression "to get
into someone else's skin" without its origin being, for all that, a rite of
human flaying. . . . There is a "technology" of symbolism, which is as
capable of evolution as the technology of tools, and in this perspective the
Spaniards are more "advanced" than the Aztecs. (*Conquest of America*,
158–60)

It is difficult to agree with Todorov wholeheartedly that the
Spanish understanding and manipulation of symbols was more
"advanced," or less literal-minded, than the Aztec. We have taken
a close look at Columbus's confusion of the symbolic and the
actual, and this was the culture, after all, that "sacrificed" those
who did not believe in a literal transubstantiation of the eucharis-
tic host. (To further complicate matters, Todorov has taken his
description of the Aztec rite from the text of a Spanish Dominican,
Diego Durán.) But the example provides a useful extreme against
which to measure the changing operation of similitudes in the
travel writing of the period.

We have seen some widening of the distance between tenor and
vehicle in the obvious rhetoricity of Columbus's statement "this
island is Tarsis, is Cythia, is Ophir and Ophaz and Cipango, and we
have named it Española." But Columbus and the humanist histo-

rians who incorporated his writings into their own act and speak as if the identity were more literal than figurative. The metaphor is accepted by many as a statement of fact.[25] And the pastoral fantasies elaborated out of Virgil and Genesis for the depiction of the Caribbean produce an imaginary flock of Indian "lambs" whose projected qualities stimulate Las Casas into an entire career of passionate but reductive shepherding. (Todorov points out that "it is as an empirical observation that Las Casas declares, and tirelessly repeats, that the Indians possess Christian traits, and that they aspire to have their 'wild' Christianity be recognized"; *Conquest of America*, 163.)

Ralegh's comparisons, analogies, similes, and metaphors manifest much more clearly the "advance" of which Todorov speaks. Although they may express a complex of desires that condition his perception and experience of the American wilderness, they are, for the most part, *consciously* expressive, and their function is (at last) aesthetic. Ralegh's similitudes do not function as exact depiction, nor as the single-minded medium of information. They do not equal fact; they do not replace the objects they represent. This is partly a matter of the length and rhetorical variety of his account. It offers other sources of information than depiction by similitude: we can in fact *extrapolate* information from the narrative unwinding of incident and detail. In Ralegh's particular case, the difference is also partly a matter of the beauty of his imagery. A good poet and a man who took marvelous advantage of the potential riches of Elizabethan prose, he constructs analogies, similes,

---

25. Peter Martyr proves the abundant presence of gold in the West Indies by means of more syllogistic similitudes: "I conjecture therefore thus by a similitude of oure houses: if among us any man of great poure were moved with the desyre to have great plentye of Iron, and woolde enter into Italye with a mayne force as did the Gothes in tyme paste, what abundance of Iron shoulde he have in their hooses. Where as he shulde fynde in one place a frying pan, in an other a chauldron, here a tryvet, and there a spytte . . . : Whereby any man may conjecture that Iren is plentifully engendred in suche regions where they have soo greate use thereof. Owre men also perceaved that the inhabitantes of these regions do no more esteeme golde than we do Iren; nor yet soo muche after they sawe to what use Iren served us" (98v). Elsewhere he says, "But lyke as by one apple taken from a tree [!], we may perceyve the tree to bee fruitful, and by one fysshe taken in a river, we may knowe that fysshe is ingendred in the same, even so, by a lytell golde, and by one stone, we ought to consyder that this lande bringeth forth great plentie of gold and pretious stones" (112v).

and implicit metaphors that are too verbally beautiful to be mistaken for merely informational figures.

One might argue that Columbus's groves of nightingales are equally harmless in their beauty. Taken alone, they are (and the country so "like Andalusia in April" or "Castile in May" is also a country forgivably imbued with the figures of *amor patriae*). But Columbus's beauty is so homogenized throughout his accounts as to acquire the appearance of objective factuality. He cannot mention any vista or topographical feature without employing the same and single category of images, so that in the end his Caribbean becomes equivalent to that category ("this island *is* Tarsis, *is* Cythia . . .") and the figure equals, point for point, what is figured. He has, in fact, replaced the—admittedly beautiful—Caribbean with the more familiar Earthly Paradise. (And replacement will be the constitutive trope of Caribbean history—a region now inhabited solely by imported peoples, whose diet and economy depend on imported plants, whose animals, architecture, religions, and languages all hail from Elsewhere, from the *orbis terrarum*, the *oikumene* of medieval geography.)

Ralegh's beauty is openly, and therefore expressively, artificial. His images take their place in a text ample enough to bear ornament and artful enough to lead us to expect it. Since we have, for instance, "broken Ilands and drowned lands" in the Orinoco's delta, and the "woods, prickles, bushes and thorns" of its tributaries, the deer parks and copses do not appear to enforce any implicit argument of wholesale identification, but merely to record singular instances of pleasure. The unlikeliness of "white Churche towers" in an inland Guiana otherwise presented as wild and uncultivated cannot be mistaken for fact or even for expository analogy: the unlikely associations provoked by the image belong to the delight of the poet's conceit rather than to the "doctrine" of the medieval traveler's simile. Although Ralegh himself kept an eye out for Mandeville's Acephali and Marco Polo's Amazons, no one would follow him to Guiana looking for churches. His similitude is not a dangerously deluded perception of identity between actually diverse natures, but a ferry between two worlds.

In a genre that attempts to represent one "world" in the terms of another, the structure of the similitude is a figure of the whole vision. The relations it sets up between the objects of the two worlds, the identities it confounds or preserves, the ratio between realities that it transmits: these things reveal and condition at once the quality of its parent culture's imaginative relations with "that othere half" which is the shadow of our own. Ralegh relies on similes, which link rather than blur identities, and the intermittence of his similitudes obeys the proportional decorum of ornament. This rhetorical chastity permits him to express difference and relation at once and without falsification. His images do not lead us to an imaginary Paradise, but to an experience of which pleasure and nostalgia are ingredients.

Ralegh's account of his quest for Guiana is among the very best of the sixteenth-century English travel relations: it is the most intricately constructed and entertaining, and also the fullest, the most knowledgeable and accurate. Although it explicitly rejects the informational imperative, it is in fact better at conveying information without distortion than most other English accounts of the period. But I chose it not because it was the best, but because, as the account of a search for something legendary and deeply desired, the situation of its writing was most nearly comparable to that of the medieval accounts of the magnificent and mythical East. And Ralegh had read every geographical work he could get his hands on, even teaching himself Spanish so he could inform himself directly about America and the conquest. His head must have been stocked with the legends and marvels of this heritage, as well as with its rhetoric, and he did not reject it, even defending Mandeville, "whose reports were held for fables many yeares, and yet since the East *Indies* were discovered, wee find his relations true of such thinges as heertofore were held incredible" (86).

With this literature behind him, El Dorado in front of him, and a "very wildernesse" around him, one might have expected from Ralegh's *Discoverie* another tissue of grotesque and narcissistic invention, and that is not what one gets. The few marvels that are included are admitted to be secondhand information, and Ralegh feels the need to buttress them with citations from a great number of sources, mostly native, until he can say of the Acephali with persuasive rationality: "for mine own part I saw them not, but I am resolved that so many people did not all combine, or forethinke to make the report" (86). His criteria for belief are rigorous, and his sense of what will induce the reader to it includes the all-important notion of context.

Ralegh was an intelligent and talented man, but not a genius.

Mandeville's complex achievement stands out from its time as a singular imaginative reaction, but Ralegh's owes a great deal to the current literary and political situation. Personal experience is the primary content of his knowledge, and narrative his primary generic obligation. Utopia, now at last named and delineated, has become the separate province of explicitly fictional works, and credibility is crucial to his success and reputation (even to his survival—treason could be read in any word or deed during Elizabeth's nervous reign, and accusations against Ralegh were circulating). Thus it is perhaps the suspiciously marvelous and paradisal El Dorado itself that functions, at the invisible and undiscoverable heart of the *Discoverie*, to make Ralegh's rendering of its approach and its borders so reasonable, so full, so true to the facts of the visible, reachable world.

Over the centuries, the marvelous and the desirable have moved from text, to margin and preface, and finally out of the book itself; on a complementary journey, their imagined existence has shifted from East to West around the margin of the *orbis terrarum*, and ultimately into what Peter Fleming still calls the "wild and woolly" Interior. The verge of the Interior is a good place to stop. Its penetration will involve European culture in a confrontation with deeper mysteries and a more terrible self than the scattered and mostly unsystematic contacts of the premodern history of travel could provoke. With Ralegh we have come to the verge of the modern world as well. He demonstrates the possibility of a responsible rhetoric, and of a more harmless and beautiful, because explicit, subjectivity. Whether any harmless advantage was taken of this possibility is another story.

Epilogue
A Brief History of the Future

Intending to present the World to the World in the most certaine view, I thought a World of Authors fitter for that purpose then any One Author writing of the World.
—Purchas His Pilgrimes

When Thomas Astley came out with the first volume of *A New General Collection of Voyages and Travels* in 1745, he confronted an English-speaking public already possessed of the collections of Hakluyt, Purchas, the Churchill brothers, and John Harris (among others). His competitive awareness of these collections led him to impugn the work of his predecessors in his preface and to devise a new editorial method that would differentiate his own collection. According to Edward Cox's note in his *Reference Guide to the Literature of Travel*, "His own method . . . is to substitute for the plan of giving each author entire the plan of separating the Journals and Adventures from the Remarks on various countries. The former he lets stand by themselves, and the latter he incorporates with the Remarks of other travellers to the same regions. His aim is to make his Collection a System of Modern History and Geography, as well as a body of Voyages and Travels" (1:15).

One could have predicted this fork in the road of the genre as early as the first of the great collections, the *Decades* of Peter Martyr. The crucial conditions for such a splitting of function were already in place by then. I have alluded to them before, but it is

255

time to examine them with an eye toward the genre's future—a future whose story can be picked up in a number of recent critical works on travel literature between the late seventeenth and early nineteenth century.[1] These conditions are (1) the vast increase in the numbers of exotic travel accounts that accompanied the Age of Discovery and (2) the newly commercial nature of the book in an Age of Print. Together, these conditions made the voyage collection both necessary and possible. They also determined formal changes in the writing *and* the reading of the "voyages" themselves. And they contributed to and participated in the taxonomic rage for order that characterizes the period in European intellectual history stretching between Hakluyt's and Astley's *Voyages*.

In the face of cornucopia, sciences rose to control the flood of data and commerce to control the flood of things. The voyage collection may well have had the psychological function of control over the ever-increasing mass of voyage literature; certainly it altered the experience of the reader. And in the context of a commercial literature, Calvino's maxim—"it is not the voice that commands the story: it is the ear"—rings especially true. What the reader learns to seek, the writer (and printer) will learn to provide. The voyage collections provided a plenitude of travel narratives arranged side by side (usually with regard to the places described, sometimes according to the writers' national affiliations), and thus an implicit, minimal taxonomy in which each separate "voyage" found a place.

In an article about the aesthetics of classification in both poetry and anthropology, Nathaniel Tarn recollects an intensely pleasurable childhood fantasy to which he traces his adult interests in philately, heraldry, bird-watching, and structural anthropology:

I am looking at a beloved or favorite object, let us say a pencil or a toy motorcar. Whatever its actual color, I imagine it in a different color, and then another, and then another. I have a yellow pencil, say, and I imagine the pencil is blue, or red, or green. I may well go on to blue with red stripes, green stripes, and so forth. . . . Around the age of eleven or so, I imagine a

1. See especially Percy Adams, *Travel Literature and the Evolution of the Novel* (1983); idem, *Travelers and Travel Liars, 1660–1800* (1962); Charles L. Batten, Jr., *Pleasurable Instruction* (1978); and Barbara Maria Stafford, *Voyage into Substance* (1984); also Wayne Franklin, *Discoverers, Explorers, Settlers* (1979), which includes some very sensitive readings of earlier accounts as well.

collection of modeler's kits which would allow me possession of a private, concrete "natural history." There are to be wooden or plastic models of sheep, dogs, camels, bears . . . in fact: all animals, all birds, all fish, perhaps all plants, etc. The collection is to be housed in a special room with thousands of drawers and closets. ("Heraldic Vision," 24)

Tarn would have been quite at home and happy among the collectors of the sixteenth and seventeenth century, who fulfilled the latter fantasy literally in their "cabinets of curiosities," and more abstractly in the geographical encyclopedias and voyage collections that housed so many data in their "special rooms." He goes on to note the precise structure of his pleasure: "I am interested in the relation of [species to family]: that is, I am thrilled by the fact of many species *in relation to each other* so as to form a family" (25).

In the family of the voyage collection, each travel account is a species, or at least a different color of pencil, to continue Tarn's exemplary instances. Thus the exotic lure of difference—once wholly located in the rhetorical presentation of the exotic place or people (and readable as a feature inherent in that unvisited place or people)—is now available among and between the accounts in a single collection. Similarly, the exotic objects in a cabinet of curiosities are no longer glamorous by virtue of their alien singularity alone but by virtue—at least in part—of their difference from each other. Margaret Hodgen's descriptions of the contents of these cabinets make for rich and strange reading. For instance, the catalog of the Anatomie-Hall at the University of Leyden contained,

along with the usual miscellany to be seen in such an exhibit, . . . a Norway house built of beams without mortar or stone . . . shoes and sandals from Russia, Siam, and Egypt; the skin of a man dressed as parchment; a drinking cup made out of the skull of a Moor killed in the beleaguering of Haarlem; warlike arms used in China; Chinese gongs, paper, and books; Egyptian mummies and idols; a petrified toadstool; and 'a mallet or hammer that the savages in New Yorke kill with.' (*Early Anthropology*, 122)

Clearly, the only family to which these particular object-species belong is the human family (with the possible exception of the toadstool): taxonomy has a long way to go before it reaches the subtlety and hierarchical complexity of Linnaeus, Buffon, and Lafitau. The collection of the Danish physician and proto-archeologist Ole Worms classified rarities "according to the substances of which they were formed . . . clay, amber, gold, silver, bronze, iron, glass, and wood" (Hodgen, 123). This is very close to Tarn's characterization of his childhood fantasy, in which he says, "I am enjoying a proliferation of objects in decorative terms, a pleasing but, as far as I can see, non-functional classificatoriness" ("Heraldic Vision," 24).

Collections of data and objects became so overwhelmingly, unnervingly large that subtler taxonomies developed almost spontaneously, from the needs of catalogers and indexers trying to maintain their accessibility. Objects did not change so rapidly as ways of classifying them did. But the travel narrative is not a found (or stolen) object, and its writer was aware of the new pressures on him, not only of the state and its colonial aspirations, but of the voyage collector and the printer.

These pressures were sometimes quite blatant. In 1620, for instance, Richard Whitbourne published his *Discourse and Discouery of New-Found-Land, with many reasons to prooue how worthy and beneficiall a Plantation may there be made*; the copy in the British Museum has a broadside attached to it "signed by the Bishop of London, authorizing the collection of funds to advance the distribution of the treatise. A command from the King to the Archbishops of York and Canterbury to order collections for the same purpose is also printed in the preface" (Wright, *Middle-Class Culture in Elizabethan England*, 541). We have seen the overt pressure of the listening State in the works of Columbus and Ralegh; in the most personal and internal of all the sixteenth-century accounts, Cabeza de Vaca's tale of eight years' wanderings in the American Southwest, that presence is equally felt: "My hope of going out from among those nations was always small; nevertheless I made a point of remembering all the particulars, so that should God our Lord eventually please to bring me where I am now, I might testify to my exertions on the royal behalf" (Proem).[2]

2. I quote from Cyclone Covey's translation of Cabeza de Vaca's *Relación* (1542), *Adventures in the Unknown Interior of America*. I cite by his chapter numbers, which are generally those of the second edition (printed in his *Commentarios*, 1555).

Such exertion was a prerequisite to social and political advancement, and it paid off for Cabeza de Vaca about as well as it did for
Columbus and Ralegh: he was awarded the governorship of the
provinces of the Rio de la Plata, from which he returned in chains,
and in 1551 he was banished to Africa.

We have already observed the effect in Ralegh's text that pressure of this sort exerts on the characterization of the writer's persona. What cannot be observed in the pages of any single account is
the effect on that account of all the others. Where do Tarn's colors
come from? How is this account different from all other accounts?
There are only so many places and there are thousands of writing
voyagers. Even if one's account does not end up in a collection, or
at least does not begin there (as so many pieces in Hakluyt did), it
still has to compete for its fame. Readers do not buy or read
indiscriminately, and there is a kind of traveler's stardom to be
won: in 1653 the market could tolerate a voyage collection devoted
entirely to the exploits of Drake and his fellow voyagers, *Sir
Francis Drake Revived*, which included as frontispiece a portrait of
the ennobled pirate. The 1729 edition of Dampier's *Voyages*
includes the accounts of Cowley, Sharp, Wood, and Roberts.
According to the bibliographers Pottick and Simpson, "Dampier
seems to have been at the mercy of his publisher, Knapton, who
used the author's saleable volumes as mules for carrying off his
unsaleable stock" (quoted in Cox, *Reference Guide*, 1:13).

The popularity of Marco Polo's book was assured in large part by
his singular access to its subject matter—as Rusticello never tires
of reminding us, "Never was Christian, Saracen, nor pagan nor
Tartar nor Indian nor any man of any kind who saw and knew or
inquired so much of the different parts of the world & of the great
wonders." When travels and wonders both became available for a
dime a dozen (along with the dimes and the dozens), part of the
reader's focus shifted from the *materia* to something else. What
else? It is a large question to answer, but Thomas Astley's editorial
decision offers some assistance: he leaves the Adventures and Journals alone, merges one author's more purely informational
"Remarks" on countries with those of another, and ends up with
both a "body of Travels" *and* "a System of [Natural] History and
Geography." In the body of Travels, the integrity of the authorial
voice is respected: it is part of what we pay for.

We have followed all along in this book a noticeable tension in
the travel account between the literary pleasures and the practical

functions of description and narration. That tension was eventually to resolve itself in the increasing separation of two spheres of discourse, the scientific and (for lack of a better word) the novelistic—a separation explicit in Astley's *Voyages* but existing de facto well before that time. A pan-European scientific community can be dated from the rise of the scientific societies in the seventeenth century, and in the pages of their journals these societies issued not only calls for data but "correspondence instructions" for its representation. "Scientific travel" grew up here, in the service of a discourse suspicious of both wonder and rhetoric. "Wonder is broken knowledge," announced Bacon in the introduction to his *Advancement of Learning* (1605). Thomas Sprat is equally dismissive of the ornaments that embody it:

Who can behold without indignation how many mists and uncertainties these specious *Tropes* and *Figures* have brought on our knowledg? . . . They [the members of the Royal Society] have therefore been most rigorous in putting in execution, the only Remedy, that can be found for this *extravagance*: and that has been, a constant Resolution, to reject all the amplifications, digressions, and swellings of style: to return back to the primitive purity, and shortness, when men deliver'd so many *things*, almost in an equal number of *words*. (*History of the Royal-Society*, 2.20:112–13)

The travelers' reports printed in the pages of the Royal Society's *Philosophical Transactions* are nothing like Ralegh's shapely quest narrative; they are generally fetishistic catalogs of that reality the philosophers referred to as *res*—things. Matters. (This is precisely the reality the American Indians were charged with being unable to account for—and on that basis they were often charged further with not being human.[3]) The ethnologists, zoologists, botanists, mineralogists, meteorologists, and astronomers who reported, or used reports of, all this natural history might be seen as following the path of *descriptio*, in a reversal of Egeria's adamant neglect of the phenomenal *res*. This positivism is not unrelated to the parallel growth of imperialism among the western European nations. Francis Bacon makes the link quite easily in describing the scientific program of the fictional Salomon House in his *New*

3. See Pagden, *Fall of Natural Man*, chap. 4, sec. 11.

Atlantis (1627): "The end of our foundation is the knowledge of causes, and secret motions of things; and the enlarging of the bounds of human empire, to the effecting of all things possible" (240). The charter of the Royal Society brought Bacon's science fiction to legal life: "We have long and fully resolved with ourselves to extend not only the boundaries of Empire but also the very arts and sciences" (quoted in Ornstein, *Rôle of Scientific Societies*, 105).

For a mentality like the one Sprat proclaims, in which words can equal things, scientific description might well come to seem identical with possession; certainly such description and commercial empire were to burgeon together. One is reminded of Lévi-Strauss's Brazilian village scribe in *Tristes Tropiques*: "his knowledge is a source of power—so much so, in fact, that the function of scribe and usurer are often united in the same human being. This is not merely because the usurer needs to be able to read and write to carry on his trade, but because he has thus a twofold empire over his fellows" (291).

The equation of words and things leads of course to a new form of the old materialism of exotic representation we first noted in *Wonders of the East*. The distant places and peoples of the world came again to be seen, through the eyes of the European specialists, as fixed substances: Matters more amenable to the aggrandizement of scientific knowledge than the dogheads and vegetable lambs, or the immortal "Khan" and Prester John, of the medieval East, but still matter—even more deeply matter, as the symbolic and fantastic overtones of the newly scientific wonders were damped and the role of wonder—"broken knowledge"—scorned.

What is left for the travel writer as we know him now is narrative, and it is indeed by his narration that he distinguishes himself from his fellow travel writer and reaches for a place in the sun of commercial publication. Nothing could offer a clearer case of Tarn's heraldic paradigm than the collection of Drake's voyages (by Drake and his fellow sailors) mentioned earlier: the subject matters of the collection are the same not only geographically but even temporally. Each mariner in his cabin writes his own account as their common ship tosses along the route of a common voyage. The pleasure of reading the collection is an orchestral pleasure in the different voices, different colors of the human instruments. But the metaphors of color and musical sound cannot get us all the way home. We are dealing with language here, structured by narrative to offer vicarious experience. "Here also," says Purchas of his collection, "both Elephant may swimme in deepe voluminous Seas, and such as want either lust or leisure, may single out, as in a Library of Bookes, what Author or Voyage shall best fit to his profit or pleasure" (*Purchas His Pilgrimes*, 1:xliii). What principle of pleasure operates in this singling out? For the reader who wants lust or leisure for the orchestral experience, what command does the *single* tale answer to? Purchas does not know whether it is the Author or the Voyage that answers—a sensible confusion for, like Yeats's dancer and dance, the narrator and narrative are hard to separate. My guess as to the operant pleasure is only a guess—a projection perhaps of my own pleasure onto the readers of the sixteenth and seventeenth century.

What all personal narratives have in common is a perspective issuing from a locatable point of view—mere grammar makes it so. Active verbs are conjugated by person and performed by subjects: Ralegh "performs" his *Discoverie* in more than one sense. By the sixteenth century, travel accounts have become generically narrative, emphatically subjective. The self-effacement that cloaks Egeria's testimony has gone out of style, as has Marco Polo's formula "There is X." More openly than he once did, the witness matters. His particularity is the very sign of his authority to speak, the seal of the truth of his speech. Conversely, his text's particulars "testify to [his] exertions," prove there is a self behind the page who was not "hidden in Cornewall . . . as was supposed."

This technical subjectivity was, I think, a good thing. As we saw in Ralegh's account, it tended to convey other peoples in the form of individually encountered people, people in action. Obviously, first-person narrative is egocentric, and thus travel narrative tends to be ethnocentric, but one can at least extrapolate a subjectivity for the alien from a narrated event in which he plays a part. This is more difficult with the grand, categorical descriptions of a writer like that amalgam we call Marco Polo.

The most extraordinary possibility held out by the newly narrative and subjective form is realized in Álvar Núñez Cabeza de Vaca's *Relación* of 1542—a narrative of events that threatened their narrator with a serious shift of identity and orientation. (This thrillingly internal aspect of travel is perhaps the ultimate source

of the *ostronemie* that lures us to its texts.[4]) After wandering for
eight years, often naked and sometimes in slavery, across the wilderness of the American Southwest in search of fellow Christians
who could send him home to Spain, Cabeza de Vaca finally finds
some at a military campsite near Culiacán in northern Mexico. By
this time he is famous among the peoples of the region as a healer,
and he arrives with a faithful escort. "They [the Christians] were
dumbfounded at the sight of me, strangely undressed and in company with Indians. They just stood staring for a long time, not
thinking to hail me or come closer to ask questions" (51).

The Spanish recover from their surprise and enlist the wanderer's help in gathering food from the local villagers—no problem
for Cabeza de Vaca and his three companions, who have been regularly receiving such tribute, unasked, in recognition of their semi-
divine status as healers. But the mind of Capt. Diego Alcaraz has
not been touched and transformed by an experience like Cabeza de
Vaca's:

After this we had a hot argument with them [the Christians], for they
meant to make slaves of the Indians in our train. We got so angry that we
went off forgetting the many Turkish-shaped bows, the many pouches,
and the five emerald arrowheads, etc., which we thus lost. And to think
we had given these Christians a supply of cowhides and other things that
our retainers had carried long distances! (52)

"These Christians," "our retainers": the perspective expressed in
the demonstrative and pronominal adjectives is a strange one for
the Spanish *hidalgo* who had come to the New World on an expedition of conquest eight years before. "To the last I could not con-
vince the Indians that we were of the same people as the Christian
slavers," says Cabeza de Vaca later in that chapter:

Alcaraz bade his interpreter tell the Indians that we were members of his
race who had been long lost; that his group were the lords of the land who

4. Roland Barthes says, about writing his account of a trip to Japan: "The author
has never, in any sense, photographed Japan. Rather, he has done the opposite: Japan
has starred him with any number of 'flashes'; or, better still, Japan has afforded him
a situation of writing. This situation is the very one in which a certain disturbance
of the person occurs, a subversion of earlier readings, a shock of meaning lacerated,
extenuated to the point of its irreplaceable void, without the object's ever ceasing to
be significant, desirable" (*Empire of Signs*, 4).

must be obeyed and served, while we were inconsequential. The Indians paid no attention to this. Conferring among themselves, they replied that the Christians lied: We had come from the sunrise, they from the sunset; we healed the sick, they killed the sound; we came naked and barefoot, they clothed, horsed, and lanced; we coveted nothing but gave whatever we were given, while they robbed whomever they found and bestowed nothing on anyone. (52)

(In the eloquence of his presentation we may sense that Cabeza de Vaca was rather more convinced by the Indian representation of his case than by the Spanish.)

Cabeza de Vaca's circumstances were of course unusual and account in part for the "internal" quality of his *Relación*—as he remarks in his opening letter to the king, it was "the most one could bring back who returned thence naked." These circumstances also drive out the traditional wonders: there is no Earthly Paradise here, no Prester John, no El Dorado, no Fountain of Youth, no Seven Cities of Cíbola (though one of Cabeza de Vaca's companions would later lead an expedition to pueblo country in search of the Seven Cities). The most "wonderful" thing in the book is Cabeza de Vaca himself, as seen through the eyes of the Indians he heals, and the book's strangest miracle is his resurrection of a dead man. It is in response to this event that the widespread cult springs up which occupies so much of his account of Indian mores. Rather than domesticate the alien land with his own language, Cabeza de Vaca is himself domesticated early on; he starts his American career as a slave to a Mariame Indian. The land he wanders in is Home to his owners and hosts, and he shares their life and dress and, eventually, six of their languages. He comes to see through their eyes, and at the moment of crisis, when he finally encounters Christians in Mexico, his language betrays his identification with the Indian escort rather than "these Christians." In a similar reversal, the only anthropophagi he offers are "five Christians quartered on the coast [who] came to the extremity of eating each other . . . . The Indians were so shocked at this cannibalism that, if they had seen it sometime earlier, they surely would have killed every one of us" (21).

What a long way we have come, in the rhetorical depiction of strange peoples, from the irresponsible glee of *Wonders of the East* or the fastidious shudders of Friar Odoric. In fact, we have come farther, in Cabeza de Vaca's *Relación*, than the genre itself has come; this book is not an epitome but an exception. There is no one like Cabeza de Vaca; his is the eye of the storm, or the still, small voice one always hopes to hear in the heart of the whirlwind.

But the world informed by the voyage reports is a world informed by their subjectivity as well, even if it rarely reaches the mystical relatedness of Cabeza de Vaca's. I am stressing this point more than it needs to be stressed, perhaps, in sad awareness of the part the voyage report was to play in the development of an extremely interventionist ethnology, now justifiably under attack from many quarters. Earlier voyage reports stocked the magazines of anthropological discourse among the stay-at-homes; later, such reports would be commissioned and finally undertaken personally by men "who insisted that . . . only such experience could guarantee the accuracy of ethnological observation" (Pagden, *Fall of Natural Man*, 200). It is the element of narrative itself, which I have been considering as the tool of an almost ethical leap in European consciousness of exotic people and places, that Johannes Fabius has condemned as inherently distancing and false.[5] In the service of ethnology, narrative reduced an alien reality to the controlling terms not simply of the narrator's and reader's exclusively shared language, but of narrative structure itself, while claiming to be in some sense equal to that reality ("so many things . . . in an equal number of words").

The argument is not easy to dismiss, especially in light of the political uses to which ethnology would be put. But it might still be said that the voyage narratives of the sixteenth and even the seventeenth century offered readers, with some frequency, the experience of imaginative entrance into the minds or points of view of alien humans; as reductive, false, and inadequate as those entrances might have been, they constituted a new opportunity for consciousness. And the opportunity was taken, the experience mimicked in strange and surprising places. When a French astronomer offered a view of the earth through the eyes of moon-men in the first volume of the *Philosophical Transactions*, one might have seen a faint reflection of Cabeza de Vaca's oscillating point of view: "Meanwhile, since we see in *the Moon*, when she is increasing or

---

5. See Johannes Fabius, *Time and the Other: How Anthropology Makes Its Object* (1983).

decreasing, the Light she receives from the Earth, we cannot doubt, but that the People of the *Moon* should likewise see in the Earth that Light, wherewith the *Moon* illuminates it, with perhaps the difference there is between their bigness" ("Monsieur Auzout's Speculations of the Changes, Likely to be Discovered in the *Earth* and *Moon*, by their respective Inhabitants").[6]

I would like to postulate a moment of innocence to match Egeria's, here, in the heart of the whirlwind—where cornucopia meets the circumnavigator, the astronomer, the delighted collector of voyages and rarities, the wandering *hidalgo* who raises the dead, the reviewer of Hooke's *Micrographia* who hopes "to improve our senses of Hearing, Smelling, Tasting, Touching, as well as we have improved that of Seeing by Optick Glasses" (*Philosophical Transactions*, 1.2:32). But the detached, prosthetic quality of the reviewer's sensuous fantasy reminds us of what is to come of all this—how the delicate balance between plenty and chaos, held in place for the moment by adventure narratives, the twenty volumes of *Purchas His Pilgrimes*, cluttered museums and unstructured curiosity, will soon be tipped by the totalizing and objectifying systems of natural history; how the interest in other people will lead to an organized ethnology that can control them for the purposes of Church and State. How, for the state, the roundness of the earth and the singleness of its nature are opportunities for empire. How, soon, among the palpable, mute rarities brought home by adventurous merchants for sale to the reading, buying, socially climbing publics of Europe—the ivory and sables, cinnamon and saffron, gongs and skull-cups—how among these there will soon be shiploads of people. How, in fact, there already are.

6. *Philosophical Transactions*, 1.7:122 (1665).

References

Adamnan. *Adamnan's "De locis sanctis."* Ed. and trans. Denis Meehan. Scriptores Latini Hiberniae, 3. Dublin: Dublin Institute for Advanced Studies, 1958.

Adams, Percy G. *Travel Literature and the Evolution of the Novel.* Lexington: University Press of Kentucky, 1983.

____. *Travelers and Travel Liars, 1660–1800.* 1962; reprint, New York: Dover, 1980.

Alcuin. Letter. In *Patrologia latina*, 100:141A. Ed. J. P. Migne. Paris, 1857–66.

Alden, John. *European Americana: A Chronological Guide to Works Printed in Europe Relating to the Americas, 1493– 1776.* 2 vols. New York: Readex Books, 1980.

Alexander's Letter to Aristotle. In *Three Old English Prose Texts in MS. Cotton Vitellius A xv.* Ed. Stanley Rypins. Early English Text Society, orig. ser., 161. London, 1924.

Allen, John L. "Lands of Myth, Waters of Wonder: The Place of the Imagination in the History of Geographical Exploration." In *Geographies of the Mind: Essays in Historical Geosophy*, 41–62. Ed. David Lowenthal and Martyn J. Bowden. New York: Oxford University Press, 1976.

Antoninus. "Of the Holy Places Visited by Antoninus Martyr." Trans. Aubrey Stewart. Library of the Palestine Pilgrims' Text Society, 2. 1896; reprint, New York: AMS Press, 1971.

Archer, Gabriel. "The Relation of Captaine Gosnols Voyage to the North Part of Virginia, begunne the sixe and twentieth of March, Anno 42. Elizabethae Reginae 1602. and delivered by Gabriel Archer, a Gentleman in the said Voyage." In Purchas, *Purchas His Pilgrimes*, 18:302–313.

Arrian. *Indica.* Trans. P. A. Brunt. Loeb Classical Library. Cambridge, Mass.: Harvard University Press, 1983.

Astley, Thomas [John Green]. *A New General Collection of Voyages and Travels.* London: Thomas Astley, 1745.

References

Auerbach, Erich. *Mimesis: The Representation of Reality in Western Literature.* Trans. Willard R. Trask. Bollingen Series, 36. Princeton, N.J.: Princeton University Press, 1953.

Augustine, Saint. *The City of God.* Trans. Henry Bettenson. Harmondsworth, England: Penguin, 1972.

———. *The City of God.* Trans. W. M. Green. Loeb Classical Library, vol. 417. Cambridge, Mass.: Harvard University Press; London: William Heinemann, 1972.

Bacon, Francis. *The Advancement of Learning.* Great Books of the Western World, vol. 30. Chicago: Encyclopaedia Britannica, 1952.

———. *The New Atlantis.* In *Famous Utopias of the Renaissance.* Ed. Frederic R. White. 1946; reprint, Putney, Vt.: Hendricks House, 1981.

Bacon, Roger. *Opus majus.* Trans. Robert Belle Burke. Philadelphia: University of Pennsylvania Press, 1928.

Baker, Ernest Albert. *The History of the English Novel.* London: H. F. and G. Witherby, 1924–39.

Baker, Robert. "Voyage to Guinie." In Hakluyt, *Divers Voyages,* 130–42.

Bakhtin, Mikhail M. *The Dialogic Imagination: Four Essays.* Trans. Caryl Emerson and Michael Holquist. Austin: University of Texas Press, 1981.

———. *Rabelais and His World.* Trans. Helen Iswolsky. Cambridge, Mass.: MIT Press, 1968.

Barthes, Roland. *The Pleasure of the Text.* Trans. Richard Miller. New York: Hill and Wang, 1975.

———. *S/Z.* Trans. Richard Miller. New York: Hill and Wang, 1975.

———. *Empire of Signs.* Trans. Richard Howard. New York: Hill and Wang, 1982.

Batten, Charles L., Jr. *Pleasurable Instruction: Form and Convention in Eighteenth-Century Travel Literature.* Berkeley: University of California Press, 1978.

Baudet, Henri. *Paradise on Earth: Some Thoughts on European Images of Non-European Man.* Trans. Elizabeth Wentholt. New Haven, Conn.: Yale University Press, 1965.

Benedetto, L. F., ed. *Il milione.* By Marco Polo. Comitato Geografico Nazionale Italiano Pubbl. 3. Florence, 1928.

Bennett, Josephine Waters. *The Rediscovery of Sir John Mandeville.* New York: Modern Language Association of America, 1954.

Bernard, J. H., trans. "Guidebook to Palestine." Library of the Palestine Pilgrims' Text Society, 6. 1896; reprint, New York: AMS Press, 1971.

Boas, George. *Essays on Primitivism and Related Ideas in the Middle Ages.* Baltimore: Johns Hopkins University Press, 1948.

Boon, James. *Other Tribes, Other Scribes: Symbolic Anthropology in the Comparative Study of Cultures, Histories, Religions, and Texts.* Cambridge: Cambridge University Press, 1982.

Bourdeaux Pilgrim. "Itinerary from Bourdeaux to Jerusalem." Trans. Aubrey Stewart. Library of the Palestine Pilgrims' Text Society, 1. 1887; reprint, New York: AMS Press, 1971.

Bourne, Edward Gaylord. "Columbus, Ramon Pane and the Beginnings of American Anthropology." *Proceedings of the American Antiquarian Society*, n.s. 17 (April 1906): 310–48.

Breiner, Laurence. "The Basilisk." In *Mythical and Fabulous Creatures*. Ed. Malcolm South. Westport, Conn.: Greenwood Press, 1986.

Brereton, John. "Notes of the Same Voyage [Bartholomew Gosnold's] taken out of a Tractate written by James Rosier to Sir Walter Raleigh ... " In Purchas, *Purchas His Pilgrimes*, 18:314–19.

Brooks, Van Wyck, trans. *Journal of the First Voyage to America*. By Christopher Columbus. New York: Albert and Charles Boni, 1924.

Brougham, John. *Columbus el Filibustero!! A New and Audaciously Original Historico-Plagiaristic, Ante-National, Pre-Patriotic, and Omni-Local Confusion of Circumstances, Running through Two Acts and Four Centuries*. N.p., 185–?. Harris Collection. Brown University, Providence, R.I.

Buck, Percy, and H. E. Wooldridge. *The Oxford History of Music*. Vol. 1. London: Oxford University Press, 1929.

Burchard of Mt. Sion. *A Description of the Holy Land by Burchard of Mount Sion*. Trans. Aubrey Stewart. Library of the Palestine Pilgrims' Text Society, 12. 1896; reprint, New York: AMS Press, 1971.

Butor, Michel. "Travel and Writing." *Mosaic* 8.1 (1974): 1–16.

Byron, Robert. *The Road to Oxiana*. 1937; reprint, New York: Oxford University Press, 1982.

Cabeza de Vaca, Alvar Nuñez. *La relación*. Zamora, 1542. In *Adventures in the Unknown Interior of America*. Trans. Cyclone Covey. 1961; reprint, Albuquerque: University of New Mexico Press, 1983.

Cabrol, Fernand, and Henri Leclercq, eds. *Dictionnaire d'archéologie chrétienne et de liturgie*. Paris: Librairie Letouzey et Ané, 1922.

Campbell, Joseph. *The Hero with a Thousand Faces*. 2d ed. Bollingen Series, 17. Princeton, N.J.: Princeton University Press, 1968.

Carroll, Lewis. *Through the Looking Glass*. Harmondsworth, England: Puffin, 1962.

Cawley, Robert R. *Unpathed Waters: Studies in the Influence of Voyagers on Elizabethan Literature*. Princeton, N.J.: Princeton University Press, 1940.

Chappuys, Gabriel. *L'estat, description et gouvernement des royaumes et républiques du monde, tant anciennes que modernes . . .* Paris, 1585.

Chiappelli, Fred, ed. *First Images of America: The Impact of the New World on the Old*. 2 vols. Berkeley: University of California Press, 1976.

"The City of Jerusalem." Trans. C. R. Conder. Library of the Palestine Pilgrims' Text Society, 6. 1896; reprint, New York: AMS Press, 1971.

References

Clifford, James, and George E. Marcus, eds. *Writing Culture: The Poetics and Politics of Ethnography.* Berkeley: University of California Press, 1986.

Cochleus, Joannis, ed. *Cosmographiae Pomponii Melae.* Nuremberg, 1512.

Columbus, Christopher. Documents from the third and fourth voyages. In de Lollis, *Scritti di Cristoforo Colombo.*

———. *Epistola de insulis nuper inventis.* Trans. Alexander de Cosco. Rome: S. Plannck, after April 29th, 1493.

———. *The Journal of Christopher Columbus.* Trans. Cecil Jane. Appendix by R. A. Skelton. New York: Clarkson N. Potter, 1960.

———. Journal of the first voyage. In de Lollis and Paz, *Raccolta . . . Columbiana,* vol. 1.

———. *Journal of the First Voyage to America.* Trans. Van Wyck Brooks. New York: Albert and Charles Boni, 1924.

———. *A New and Fresh English Translation of the Letter of Columbus Announcing the Discovery of America.* Trans. Samuel Eliot Morison. Madrid: Graficas Yagues, 1959.

———. *Select Documents Illustrating the Four Voyages of Columbus.* 2 vols. Ed. and trans. Cecil Jane. Hakluyt Society, 2d ser., 65 and 70. London, 1930–33 (bilingual edition).

———. Various documents. In Navarrete, *Colección de los viages,* vols. 1–3.

Cook, Sherburne, and Woodrow W. Borah. *Essays in Population History: Mexico and the Caribbean.* Berkeley: University of California Press, 1971.

Córdoba, José Maria Gárate. *La poesia del descubrimiento.* Madrid: Ediciones Cultura Hispanica, 1977.

Cosmas Indicopleustes. *The Christian Topography of Cosmas, an Egyptian Monk.* Trans. and ed. J. W. McCrindle. Hakluyt Society, o.s. 98. London, 1897.

Cox, Edward G. *A Reference Guide to the Literature of Travel.* 3 vols. University of Washington Publications in Language and Literature, vols. 9–11. Seattle: University of Washington, 1938.

Ctesias. *La Perse, L'Inde: Les sommaires de Photius.* Trans. R. Henry. Collection Lebègue, 7th ser., 84. Brussels: J. Lebègue, 1947.

Cunningham, William. *The Cosmographical Glasse.* London, 1559.

Curtius, Ernst Robert. *European Literature and the Latin Middle Ages.* Trans. Willard R. Trask. Bollingen Series, 36. Princeton, N.J.: Princeton University Press, 1953.

Dante. Letter to Can Grande. See Toynbee.

David-Neel, Alexandra. *Magic and Mystery in Tibet.* 1932; reprint, New York: Dover, 1971.

Dawson, Christopher, ed. *Mission to Asia.* 1955; reprint, Toronto: University of Toronto Press for the Medieval Society of America, 1980.

270

De Lollis, Cesare, ed. *Scritti di Cristoforo Colombo.* In *Raccolta di documenti e studi pubblicati dalla R. Commissione Columbiana.* Part 1 (vols. 1 and 2). Rome: Ministero della pubblica istruzione, 1892–96.

De Lollis, Cesare, and Julian Paz, eds. Journal of Christopher Columbus. In *Raccolta di documenti e studi pubblicati dalla R. Commissione Columbiana.* Vol. 1. Rome: Ministero della pubblica istruzione, 1892–96.

Douglas, Mary. *Purity and Danger: An Analysis of the Concepts of Pollution and Taboo.* 1966; reprint, London and Boston: ARK Paperbacks, 1984.

Dudley, Robert, Capt. Wyatt, and Abram Kendall. *The Voyage of Robert Dudley afterwards styled Earl of Warwicke and Leicester and Duke of Northumberland, to the West Indies, 1594–1595, Narrated by Capt. Wyatt, by Himself, and by Abram Kendall, Master.* Ed. George F. Warner. The Hakluyt Society, 2d ser., 3. London, 1899.

Eden, Richard, trans. *The Decades of the New Worlde or West India.* By Pietro Martire d'Anghiera. London, 1555.

———. *A Treatyse of the Newe India.* By Sebastian Münster. London, 1553.

Egeria. *Egeria: Diary of a Pilgrimage.* Ed and trans. George E. Gingras. Ancient Christian Writers: The Works of the Fathers in Translation, 38. New York: Newman Press, 1970.

———. *Itinerarium Egeriae.* Ed. E. Franceschini and R. Weber. Corpus Christianorum, Series Latina, 175. Turnhout and Paris: Brepols, 1953.

Eusebius. *Historia ecclesiastica.* Extracts in "The Churches of Constantine at Jerusalem: Being Translations from Eusebius and the Early Pilgrims." Ed. and trans. John H. Bernard. Library of the Palestine Pilgrims' Text Society, 1. 1890; reprint, New York: AMS Press, 1971.

———. *Vita Constantini.* Extracts in "The Churches of Constantine."

Fabius, Johannes. *Time and the Other: How Anthropology Makes Its Object.* New York: Columbia University Press, 1983.

Fabri, Felix. *The Wanderings of Felix Fabri.* Trans. Aubrey Stewart. Library of the Palestine Pilgrims' Text Society, 7–10. 1893; reprint, New York: AMS Press, 1971.

Fleming, Peter. *Brazilian Adventure.* 1933; reprint, Los Angeles: J. B. Tarcher, 1983.

Fletcher, Angus. *Allegory: The Theory of a Symbolic Mode.* Ithaca, N.Y.: Cornell University Press, 1964.

Franklin, Wayne. *Discoverers, Explorers, Settlers: The Diligent Writers of Early America.* Chicago: University of Chicago Press, 1979.

Friedman, John Block. *The Monstrous Races in Medieval Art and Thought.* Cambridge, Mass.: Harvard University Press, 1981.

Fulcher of Chartres. *A History of the Expedition to Jerusalem, 1095–1127.* Trans. Frances Rita Ryan. Ed. Harold S. Fink. Knoxville: University of Tennessee Press, 1969.

References

Galinsky, Hans. "Exploring the 'Exploration Report' and Its Image of the Overseas World: Spanish, French and English Variants of a Common Form Type in Early American Literature." *Early American Literature* 12 (1977): 5–24.

Gardiner, F. C. *The Pilgrimage of Desire*. Leiden: E. J. Brill, 1971.

Genette, Gérard. *Narrative Discourse: An Essay in Method*. Trans. Jane E. Lewin. Ithaca, N.Y.: Cornell University Press, 1980.

Gibb, Paul Allen, ed. and trans. "*Wonders of the East*: A Critical Edition and Commentary." Ph.D. diss., Duke University, 1977.

Gilbert, Humphrey. *Discourse of a Discoverie for a New Passage to Cataia*. London, 1576.

Gingras, George E., ed. and trans. *Egeria: Diary of a Pilgrimage*. Ancient Christian Writers: Works of the Fathers in Translation, 38. New York: Newman Press, 1970.

Goldschmidt, E. P. "Not in Harrisse." In *Essays Honoring Lawrence C. Wroth*, 129–41. Portland, Maine: Anthoensen Press, 1951.

Gombrich, Ernst. *Art and Illusion: A Study in the Psychology of Pictorial Representation*. 2d ed. Bollingen Series, 35.5. Princeton, N.J.: Princeton University Press, 1961.

Gove, Philip. *The Imaginary Voyage in Prose Fiction: A History of Its Criticism and a Guide for Its Study, with an Annotated Check List of 215 Imaginary Voyages from 1700 to 1800*. London: Holland Press, 1961.

Greenblatt, Stephen J. "Learning to Curse: Aspects of Linguistic Colonialism in the Sixteenth Century." In Chiappelli, *First Images of America*, 2:561–80.

"Guidebook to Palestine." Trans. J. H. Bernard. Library of the Palestine Pilgrims' Text Society, 6. 1894; reprint, New York: AMS Press, 1971.

Hakluyt, Richard, ed. *Divers Voyages Touching the Discovery of America . . .* London, 1582.

——. *The Principall Navigations, Voiages and Discoveries of the English Nation . . .* 1589; rev. ed., 1598–1600; reprint (Hakluyt Society, extra series), Glasgow: James MacLehose and Sons, 1903–5.

Hamelius, P., ed. *Mandeville's Travels*. 2 vols. Early English Text Society, o.s. 153 and 154. 1919; reprint, Millwood, N.Y.: Kraus Reprint, 1974.

Hanke, Lewis. *Aristotle and the American Indians*. London: Hollis and Carter, 1959.

Harcourt, Robert. *A Relation of a Voyage to Guiana . . .* London, 1613.

Harley, J. B., and David Woodward, eds. *Cartography in Prehistoric, Ancient, and Medieval Europe and the Mediterranean*. In *The History of Cartography*. Vol. 1. Chicago: University of Chicago Press, 1987– .

Harpham, Geoffrey. *On the Grotesque: Strategies of Contradiction in Art and Literature*. Princeton, N.J.: Princeton University Press, 1982.

Henry, R., ed. and trans. *La Perse, L'Inde: Les sommaires de Photius*. Collection Lebègue, 7th ser., 84. Brussels: J. Lebègue, 1947.

Herodotus. *The History.* Trans. George Rawlinson. Great Books of the Western World, 6. Chicago: Encyclopaedia Britannica, 1952.

Hippocrates. *Hippocrates with an English Translation.* Trans. and ed. W. H. S. Jones. Loeb Classical Library. Cambridge, Mass.: Harvard University Press, 1948.

Hodgen, Margaret. *Early Anthropology in the Sixteenth and Seventeenth Centuries.* Philadelphia: University of Pennsylvania Press, 1964.

Howard, Donald R. "The World of *Mandeville's Travels.*" *Yearbook of English Studies* 1 (1971): 1–17.

_____. *Writers and Pilgrims: Medieval Pilgrimage Narratives and Their Posterity.* Berkeley: University of California Press, 1980.

Huxley, Aldous. *Heaven and Hell.* New York: Harper and Row, 1955.

Jane, Cecil, trans. *The Journal of Christopher Columbus.* Appendix by R. A. Skelton. New York: Clarkson N. Potter, 1960.

_____, trans. and ed. *Select Documents Illustrating the Four Voyages of Columbus.* 2 vols. Hakluyt Society, 2d ser., 65 and 70. London, 1930–33.

Jerome, Saint. "The Pilgrimage of the Holy Paula." Trans. Aubrey Stewart. Library of the Palestine Pilgrims' Text Society, 1. 1887; reprint, New York: AMS Press, 1971.

Joinville, Jean, sire de. *La vie de Saint Louis.* Ed. Noel L. Corbett. Sherbrook, Quebec: Editions Naaman, 1977.

Kappler, Claude, and René Kappler, trans. *Voyage dans l'empire mongol.* By William of Rubruck. Paris: Payot, 1985.

Kayser, Wolfgang. *The Grotesque in Art and Literature.* Trans. Ulrich Weisstein. Bloomington: Indiana University Press, 1963.

Keymis, Lawrence. *A Relation of the Second Voyage to Guiana . . .* London, 1596.

Klamroff, Manuel, rev. and ed. *The Travels of Marco Polo the Venetian.* Trans. William Marsden. New York: Liveright Publishing, 1953.

Ladner, Gerhart B. "*Homo Viator*: Medieval Ideas on Alienation and Order." *Speculum* 42.2 (1967): 233–59.

Las Casas, Bartolomé de. *The Spanish Colonie, Or Brief Chronicle of the Actes and gestes of the Spaniards in the West Indies, called the newe World . . .* Trans. "M. M. S." 1583; reprint, Readex Microprint, 1966 (photocopy).

Latham, Ronald, ed. and trans. *The Travels of Marco Polo.* Harmondsworth, England: Penguin, 1958.

Letts, Malcolm. *Sir John Mandeville: The Man and His Book.* London: Batchworth Press, 1949.

Lévi-Strauss, Claude. *Tristes Tropiques: An Anthropological Study of the Primitive Societies in Brazil.* Trans. John Russell. 1955; trans. 1961; reprint, New York: Atheneum, 1968.

Lilius, Zacharius. *Contra antipodes.* Florence, 1496.

López de Gómara, Francesco. *La historia general de las Indias.* Antwerp, 1554.

References

———. *La istoria de las Indias. Y la conquista de Mexico.* Saragosa, 1552.

Lowes, John Livingston. *The Road to Xanadu: A Study in the Ways of the Imagination.* Boston: Houghton Mifflin, 1927.

Ludolph von Suchem. *Ludolph von Suchem's Description of the Holy Land, and of the Way Thither.* Trans. Aubrey Stewart. 1896; reprint, New York: AMS Press, 1971.

McDougall, Walter Hugh. *The Un-authorized History of Columbus, Composed in Good Faith by Walt McD.; Containing No Maps, References or Facts . . .* N.p., 1892. Harris Collection. Brown University, Providence, R.I.

McGurk, Patrick, Anne Knock, et al. *An Eleventh-Century Anglo-Saxon Miscellany.* Early English Texts in Facsimile, vol. 21. Baltimore: Johns Hopkins University Press, 1985.

Mâle, Emile. *The Gothic Image: Religious Art in France of the Thirteenth Century.* Trans. Dora Nussey. New York: Harper, 1958.

Mandeville, John. *Mandeville's Travels.* Ed. P. Hamelius. 2 vols. Early English Text Society, o.s., 153 and 154. 1919; reprint, Millwood, N.Y.: Kraus Reprint, 1974.

Martin, Terence. "The Negative Structures of American Literature." *American Literature* 57.1 (March 1985): 1–22.

Martire d'Anghiera, Pietro [Peter Martyr]. *The Decades of the Newe Worlde or West India.* Trans. Richard Eden. London, 1555.

Matthews, W. H. *Mazes and Labyrinths: Their History and Development.* 1922; reprint, New York: Dover, 1970.

Meehan, Denis, trans. and ed. *Adamnan's "De locis sanctis."* Scriptores Latini Hiberniae, 3. Dublin: Dublin Institute for Advanced Studies, 1958.

Mézières, Philippe de. *Le songe du vieil pèlerin.* Ed G. W. Coopland. 2 vols. Cambridge: University Press, 1969.

Milani, Virgil I. "The Written Language of Christopher Columbus." *Forum Italicum* 7, supp., 1973.

Miller, Christopher. *Blank Darkness: Africanist Discourse in French.* Chicago: University of Chicago Press, 1985.

Minto, William. *A Manual of English Prose Literature.* 1872; reprint, Boston: Ginn, 1891.

Montaigne, Michel de. *The Essayes of Michael Lord of Montaigne.* Trans. John Florio. 3 vols. London: David Nutt, 1892.

———. *Montaigne's Travel Journal.* Trans. Donald M. Frame. 1957; reprint, San Francisco: North Point Press, 1983.

More, Thomas. *Utopia.* Trans. Ralphe Robynson. In *Famous Utopias of the Renaissance.* Ed. Frederic R. White. Putney, Vt.: Hendricks House, 1981.

Morgan, Wendy. "Constructing the Monster: Notions of the Monstrous in Classical Antiquity." Ph.D. diss., Deakin University, Australia, 1984.

Morison, Samuel Eliot. *Admiral of the Ocean Sea*. Boston: Little, Brown, 1949.

Moseley, C. W. R. D. "The Metamorphosis of Sir John Mandeville." *Yearbook of English Studies* 4 (1974): 5–25.

Moule, A. C., and Paul Pelliot, eds. and trans. *Marco Polo: The Description of the World*. Vol. 1. London: G. Routledge and Sons, 1938.

Münster, Sebastian. *A Treatyse of the New India*. Trans. Richard Eden. London, 1553.

Navarrete, Martin Fernández de, ed. *Colección de los viages y descubrimientos*. 5 vols. Madrid: En la Imprenta Real, 1825–37.

Odoric of Pordenone. *The Travels of Friar Odoric*. In *Cathay and the Way Thither*. Vol. 2. Ed. and trans. Henry Yule. 2d ed. Hakluyt Society, 2d ser., 33. London, 1913.

O'Gorman, Edmundo. *The Invention of America*. Bloomington: Indiana University Press, 1961.

Olschki, Leonardo. *Marco Polo's Asia: An Introduction to His "Description of the World" Called "Il Milione."* Trans. John A. Scott. Berkeley: University of California Press, 1960.

Ornstein, Martha. *The Rôle of Scientific Societies in the Seventeenth Century*. 1913; reprint, Chicago: University of Chicago Press, 1928.

Pagden, Anthony. *The Fall of Natural Man: The American Indian and the Origins of Comparative Ethnology*. Cambridge: Cambridge University Press, 1982.

Parmenius, Stephen. *The New Found Land of Stephen Parmenius: The Life and Writings of a Hungarian Poet, Drowned on a Voyage from Newfoundland, 1583*. Ed. and trans., with commentaries, David B. Quinn and Neil M. Chesire. Toronto: University of Toronto Press, 1972.

Patch, Howard. *The Other World according to Descriptions in Medieval Literature*. Cambridge, Mass.: Harvard University Press, 1950.

Patrologia latina. Ed. J. P. Migne. See Alcuin.

Paula (and Eustochium). "The Letter of Paula and Eustochium to Marcella, about the Holy Places." Trans. Aubrey Stewart. Library of the Palestine Pilgrims' Text Society, 1. 1889; reprint, New York: AMS Press, 1971.

The Periplus of the Erythraean Sea. Trans. and ed. G. W. B. Huntingford. Hakluyt Society, 2d ser., 151. Cambridge: Cambridge University Press, 1980.

Philosophical Transactions. Vol. 1, nos. 2 and 7. London: Royal Society of London, 1665.

Pliny the Elder. *Natural History*. Trans. H. Rackham. Loeb Classical Library. Cambridge, Mass.: Harvard University Press, 1969.

Polo, Marco. *The Book of Ser Marco Polo the Venetian Concerning the Kingdoms and Marvels of the East*. 3rd ed. rev. Henri Cordier. 2 vols. London: John Murray, 1921.

References

_____. *Marco Polo: The Description of the World*. Ed. and trans. A. C. Moule and Paul Pelliot. London: G. Routledge and Sons, 1938.

_____. *Il milione*. Ed. L. F. Benedetto. Comitato Geografico Nazionale Italiano Pubbl. 3. Florence, 1928.

_____. *Il milione*. In *Viaggiatori Antichi*. Marciana Cl. VI codd. ital. 208, 22–100.

_____. *The Travels of Marco Polo*. Ed and trans. Ronald Latham. Harmondsworth, England: Penguin, 1958.

Poloner, John. *John Poloner's Description of the Holy Land*. Trans. Aubrey Stewart. Library of the Palestine Pilgrims' Text Society, 6. 1894; reprint, New York: AMS Press, 1971.

Purchas, Samuel. *Hakluytus Posthumus, or Purchas His Pilgrimes*. 20 vols. Glasgow: James MacLehose and Sons, 1905.

The Quest of the Holy Grail. Trans. P. M. Matarasso. Harmondsworth, England: Penguin, 1969.

Ralegh, Walter. *The Discoverie of the Large, Rich, and Bewtiful Empire of Guiana, with a Relation of the Great and Golden City of Manoa (which the Spaniards call El Dorado) . . .* 1596; reprint (ed. Robert H. Schomberg) for Hakluyt Society, 1848; reprint, New York: Lenox Hill, 1970.

Rockhill, William, ed. and trans. *The Journey of Friar William of Rubruck*. The Hakluyt Society, 2d ser., 4. London, 1900.

Roger, Francis M. *The Quest for Eastern Christians: Travels and Rumor in the Age of Discovery*. Minneapolis: University of Minnesota Press, 1962.

Romm, James S. "The Edges of the Earth in Ancient Thought: Distance and the Literary Imagination." Ph.D. diss., Princeton University, 1988.

Rosier, James. "Extracts of a Virginian Voyage made An. 1605 by Captaine George Waymouth, in the Archangell, Set forth by the Right Honorable Henry Earle of South-hampton, and the Lord Thomas Arundel, written by James Rosier." In Purchas, *Purchas His Pilgrimes*, 18:335–359.

Ryan, Frances Rita, trans. *A History of the Expedition to Jerusalem, 1095–1127*. By Fulcher of Chartres. Ed. Harold S. Fink. Knoxville: University of Tennessee Press, 1969.

Rypins, Stanley, ed. *Three Old English Prose Texts in MS. Cotton Vitellius A xv*. Early English Text Society, orig. ser., 161. London, 1924.

Said, Edward. *Orientalism*. 1978; reprint, New York: Vintage Books, 1979.

Sarton, George. "The Scientific Information Transmitted through the Incunabula." *Osiris* 5 (1938): 43–230.

Seneca. *Medea*. In *Tragedies*. Vol. 1. Ed. and trans. Frank Justus Miller. Loeb Classical Library, vol. 142. Cambridge, Mass.: Harvard University Press, 1917.

Skelton, R. A. *Explorers' Maps*. London: Routledge and Kegan Paul, 1958.

Skelton, R. A., D. B. Quinn, and W. P. Cumming. *The Discovery of North America*. New York: American Heritage Press, 1972.

Spearing, A. C. *Medieval Dream-Poetry.* Cambridge: Cambridge University Press, 1976.

Spitzer, Leo. "The Epic Style of the Pilgrim Aetheria." *Comparative Literature* 1.3 (1949): 225–58.

Sprat, Thomas. *The History of the Royal-Society of London for the improving of natural knowledge.* London, 1667.

Stafford, Barbara Maria. *Voyage into Substance: Art, Science, Nature and the Illustrated Travel Account, 1760–1840.* Cambridge, Mass.: MIT Press, 1984.

Stamler, Johannus. *Dyalogus . . . de diversarum gencium sectis et mundi religionibus.* N.p., 1508.

Sumption, Jonathan. *Pilgrimage: An Idea of Medieval Religion.* Totowa, N.J.: Rowman and Littlefield, 1975.

Swift, Jonathan. *Gulliver's Travels.* Ed. Robert A. Greenberg. 2d ed. New York: W. W. Norton, 1970.

Swigger, Ronald T. "Fictional Encyclopedism and the Cognitive Value of Literature." *Comparative Literature Studies* 12 (1975): 351–66.

Tarn, Nathaniel. "The Heraldic Vision." *Alcheringa,* n.s. 2.2 (1975): 23–41.

Todorov, Tzvetan. *The Conquest of America.* Trans. Richard Howard. New York: Harper and Row, 1984.

_____. "The Origin of Genres." *New Literary History* 8.1 (Autumn 1976): 159–70.

Toynbee, Paget, ed. and trans. *Dantis Aligherii epistolae: The Letters of Dante.* 2d ed. 1920; reprint, Oxford: Clarendon Press, 1966.

Tuan, Yi-fu. "Geography, Phenomenology, and the Study of Human Nature." *Géographe Canadien* 15.3 (1971): 181–92.

Turner, Victor, and Edith Turner. *Image and Pilgrimage in Christian Culture: Anthropological Perspectives.* New York: Columbia University Press, 1978.

Tutuola, Amos. *The Palm-Wine Drinkard.* New York: Grove Press, 1953.

Valerius. "Letter in Praise . . . of the Most Blessed Egeria." In *Analecta Bollandiana* 29 (1910): 394–95.

Vespucci, Amerigo. *Navigationes.* In Martin Waldseemüller, *Cosmographiae introductio.* Saint Die, 1507; reprint, Readex Microprint, 1966 (photocopy).

Vignaud, Henry. *Toscanelli and Columbus: The Letter and Chart of Toscanelli.* London: Sands, 1902.

Villehardouin, Geoffroi de. *La conquête de Constantinople.* Ed. Edmond Faral. 2 vols. Paris: Société d'Edition "Les Belles Lettres," 1961.

Waldseemüller, Martin. *Cosmographiae introductio. . . .* Saint Die, 1507; reprint, Readex Microprint, 1966 (photocopy).

Washburn, Wilcomb E. "The Meaning of 'Discovery' in the 15th and 16th Centuries." *American Historical Review* 68 (1962): 1–21.

References

Watts, Pauline Moffitt. "Prophecy and Discovery: On the Spiritual Origins of Christopher Columbus's 'Enterprise of the Indies.'" *American Historical Review* 90.1 (February 1985): 73–102.

White, Hayden. *Tropics of Discourse: Essays in Cultural Criticism.* Baltimore: Johns Hopkins University Press, 1978.

Wilkinson, John, trans. *Egeria's Travels in the Holy Land.* Rev. ed. Jerusalem: Ariel Publishing House; Warminster, England: Ares and Phillips, 1981.

William of Rubruck [Guilielmi Rubruquis]. *Itinerarium.* Ed. Anastasius van den Wyngaert. In *Sinica Fransiscana.* Vol. 1. Karachi and Florence: Collegium S. Bonaventurae, 1929.

——. *The Journey of Friar William of Rubruck.* Ed. and trans. William Rockhill. Hakluyt Society, 2d ser., 4. London, 1900.

——. *The Journey of William of Rubruck.* Trans. "a nun of Stanbrook Abbey." In Dawson, *Mission to Asia.*

——. *Voyage dans L'empire mongol.* Trans. Claude and René Kappler. Paris: Payot, 1985.

Wittkower, Rudolf. "Marvels of the East: A Study in the History of Monsters." *Journal of the Warburg and Courtauld Institutes* 5 (1942): 159–97.

Wonders of the East. Ed. and trans. Paul Allen Gibb. In *"Wonders of the East*: A Critical Edition and Commentary." Ph.D. diss., Duke University, 1977.

——. Facsimile. In *An Eleventh-Century Anglo-Saxon Miscellany.* See McGurk, Knock, et al.

——. Ed. Stanley Rypins. In *Three Old English Prose Texts.* See Rypins.

Wren, Robert M. *Achebe's World: The Historical and Cultural Context of the Novels of Chinua Achebe.* Washington, D.C.: Three Continents Press, 1980.

Wright, Louis B. *Middle-Class Culture in Elizabethan England.* 1935; reprint, Ithaca, N.Y.: Cornell University Press, 1958.

Wright, Thomas, ed. and trans. *Early Travels in Palestine.* 1848; reprint, New York: AMS Press, 1969.

Wyngaert, Anastasius van den, ed. *Itinerarium Guilielmi Rubruquis.* See William of Rubruck.

Wynter, Sylvia. "Ethno or Socio Poetics." *Alcheringa,* n.s. 2.2 (1976): 78–94.

Yule, Henry, ed. and trans. *The Book of Ser Marco Polo the Venetian concerning the Kingdoms and Marvels of the East.* 3rd ed. rev. Henri Cordier. 2 vols. London: John Murray, 1921.

——. *Cathay and the Way Thither.* Vol. 2. 2d ed. Hakluyt Society, 2d ser., 33. London, 1913.

Zacher, Christian K. *Curiosity and Pilgrimage: The Literature of Discovery in Fourteenth-Century England.* Baltimore: Johns Hopkins University Press, 1976.

Index

Boldface numbers indicate principal discussions.

Index

Index

Louis IX, King, 112, 134–136
Lovecraft, H. P., 72
Lowes, John Livingston, 211
Lucian of Samosata, *True Story*, 48, 65, 141
Ludolph von Suchem, *Description of the Holy Land*, 131, 142, 143

Macrobius, 65, 66 (fig. 3)
Mâle, Emile, 83
Mandeville's Travels, 3, 7, 9, 31, 34, 48, 49, 57, 183, 191, 192, 221, 223n, 250; and Columbus, 169, 171; fact and fiction in, 136–148; and genre, 122–127; in Hakluyt, 218; and inexpressibility topos, 179; and irony, 149–153; monsters and wonders in, 154–161, 177, 224; and Ralegh, 252–253
Mappae mundi, frontispiece, 55n, 56 (fig. 1), 65, 66 (fig. 3), 67 (fig. 4), 150, 214. *See also* Ebsdorf map
Martyr, Peter (Pietro Martire d'Anghiera), *Decades*, 214–218, 222, 225, 246, 251n, 255
Marvels. *See* Wonders
Matter of the East, 8, 10, 15, 47–58, 124–126
Metaphor, 1, 178–179, 249–252
Mézières, Philippe de, *Le songe du vieil pèlerin*, 132
Milani, Virgil I., "Written Language of Christopher Columbus," 172, 200
Milione, Il (Marco Polo), 9, 97n, 236. *See also* Polo, Marco
Miller, Christopher, *Blank Darkness*, 3
Minto, William, *Manual of English Prose Literature*, 136
Miracles, 37–39, 81
Missionary accounts, 7, 112–113, 116. *See also* Odoric of Pordenone; William of Rubruck
Monsters, 46 (ill.), 53, 58 (fig. 2); and allegory, 75–84; in Cabeza de Vaca, 264; in Columbus, 180, 183; in *Mandeville's Travels*, 154–158; in Ralegh, 239; in Renaissance cosmography, 214, 216n; representations of, 71–75; as species, 64; and theology, 77–86. *See also names of individual monsters and monstrous species*
Montaigne, Michel de, 61n, 133n, 167, 186, 194–195
Montezuma, 185

More, Sir Thomas, *Utopia*, 211, 217, 218n, 245
Morgan, Wendy, 53n
Morison, Samuel Eliot, 180n, 202n
Moseley, C. W. R. D., 140n, 154
Moule, A. C., and Paul Pelliot, *Marco Polo: The Description of the World*, 87–88n, 92
Münster, Sebastian, *Cosmographiae Universalis*, 9, 134 (fig. 4), 214–215, 225

Names and naming, 196, 200–204, 226
Narrative: and crusade chronicles, 131–136; first person, in Renaissance travel accounts, 218, 227–228; and guidebooks, 127–129; travel literature defined as, 5
Narrator: as intercessor, 25, 82–83; and personal voice, 113–115; as protagonist, in Ralegh's *Discoverie*, 235–238; as romance hero, 188–204; as witness, 18–20, 36, 38–39, 93–95
Native Americans. *See* Indians (American)
Nearchus, 49, 195
Negative description, 159, 223–225
New World: as East, 173; European relations with, 6; heroes in, 189; interpretations of, 204–209; Matter of, 167–168, 169; naming in, 202–203; and Other World, 222; and vocabulary, 222–228
Noble Savage, 177, 242
Novel, 132; and Joinville, 135–136; and Marco Polo 98–102; and Ralegh's *Discoverie*, 234–235; and science, 261; and travel romance, 122–123
Novus mundus, 169, 176

Occupatio, 30, 142, 207, 239
Ocean Stream, 52
Odoric of Pordenone, 49, 102, 106, 112, 126n, 148, 154–159, 264
Odyssey, 53, 68
O'Gorman, Edmundo, *Invention of America*, 167, 172, 176n, 192, 225
Olivet, Mount, 38, 130
Olschki, Leonardo, 97n, 103, 110n, 112, 133n
Ophir, 178, 204–205, 215
Orbis terrarum, 52, 55, 172–173, 176, 252

Index

Library of Congress Cataloging-in-Publication Data

Campbell, Mary B., 1954–
  The witness and the other world.

  Bibliography: p.
  Includes index.
  I. Geography, Medieval.   I. Title.
G89.C3   1988   809′.93591   88-47720
ISBN 0-8014-2137-3 (alk. paper)